SWEDISH CAKES

SWEDISH CAKES

Jan Hedh

photography
Charlotte Gawell

Skyhorse Publishing

Originally published by ICA bokförlag, Forma Books AB
Translated by Monika Romare

Skyhorse Publishing books may be purchased in bulk at special discounts for sales
promotion, corporate gifts, fund-raising, or educational purposes. Special editions can
also be created to specifications. For details, contact the Special Sales Department,
Skyhorse Publishing, 307 West 36th Street, 11th Floor, New York, NY 10018
or info@skyhorsepublishing.com.

Skyhorse® and Skyhorse Publishing® are registered trademarks of
Skyhorse Publishing, Inc.®, a Delaware corporation.

www.skyhorsepublishing.com

Library of Congress Cataloging-in-Publication
Data is available on file.

ISBN: 978-1-62087-099-0

Printed in China

he cake is the highlight of a birthday or any celebration, not to mention weddings. The word derives from the Latin word tortus; in Italian it's called torta, in French it's called tourte and gâteau, in German it's called torten, lagkake in Denmark and blötkage in Norway.

The cake is round in shape and will remain that way, although we've tried making various shapes over the years. It's easy to portion and it looks good on the plate.

When I decided to write a book about cakes, a colleague said to me: "Are you not adding pastries to it too?" He thought that it would be hard to fill an entire book with cake recipes.

But when I began writing down the cakes I wanted to include in the book, I immediately realized that it was the opposite. I would've needed five volumes to include all the important cakes. However, I've published some recipes in previous books and they won't be included in this book.

When I was 15 years old, I started working as a pastry apprentice at the pastry shop Heidi in Limhamn. The most popular cakes were Cream Cake, Raspberry Cake, Strawberry Cake, Princess Cake, Black Forest Gateau, Walnut Cake, Napoleon Cake, Casablanca Cake, Fragilité Cake, Alexander Cake, French Mocha Cake, Almond Cake, Tosca Cake, Florentine Cake, Saint Honoré Cake, Swedish Mocha Cake, Sans Rival Cake, Scottish Cake, Bananza Cake, Boston Cake, Zola Cake, Thousand Leaf Cake, Queen Cake, King Cake, Sacher Cake, Truffel Cake and Dobos Cake, Arrack Cake with Nougat.

Dessert cakes, such as Lemon Fromage and Orange Fromage cakes, were made in a circle. On Saturdays and Sundays, there were always many orders for Swiss Merengue Cakes and also sometimes the finest of them all: Charlotte Russe.

As an apprentice, I was responsible for making all the cake bottoms. Head Pastry Chef Kurt Lundgren treated apprentices well, but demanded that everything was perfect, which I am grateful for. Kurt had worked at many pastry shops all over Sweden and was a skilled craftsman. The manager, pastry chef Jan Gunnar Malmberg, was also a skilled craftsman who, among other places, had worked at the famous pastry shop Kellermans in Ystad and at Sundets bröd in Malmö. Jan, Gunnar's father, was also a baker, and the brother, Olle Malmberg, is a pastry chef as well as a baker in Jönköping. He occasionally comes with me on a bread tour to spread knowledge about our beloved profession.

Kurt's brother, pastry chef and master baker Birger Lundgren, was a teacher at The Pastry School in Gothenburg and is one of Sweden's best confectioners. He worked as head pastry chef at the Swedish American programme at the Savoy Hotel in Malmö and the famous Hotel Knaust in Sundsvall, among other places. Birger and his students visited bakeries and schools and during summer vacations he worked as an intern at famous pastry shops in Europe. I especially remember when he told me about Pasticceria Motta in Milan, where he learned how to make panettone.

Many Swedish pastry chefs have taken the journeyman baker exam with Birger as a teacher. He provided me with a lot of educational knowledge, such as the chemistry of baking, professional subscription, sketching, recipe and professional counting and calculation.

Another one of my teachers that I often talk to is master confectioner Walter Härtfelder, who was one of my teachers at Pastry Trade School in Uppsala. Walter always baked amazing stollen cake and when I recently visited him in Uppsala, he had just baked Nürnberger lebkuchen on chocolate dipped wafers.

Being responsible for the bottoms was pretty cumbersome when you were working as an intern; there were a lot of different cake bottoms at that time. We apprentices weren't allowed to go home until we were done with all the preparations for the next day. Each day we whisked fresh cake bottoms and while we washed mountains of dishes and cleaned up after the other confectioners, we were always cooking creams, jellies for cakes, apple compote, tosca mixtures and other fillings. Shortcut pastry and molds were lined and we lubricated baking pans. Toffee pastries were dipped in toffee and were filled with cream the next day. When I finished everything I started to practice piping and writing, and making marzipan flowers and figures.

The second year as an apprentice I helped to make pies and cakes, which was much more exciting than making bread buns and biscuits and cookies. The third

year we got to make ice cream, pudding and cotton candy and eventually became trusted with croquembouche and cornucopia. These were packed in special boxes so that they wouldn't fall, and ice cream was shipped in tubs of ice and salt.

I carefully took notes on the recipes and prices in my recipe book, which grew with time. At the time, you had to study for five years to become a pastry chef and four years to become a baker. However, if you were good enough, you could take the journeyman bakery test after only three years of learning. Nevertheless, you had to wait for five years before getting full salary. Things were quite different back then.

I took my journeyman test in 1969 at The Pastry Trade School in Uppsala, which was a private pastry chef school owned by the Sweden Confectioners Association. I was ready to become a restaurant pastry chef. Cakes in a restaurant were more exclusive than the ones in the pastry shops, and it was particularly gratifying to learn how to make ice cream cakes and desserts.

When I obtained my master's in professional pastry cooking, beautiful cakes and croquembouche played a major part. The censors were the master confectioner Hans Eichmüller and master confectioner Calle Widell. Both are my good friends to this day, and their professional achievements live on through all the students they had over the years.

The cake. This amazing pastry that brightens up our existence and is made for baptisms, confirmations, weddings, birthdays and other festivities. The cake is also a pleasure in everyday life and it provides a necessary break in life. Sitting at a bakery café with a delicious cup of coffee with a slice of a tasty cake is one of life's virtues.

I remember how I would enjoy a slice of cake for breakfast the morning after my birthday.

My mother would often bake cakes, both for dessert and for parties. If we wanted Princess cake, she would order one, usually from the Braun Conditori in Malmö, since my mom found it difficult to roll out the marzipan. The Princess cake really is a Swedish specialty. The recipe was first published in *The Princesses Cookbook* and became a Swedish classic. Some pastry chefs called it the Opera Cake, but in that case there was no raspberry jam on the first layer. Black Forest cake is another Swedish classic, even though it's of foreign origin.

As a pastry chef, Switzerland was my dream country to visit and work in. The best schools in the world were located there. When I visited the Richemont School in Lucerne on a 14-day pastry course and met with the head of the pastry department, master confectioner Joseph Mattle, I realized how much I had left to learn about the profession. Mr. Mattle was a great teacher and he always laughed when I visited the school and took new courses while working in Switzerland. He

told me that he'd just spoken with the Director of the Coba School in Basel and had heard that I had taken all the courses at that school too. The school is still one of the world's best pastry schools.

Just a stone's throw away from the Richemont School was the restaurant school Montana, where I also studied with the guidance of the dessert master, Chef Pâtissière François Gatti, a great teacher who with lots of humor taught us how to make beautiful desserts. The gastronomy professor, Gert Klötzke, was also a student at the school prior to me. In the evenings after work I took an evening class at the International Sugar School of Zurich, where Willy Pfund, the chief of the décor department at the world famous Confiserie Sprüngli, was the teacher. The pastry shop is located at Paradeplatz by Bahnhofstrasse. Try a Zuger Kirsch torte or Japonaise torte at Sprüngli if you visit, I almost always do when I visit Zurich. Or I'll have a piece of Saint Honoré cake, or a Honold birnen torte at Confiserie Honold series on Rennweg, which is a side street of Bahnhofstrasse. They always taste as good, as if time stands still.

The students at the International Sugar School came from all over the world. Willy worked fantastically with caramel, and I had great admiration for him. He always gave me difficult tasks to solve, which turned out well most of the time. He laughed a lot and was easy to get along with. I interned with him for 14 days at the decor department at Sprüngli, and it meant a lot for a young professional to see how the pastry worked. All departments were entrusted to various station managers and Mr. Sprüngli himself kept an eye on all the departments.

In Zurich, I took a cake-decorating class in the evenings that was held by master confectioner Charles Thanz, who is among other things a specialist in cake decorating and cocoa painting. He worked only with cake decoration at Confiseries Sprüngli.

When I was working making cake bottoms at Confiseries Honold in Zurich, we were two men who baked bottoms from dawn to dusk. We had four whipping machines with gas flames below, so that we could quickly warm the eggs for the hot whipped bottoms. After three months, I started working in the crèmerie, where we worked with cream cakes and pastries. The cake station was located in the pâtissérie department, where the most advanced cakes were made. One whole section only baked meringue and japonaise bottoms. On Fridays and Saturdays the cake orders culminated, and I remember that the worst day was on Christmas Eve, just like in Sweden.

The art of making cake bottoms and biscuits was first developed in the early 1300's, when they whipped the first biscuit in the city of Joinville in France. During the 1500s, the techniques of making various kinds of bottom and fillings further developed. The pastry bag nozzle

was invented in 1710 which meant that there were now more ways of shaping pastry. During the 1700 and 1800s people began to make cake bottoms with warm whipped batter, and during the 1900's most of the cakes that we have today were developed.

At first, they were mostly filled with jam, and then came the vanilla cream and buttercream. In the 1900s came the whipped cream, mousse, fromage and bavaroise. The buttercream cake isn't very common anymore, which is a shame - a Mocha cake made with the right buttercream is always delicious.

I remember when the Pastry Chef of the bakery at NK department store, Stefan Johnson Petersén, and I toured Sweden and we presented modern French cakes. Following that occasion, many bakeries started to create easy and beautiful cakes using fruit mousse, jelly mirrors and light almond bottoms. At the time, a lot of pastry shops would work with ready-made cake bottoms, cold whipped vanilla cream, canned tangerines and cherries for garnishing, untempered chocolate and artificial chocolate made without cocoa butter, instead of real chocolate (yuck!). It's much better today.

Confectioners Karin Ludorowski and Jessica Larsson from the Olof Viktor's bakery in Glemminge make all the cakes from scratch, and special cake orders, such as wedding cakes, make Saturdays chaotic. All cakes that one eats with coffee must be freshly baked every day.

Christer Alfredsson from Olof Viktor's likes pastry just like I do, but we try not to eat many of them, as we have to be able to tighten our belts. On the contrary, we often see our CEO, Mårten Götberg, munching on a pastry in his hand. But after all, he is from Gotland ...

As I sit and read my script and taste all the cakes that I baked, I would obviously also have wanted to include Zuger Kirsch torte from Switzerland, Solothurner torte, Thusnelda torte and Spanischer torte from Germany and Prinz Regent torte, Käsetorte, Mohntorte and Linzer torte from Austria. Maria Escalante and her sister would also include a tasty cake from Peru, but all of those recipes I will have to save for the next time. You have to draw the line somewhere.

I hope you get a lot of use out of this book. Like all of my previous books, I dedicate it to my mother, whom I greatly miss, and who taught me so much about food.

I want to thank property manager Bertil Forsberg and his wife Kerstin, who always are helpful for letting me use their space at Kronprinsen in Malmö. Bertil knows much about a lot of things and he helps me out, and he even gives the photographer good advice. Thank you also to property owner Ulla Åberg, who lets me stay in her facilities when I'm working on my books, and thank you to Tårtateljé in Malmö, who contributed their pretty cake stands.

Jan Hedh

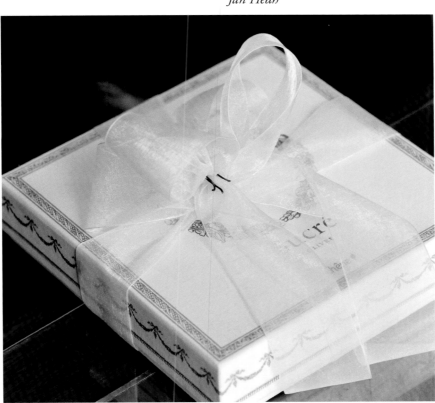

SPONGE CAKE BOTTOMS

In Sweden, cake bottoms are primarily of the sponge cake kind.

In French these are called *genoise* or *bisquit*. Eggs are the basis of cake and Swiss roll bottoms, with the addition of granulated sugar and all-purpose wheat flour. Bottoms should be light, firm, and porous. They should be baked through, but never dry. A rule of thumb is to get them into the oven as soon as possible; otherwise, they risk collapsing and becoming compact and heavy. As always, practice makes perfect.

Cake bottoms are the fundament of most cakes. In the recipes in this book, I use a 2-inch-high (5 cm) cake ring or springform pan with a 9-inch (22 cm) diameter. A cake of this size is simple to cut into 10 or 12 pieces. Portion size varies with country: in America and Germany, for instance, a slice is larger. In my experience, a perfect portion of cake weighs 3 to 4 oz (100–125 g).

Building blocks of bottoms

Eggs

Of the total weight of an egg, the shell makes up 10½ %, the egg white 57½ %, and the yolk 32 %. Of the liquid weight, the egg white makes up 64 %, the yolk 36 %. To achieve consistent results when baking cake bottoms, always weigh the eggs, egg whites, and egg yolks, rather than relying on the number of each, since the size of eggs can often vary.

The pastry chef's simple egg converter:
One egg white weighs 1 oz (30 g)
One egg yolk weighs 2/3 oz (20 g)
One egg weighs 1 2/3 oz (50 g)

The air that is beaten into the egg mixture expands, making the bottom light and porous. For best results, the egg mixture must be whipped to the maximal volume. However, since fatty residues negatively impact the volume of the egg foam, it is of the utmost importance that all vessels are spotless. Herein lies a paradox: an entire egg can be beaten to foam despite the fat contained in the yolk, since this emulsified fat does not inhibit foaming as do fatty residues.

Warm-beating is the best technique for baking classic bottoms. For increasing the volume of the batter, warm the egg and sugar mixture to 105° F (40° C), then

Eggs should come from free-ranging hens.

beat until it cools to 68° F (20° C); the egg foam swells as the eggs expand and bind better.

The thin deposits that remain as a result of the sugar dissolving in the water of the eggs are less prominent when warm-beating. Warm-beating also spares you the trouble of beating the yolks and whites separately. Whisking in a lot of air both stabilizes the mixture and keeps it from collapsing when adding flour, and helps to allow the batter to rise. For 5 eggs (250 g), you will need a 2½-liter mixing bowl to beat the mixture to full volume.

Adding more yolks than whites to the mixture will make the bottom more compact. Egg yolks allow the batter to emulsify better and become creamier, due to the lecithin. The bottoms achieve a richer color and greater stability. Egg yolks do not increase in volume the way that egg whites do, since they contain 33 % fat and no albumin. However, these bottoms turn out moister.

Egg whites can be beaten to foam, making the batter lighter, fluffier, and stabler. By whisking in some sugar, the foam will not turn flocculent, or wooly, and its volume will be better maintained.

The pastry chef's advanced egg converter
Twenty (20) eggs = 1 liter
Thirty-three (33) egg whites = 1 liter
Fifty (50) egg yolks = 1 liter

2 ¼ lbs of eggs (1 kg) requires a 10-liter mixing bowl
4 ½ lbs of eggs (2 kg) requires a 20-liter mixing bowl

One liter of eggs yields
four Swiss rolls on a 16x24-inch baking sheet (400 x 600 mm)
or one 16x24x2-inch capsule (400 x 600 x 50 mm)
or four cake bottoms, 2x11 inches

Sugar

Sugar has several important functions in the batter: it allows the bottoms to stay fresh longer, provides flavor and aroma, and makes the bottoms succulent and moist.

Flour

The glutens and starches in the flour gelatinate and coagulate during baking, making the cake bottoms firm and easy to cut. All-purpose baking flour is ideal, and better than bread flour, which is high in gluten and results in dry, swollen cake bottoms. Up to half the flour may be substituted with potato starch or corn starch, which results in lighter bottoms with a crustier structure, but these are often more crumbly.

Make it a habit to sift the dry ingredients together onto a sheet of paper for a better mix. Carefully fold in the flour with a rubber spatula without puncturing the tiny air bubbles in the egg mixture. Pastry chefs usually use their hand, gently rolling up from the base of the bowl and along the sides. Mixing the sifted flour into the beaten egg mixture is called *folding*.

Baking powder

It is not a requirement to use baking powder when baking cake bottoms; but for a lighter bottom, add baking powder to the flour before sifting. Whereas baking powder gives a greater volume, this likewise means that the pastry dries out more quickly. Use 1 tsp baking powder (5 g) for 9 oz eggs (250 g), (that is, 1 g per egg). For Swiss rolls, use instead 1½ tsp (7 g) for 9 oz eggs (250 g).

At the Confiserie Brändli in Basel, we always used to make our own baking soda.
Here is the recipe.
7 oz bicarbonate (200 g)
18 oz cream of tartar (500 g)
2/3 lb wheat starch (300 g)
Combine the ingredients, sift twice, and store in a can - the results will impress you.

Flavor enhancers

Many people appreciate the taste of lemon zest in a cake bottom. Aim for 1–2 % of the weight of the batter; otherwise, the flavor might be overwhelming.

If you wish to add vanilla sugar, use the same proportions. Mix your own vanilla sugar from 1/3 oz vanilla beans (10 g) and ½ cup sugar (100 g). Grind the beans and the sugar in a blender.

Chopped nuts, walnuts, coconut, or almonds are then combined with the flour before folding into the mixture. Coarsely chopped nuts may be added to a bottom without altering the recipe, while finely ground nuts absorb liquids. Consider that 3 parts finely ground nuts, or almond flour, has the same effect on the consistency of the bottom as ¾ cup wheat flour (100 g) does in binding ability.

Even when you add cocoa powder, subtract its weight from that of the flour; otherwise, the bottoms may turn out dry, as cocoa powder is hygroscopic, absorbing as much water as does flour. Replace ¼ cup flour (25 g) with cocoa powder for a classic Swedish bottom. Cocoa in cake bottoms should contain 20–22 % cocoa fat (20/22). Never use cocoa 10/12, which is too lean and gives a thin taste. The best cocoa for our purposes comes from Valrhona.

For a coffee bottom, beat 2½ tsp instant coffee (12 g) with the eggs.

For a pistachio, walnut, hazelnut, or almond bottom, blend 3½ oz pistachio nuts (100 g), walnuts, hazelnuts, or almonds to a paste, and fold into the batter.

For a coconut bottom, fold 2 oz grated coconut (60 g) into the batter. Begin by oven-roasting the dried coconut to a golden-brown color.

Important when baking bottoms

Make sure that your oven is preheated and that your batter is baked immediately; otherwise, your cake bottom could collapse, becoming compact and heavy.

Pastry chefs never grease their cake rings. The batter is meant to stick to the ring, in order to give the bottom the right shape; greasing the ring only leads to the edges shrinking, which deforms the bottom. When the cake is prepared, cut the bottom out with a sharp knife, after which three equally thick layers may be cut with a serrated knife.

Fill the cake ring to two-thirds.

Always line cake rings with wax paper to keep the batter from seeping out. Never use silicon-treated papers, such as bakery release paper, as the batter will seep out. Pastry chefs usually use an ungreased maculater, or blotting, paper.

The paper must be properly secured, (see the illustration on page 18), unless you are using a springform pan, in which case you need to first grease the base.

Always bake cake bottoms with an open oven vent (if available), and as soon as they are done, turn them onto a baking sheet covered with parchment paper and sprinkled with sugar to keep the skin from sticking. The parchment paper will bind the bottom and keep it

from collapsing. A bottom is easier to slice the day after baking. If you need to slice it immediately, after cooling, let it stand for an hour in the freezer. Cake bottoms may be stored in the refrigerator for up to three days, or for longer in the freezer. Wrap well to prevent freezer burn.

Troubleshooting cake bottoms

- If your cake bottoms have peaks, you are using the wrong flour. Use standard all-purpose flour, or combine in equal parts high-gluten bread flour with potato or corn starch.
- If your bottoms tend to sink in the middle, you have beaten the batter for too long. Try instead to stop once deep tunnels appear in the batter, which should be enough.
- If your bottoms are not light and airy, you might need to beat the batter more thoroughly. Or, your mixing bowl had residues of fat. Or, your oven temperature may be too low.
- If your bottoms are sticky in the middle, you need to make sure that they bake through. Test with a toothpick.
- If your bottoms contain lumps of flour, you have either not sifted the flour properly or not carefully folded the flour into the egg mixture.

Slices in a cake ring

8 pieces:	7-in (180-mm) ring
10 pieces:	8-in (200-mm) ring
12 pieces:	9-in (220-mm) ring
14–16 pieces:	9½-in (240-mm) ring
16–20 pieces:	10-in (260-mm) ring

Light and heavy bottoms

Cake bottom recipes are based on egg weight.

The steam from the eggs increases the volume of the batter. Light bottoms contain as much as 45 % water, while heavy bottoms contain about 30 %. The volume weight of a light bottom should be 12–13 oz/quart (360–380 g/liter) of batter.

The following guidelines are useful when creating your own recipe.

Light bottoms:
Oven temperature 375–400 °F (190–200 °C)
1 egg (50 g), 5 tsp sugar (20 g) and at least 8 tsp flour (20 g)
1 egg (50 g), 6 tsp sugar (25 g) and 10 tsp flour (25 g)
1 egg (50 g), 7 tsp sugar (30 g) and 10 tsp flour (25 g)

Moderately heavy bottoms:
Oven temperature 375–400 °F (190–200 °C)
1 egg (50 g), 9 tsp sugar (35 g) and 13 tsp flour (35 g)
1 egg (50 g), 10 tsp sugar (40 g) and 1/3 cup flour (40 g)

Heavy bottoms:
Oven temperature 390–410°F (200–210°C)
1 egg (50 g), 11 tsp sugar (45 g) and 6 tbsp flour (45 g)
1 egg (50 g), ¼ cup sugar (50 g) and 3/8 cup flour (50 g)

Classic Swedish bottom

This light and fluffy bottom is suitable for Swedish cakes such as princess cakes, cream cakes, raspberry cakes, and strawberry cakes. A pinch of vanilla sugar provides extra body, and if desired, you may add the zest of half a lemon to the eggs. German, Swiss, and Austrian pastry chefs commonly use lemon in their bottoms, whereas Swedish pastry chefs rarely do.

Use the following proportions: for each egg (50 g), add 2 tbsp sugar (30 g) and ¼ cup flour (30 g). For an even lighter bottom, you can use 1 tsp less each of sugar and flour, but these tend to dry out sooner. You may also add 1 tsp baking powder (5 g), but they too will dry out sooner.

One 2x9-inch cake ring or springform pan

9 oz, or about 5, eggs (250 g)
2/3 cup sugar (135 g)
1 tbsp natural vanilla sugar (15 g)
1 ¼ cups flour (150 g)

1. Preheat the oven to 375°F (190°C).
2. Lightly beat the eggs, sugar, and vanilla sugar.
3. Set the bowl over a pot of simmering water, or a double boiler, making certain that the temperature never exceeds 195°F (90°C), which will coagulate the egg mixture. Whip energetically, preferably with an electric egg mixer, until the temperature reaches 104°F (40–45°C). Whip for another 10 minutes until the mixture cools, and has become light and porous. If you whip at too high a speed, the mixture will lose volume. The batter is ready when deep tunnels appear. If none appear, the mixture is overbeaten.
4. Sift the flour (optionally, along with the starch or baking powder) onto a sheet of paper and fold into the egg foam with a rubber spatula – gently and carefully so that the batter maintains its volume.
5. Pour the batter into a cake ring wrapped in parchment paper, (see the illustration on page 18), or use a greased springform pan. Spread the batter along the inside of the ring, for evener baking.
6. Bake the bottom for 25–30 minutes until it is golden brown. Test with a toothpick that it is done.
7. Sprinkle sugar on top and lay it on a sheet of parchment paper. Cover with a baking sheet and turn upside down to even out the top. Letting the bottoms cool between the sheets will keep them from drying out.
8. Let the bottoms stand this way overnight, as confectioners usually do, and they will not crumble when cut.

STORAGE

Sealed in a proper bag, bottoms will stay fresh for weeks in the freezer.

Gluten-free bottoms

See the classic Swedish bottom, but replace the flour with 1 ¼ cup potato starch (150 g). The bottom will have a slightly crumbly, but fully acceptable, consistency. Freezing the bottoms will make them easier to cut.

Génoise

A warm-beaten bottom with butter, the génoise is a building block of French baking. This bottom is a bit firmer than a classic Swedish bottom, and somewhat crustier in consistency on account of the butter. This is how we baked them at the Pâtissérie Dupont in Paris.
One 2x9-inch cake ring or springform pan

9 oz, or about 5, eggs (250 g)
¾ cup sugar (150 g)
1 tbsp natural vanilla sugar (15 g)
1 1/3 cup flour (165 g)
¼ cup unsalted butter (50 g)

Prepare a classic Swedish bottom, but melt the butter and stir into a scoop of the egg mixture, before folding into the batter.

Chocolate génoise

As above, but replace the flour with:
1 oz cocoa powder (25 g), preferably Valrhona 20/22
¾ cup flour (95 g)
1/3 cup potato starch (45 g)

Sift all the ingredients onto a sheet of paper.

1 Weighing the ingredients.
2 Warm-beating the ingredients.
3 The beaten mixture.

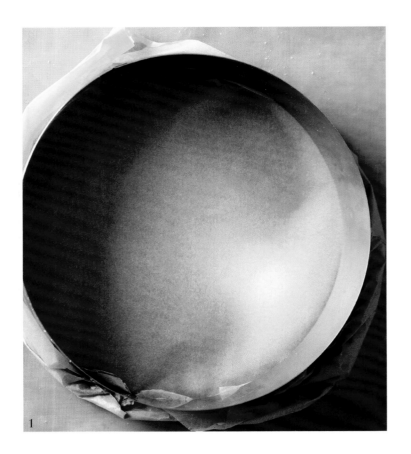

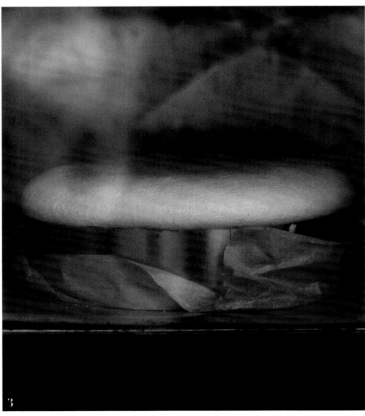

1 *Line the ring with wax paper.*
2 *Fill the ring with the mixture.*
3 *Bake the cake bottom.*
4 *Sprinkle sugar over the cake bottom.*
5 *Turn the bottom upside down.*
6 *Cut the bottom out.*
7 *Cut the cake using a serrated knife.*

Swiss cake bottom

A tad softer and moister in consistency than the classic Swedish bottom, and somewhat lighter, with more egg yolks and lemon. This is how we baked them at the Honold Confiserie in Zürich.

6 1/2 oz, or about 4, eggs (190 g)
2 oz, or about 3, egg yolks (60 g)
½ cup + 1 tbsp sugar (115 g)
2 tsp natural vanilla sugar (10 g)
1 cup flour (125 g)
Peel of ½ lemon, grated

Prepare a classic Swedish bottom, see page 16, but add the grated lemon to the beaten eggs.

Viennese cake bottom

This recipe is particularly suitable for cakes that will be frozen, since the bottom will not dry out in the same way as with the classic Swedish bottom. Butter and milk make them wonderfully moist. In Germany it is known as *Sandmasse*.

7 oz, or about 4, eggs (200 g)
2 oz, or about 3, egg yolks (60 g)
¾ cup + 1 tbsp sugar (165 g)
2 tsp natural vanilla sugar (10 g)
Peel of ½ lemon, grated
1 ¼ cups flour (150 g)
¼ cup potato starch (25 g)
2 tbsp unsalted butter, melted (25 g)
1/8 cup milk 3 % (25 g)

Prepare a classic Swedish bottom, see page 16, and as a last step mix the butter, milk and lemon peel with a scoop of the batter and fold into the egg mixture.

For a chocolate bottom, replace ¼ cup flour (30 g) with cocoa powder 20/22.

Classic Swedish Viennese bottom

This delicious bottom is moist and keeps well.

One 2x9-inch cake ring or springform pan

9 oz, or about 5, eggs (250 g)
¾ cup + 1 tbsp sugar (165 g)
¾ cup + 1 tbsp flour (150 g)
¾ cup potato starch (85 g)
¼ cup unsalted butter (65 g), melted

Prepare a classic Swedish bottom, see page 16, but stir the butter with a scoop of the egg mixture and fold into the batter.

Richer Swedish Viennese bottom

This tasty bottom uses more egg yolks, which gives it a softer structure. The addition of butter refines the taste, and it will keep longer. This bottom is suitable for richer cakes with buttercream and ganache fillings, as well as for wedding cakes.

One 2x9-inch cake ring or springform pan

9 oz, or about 5, eggs (250 g)
3 oz, or about 4, egg yolks (80 g)
½ cup + 1 tbsp sugar (115 g)
2 tsp natural vanilla sugar (10 g)
1 cup flour (125 g)
¼ cup unsalted butter (60 g), melted

Prepare a classic Swedish bottom, see page 16, but stir the butter into a scoop of the egg mixture and fold it into the batter.

Chocolate Viennese bottom

As above, but replace 1 oz of the flour (25 g) with cocoa powder, preferably Valrhona 20/22.

Grillage bottom

Very common in Switzerland and Austria, and often filled with chocolate ganache, this is the bottom for a grillage cake.

Prepare a classic Swedish bottom, see page 16, but add 1 oz finely chopped nougat (25 g), see page 79, and 1 oz chopped, roasted nuts (25 g) together with the flour.

Dobos bottom

This recipe comes from the renowned confectionery Gerbaud in Budapest, which I helped to represent in the atrium of the NK department store in Stockholm. It is one of the world's most beautiful coffeehouses. Don't miss it if you are ever in Budapest.

4 oz, or about 6, egg yolks (120 g)
6 1/2 oz, or about 6, egg whites (180 g)
1 vanilla bean
3/4 cup unsalted butter (180 g), at room temperature
3 tbsp sugar (40 g)
1 tsp salt (5 g), preferably fleur de sel
1 tsp lemon juice (5 g)
2/3 cup sugar (120 g)
1 cup flour (120 g)

1. Preheat oven to 425°F (220°C).
2. Draw 6 circles, each 9 inches (23 cm) in diameter, on parchment paper.
3. Separate the egg yolks from the whites.
4. Split the vanilla bean lengthwise. Remove the seeds and add them to the butter, salt, and sugar. Whip gently for 5 minutes. Add the egg yolks one at a time and stir until smooth.
5. Pour the egg whites and lemon juice into an immaculate metal mixing bowl, and beat to foam at medium speed. Gradually add the sugar and whisk to a stiff meringue.
6. Fold the egg foam into the butter mixture along with the sifted flour to form a light, fluffy batter.
7. Pour out the batter in circles and spread it evenly with a palette knife. Bake until golden brown, 12–15 minutes.
8. Cut evenly circular bottoms with a 9-inch cake ring as soon as they leave the oven; otherwise, they will crack. Immediately remove the parchment paper so that they become brittle.

Duchesse bottom

This Belgian almond cake bottom is moist and delicious and suitable for mousse cakes. This recipe comes from Pâtissérie Wittamer, Place Sablon, in Brussels. Don't miss the Wittamer or Pierre Marcolini if you are ever in Brussels.

One 2x9-inch cake ring or springform pan

1 ¼ cups flour (150 g)
2 oz almond flour (60 g)
9 oz, or about 5, eggs (250 g)
2 oz, or about 3, egg yolks (60 g)
2/3 cup + 1 tbsp sugar (140 g)

Preheat oven to 360°F (180°C).

Prepare a classic Swedish bottom, see page 16, but mix the sifted flour with almond flour.

Cold-beaten bottoms

For cold-beaten bottoms, the egg yolks and the egg whites are beaten separately. The whites are first beaten to meringue and then folded into the yolk mixture, followed by the sifted flour. The egg whites add air to

Folding the sifted flour into the batter.

the batter, making it light and fluffy; therefore, baking powder is seldom required. Half the flour may be replaced with an equal amount of potato or corn starch, resulting in an even lighter batter. This batter can be piped into ladyfingers, as well as chocolate cakes. They will have a drier consistency, which makes them perfect for soaking in syrup, as for example tiramisu.

The guidelines used for warm-beating apply equally to cold-beating. In certain recipes, such as for the joconde bottom made with almond flour, butter is added.

Since fatty residues negatively impact the volume of the egg foam, always use perfectly clean vessels. Use mixing bowls of stainless steel or copper not lined with tin, but never plastic bowls. Wash your mixing bowls with 2 tbsp acetic acid mixed with 1 tsp salt, to remove the fatty residues, and rinse thoroughly in cold water.

On the art of beating

Aerate the egg whites as much as possible. When beating by hand, tip the mixing bowl and use large strokes. Use a clean, large whisk suitable for egg whites. If you use an electric mixer, always start at medium speed until the foam swells. Only then should you increase the speed, while adding sugar for cohesion and consistency.

Now whisk to a firm meringue, but not for *too* long, or it will turn stiff. If the meringue has a creamy consistency, the bottom will be perfect. Adding something sour, such as lemon juice, acetic acid, or vinegar, will affect the pH of the egg white and firm it up during beating.

The air beaten into the whites expands during baking, while the steam in the eggs causes the batter to increase in volume.

Classic Swedish cold-beaten bottom

One 2x9-inch cake ring or springform pan

5 oz, or about 5, egg whites (150 g)
1 tsp lemon juice (5 g)
½ cup sugar (100 g)
3 1/2 oz, or about 5, egg yolks (100 g)
3 tbsp sugar (40 g)
2 tsp natural vanilla sugar (10 g)
1 ¼ cups flour (150 g), or, half flour, half potato starch or corn starch

1. Preheat oven to 375° F (190° C).
2. Beat the egg yolks, sugar, and vanilla sugar until frothy.
3. Sift the flour onto a sheet of paper.
4. Beat the egg whites with the sugar and lemon juice to a stiff meringue.
5. Fold the egg yolk foam into the meringue, followed by the remaining flour.
6. Fill the cake ring with the batter and bake as for a warm-baked Bottom, see page 16.

Ladyfinger sponge (spoon biscuits)

Tulle netting for pastry bags was supposedly invented in 1710, the year the piped pastry began to appear. In French they are known as *bisquit cuillière*. They should be served fresh with desserts and with zabaione.

This batter also serves as the basis of Charlotte cakes and portioned desserts.

Cold-beaten bottoms are usually drier; accordingly, they are suitable for soaking in spirits or sugar syrups.

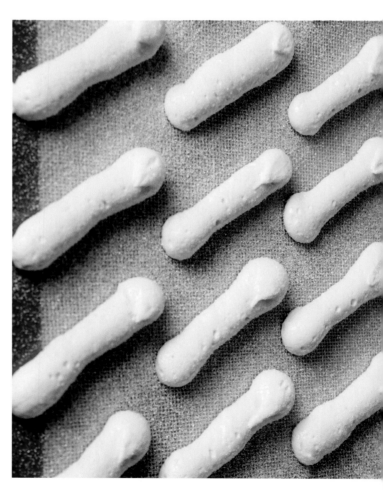

Piped ladyfingers (spoon biscuits).

About 32 piped ladyfingers for lining cake rings

4 oz, or about 6, egg yolks (120 g)
¼ cup sugar (50 g)
2 tsp natural vanilla sugar (10 g)
1 cup flour (120 g)
6 1/2 oz, or about 6, egg whites (180 g)
1 tsp lemon juice (5 g)
5 tbsp sugar (60 g)

1. Preheat oven to 440° F (225° C).
2. Beat the yolks, ¼ cup sugar, and vanilla sugar until foamy.
3. Sift the flour onto a sheet of paper.
4. Beat egg whites, lemon juice, and 5 tbsp sugar to a stiff meringue.
5. Fold the egg foam and flour into the meringue with a rubber spatula.
6. With a pastry bag, pipe the mixture to 4-inch long ladyfingers, and sprinkle sugar on top. Let stand for 5 minutes.
7. Bake the ladyfingers for 8–12 minutes until the surface starts to caramelize, and tiny sugar pearls are formed. Let cool on an oven rack.

Hazelnut Bottom for Fritz Honolds Nüsstorte
One 2x9-inch cake ring or springform pan

5 tbsp unsalted butter (70 g)
3/4 cup + 2 tbsp flour (105 g)
5 1/2 oz, or about 8, egg yolks (160 g)
½ cup + 1 tbsp sugar (110 g)
6 1/2 oz, or about 6, egg whites (190 g)
10 g lemon juice (2 tsp)
1/3 cup sugar (70 g)
4½ oz finely chopped, roasted hazelnuts (125 g)

1. Preheat oven to 375° F (190° C).
2. Melt butter and set aside.
3. Sift the flour onto a sheet of paper.
4. Beat the yolks along with the heaping ½ cup sugar for about 10 minutes to a firm foam with deep tunnels.
5. Beat the egg whites and lemon juice to foam at medium speed while gradually adding 1/3 cup sugar.
6. Increase the speed and whip to a firm meringue.
7. Fold the yolk foam into the meringue using a rubber spatula.
8. Fold in the hazelnuts and flour.
9. Mix the butter with a little of the batter, and then fold this into the rest of the batter.
10. Fill the cake ring and bake for 24 minutes. Test

Baked ladyfingers.

using a toothpick.

11. Sprinkle sugar on top, cover with parchment paper, and turn the cake bottom upside down without removing the ring.

Kadix almond bottom

A wonderfully moist and tasty bottom that can be eaten unadorned.

One 2x9-inch cake ring or springform pan

7 tbsp unsalted butter (100 g)
3/4 cup + 1 tbsp flour (100 g)
barely 1 tsp baking powder (4 g)
1 lemon
4 oz almond paste (100 g) 50/50
7 oz, or about 8, egg yolks (200 g)
2 tbsp sugar (25 g)
5 oz, or about 5, egg whites (150 g)
5 g lemon juice (1 tsp)
6 tbsp sugar (75 g)

1. Melt butter and set aside.
2. Sift the flour and baking powder onto a sheet of paper.
3. Wash the lemon, then grate it and press its juice out.
4. By hand, blend the almond paste with the egg yolks until smooth.
5. Beat the almond paste and egg yolks along with 2 tbsp sugar and the lemon peel and juice for 10 minutes to a firm foam.
6. Beat the egg whites with lemon juice to foam at medium speed. Add the 6 tbsp sugar, increase the speed and whip to a firm foam.
7. Fold the egg yolk mixture into the meringue with a rubber spatula, followed by the flour and baking powder.
8. Stir the butter with a scoop of the batter, and fold into the batter.
9. Spread the batter, wiping the inside of the cake ring. Bake until golden brown, or for 30–35 minutes. Test with a knife that it is baked through.
10. Sprinkle sugar on top, cover with a sheet of parchment paper, and turn it upside down. Cover with a baking sheet to prevent it from drying out.

Chocolate bottom without flour

A moist and tasty bottom suitable for rich chocolate cakes. In France it is known as *bisquit chocolat sans farine*.

5 oz dark chocolate (125 g), preferably Valrhona Grand Cru Guanaja 70 %
2 tbsp unsalted butter (30 g)
about 2 tbsp egg yolks (20 g)
4 1/2 oz, or about 4–5, egg whites (125 g)
5 g lemon juice (1 tsp)
a bare ¼ cup sugar (45 g)

1. Preheat oven to 360° F (180° C). Trace two circles, 9 inches in diameter, onto sheets of parchment paper.
2. Finely chop the chocolate and heat to a temperature of 125° F (50–55° C). Stir in the butter with a whisk, followed by the egg yolks, to form a smooth ganache.
3. Beat the egg whites and lemon juice at medium speed with a third of the sugar to a meringue. Add the remaining sugar, increase the speed and whip to a firm meringue.
4. Fold the chocolate ganache into the meringue with a rubber spatula and pour into a pastry bag.
5. Pipe out two bottoms, 9 inches in diameter, from the center outwards.
6. Bake until golden brown, about 15 minutes, and cool on an oven rack.

Swiss roll bottom

The international name for a jelly roll cake bottom is *Swiss roll,* since the Swiss lay claim to its invention. In France we called it, suitably, a *bisquit roulé*.

The bottoms may be either warm beaten or cold beaten; optionally, the yolks and whites may be beaten separately.

For Swiss rolls, increase the amount of sugar and decrease the flour. Apply the following proportions: one egg (50 g) to 3 tbsp sugar (35 g) to ¼ cup flour (30 g). For a lighter bottom, you may add 5–7 g baking powder, but this will cause it to dry out sooner. For a crustier consistency, substitute half the flour with potato or corn starch.

The batter is spread out to a thickness of ½ inch onto a sheet with a baking mat, paper, or linen.

Troubleshooting Swiss rolls

• If your Swiss roll bottoms are dry, either your oven temperature is too low or they have been in the oven for too long. Or, perhaps they have had to cool on the same sheet they were baked on. Bake at high heat, 450–480° F (230–250° C), sprinkle sugar on top, and turn onto a sheet of parchment paper. Immediately turn them onto a cold baking sheet to cool.
• If your bottoms have lumps of flour, you have either neglected to sift the flour, or you have folded the flour carelessly.

- If your bottoms are flat, you have waited too long before getting them into the oven, and your batter has had time to collapse. Or, you have overbeaten the eggs, which have lost their volume.

If they are stored right, wrapped in plastic film, Swiss roll bottoms can be frozen or refrigerated, and then rolled without cracking.

Classic Swiss roll
9 oz, or about 5, eggs (250 g)
¾ cup + 1 tbsp sugar (160 g)
1 tbsp natural vanilla sugar (15 g)
1 ¼ cup flour (150 g)

1. Preheat oven to 450–480° F (230–250° C).
2. Sift the flour onto a sheet of parchment paper.
3. Beat the eggs and sugars to foam, about 10 minutes. The egg mixture must not be overbeaten, that is, the air bubbles in the batter must not burst, or the Swiss roll will end up too flat and compact.
4. Fold in the flour with a rubber spatula.
5. Spread the batter to a thickness of ½ inch onto a baking sheet.
6. Bake until golden brown for 7–8 minutes.
7. Sprinkle sugar on top and turn immediately onto a sheet of parchment paper covering a cold baking sheet, to prevent it from drying out.

Swiss roll as baked at confectionery school in Uppsala
This recipe is similar to the one above, but has a thicker consistency.

7 oz, or about 4, eggs (210 g)
1 1/2 oz, or about 2, egg yolks (40 g)
¾ cup sugar (150 g)
1 tbsp natural vanilla sugar (15 g)
1 cup + 1 tbsp flour (135 g)

Swiss rolls can be frozen or refrigerated for garnishing

Baked bisquit joconde.

later.

Hazelnut bottom

According to the classic Swiss wisdom, using twice as much egg yolk to egg white results in a velvety inner cream. Josef Mattle at the Richemont School sent me to learn firsthand at the Pallas Hotel in Luzern, where we made ice cream cakes with this outstanding bottom.

One baking sheet

6 1/2 oz, or about 6, egg whites (180 g)
1 cup flour (125 g)
4 ½ oz finely ground roasted nuts (125 g)
8 1/2 oz, or about 12, egg yolks (240 g)
¼ cup water (60 g)
1/3 cup sugar (65 g)
¾ cup + 2 tbsp sugar (175 g)
2 tsp lemon juice (10 g)

1. Preheat oven to 450° F (230° C).
2. Sift the flour onto a sheet of paper and mix in the nuts.
3. Beat the egg yolks, water and 1/3 cup sugar for 10 minutes to a firm foam.
4. Beat the egg whites, ¾ cup + 2 tbsp sugar, and lemon juice to a firm meringue.
5. Fold the yolk foam into the meringue with a rubber spatula, followed by the ground nuts.
6. Pour the batter onto a sheet, and bake for 12 minutes until baked through. Test with a toothpick.
7. Turn onto a paper sprinkled with sugar.

Bisquit joconde

This French almond bottom will stay moist longer, it is pliable, and it has become a modern confectionery staple.

2 baking sheets

6½ oz almond flour (175 g)
1¾ cups confectioners' sugar (175 g)
9 oz, or about 5, eggs (250 g)
6 tbsp flour (50 g)
3 tbsp unsalted butter (40 g)
11 oz, or about 11 oz, egg whites (325 g)
1 tsp lemon juice (5 g)

6 tbsp sugar (80 g)

1. Preheat oven to 440° F (225° C).
2. Prepare a tpt by blending the almond flour and confectioners' sugar in a blender or food processor.
3. Beat the eggs along with the tpt for 10 minutes with an electric mixer.
4. Sift the flour onto a sheet of paper. Melt the butter.
5. Beat the egg whites, lemon juice and sugar to a firm meringue.
6. Fold the egg and tpt batter into the meringue with a rubber spatula, followed by the sifted flour.
7. Carefully stir the butter with a scoop of the batter, and fold it into the batter with a rubber spatula.
8. Spread out evenly with a palette knife.
9. Bake for 7–8 minutes. Remove the sheets from the oven, and immediately lift off the bottoms to prevent them from drying out, since the baking process will continue until cool.
10. Sprinkle with plenty of confectioners' sugar, lay on parchment and cool completely.

If wrapped well, this bottom will keep for several weeks

Pâte à cigarette: thinly spreading sugarpaste onto a non-stick baking mat or linen towel.

in the freezer.

Two-colored charlotte bisquit

This recipe was given me by master pastry chef Jean Millet at the Pâtissérie Millet on rue de Saint Dominique in Paris. This bottom is suitable for lining cake and pastry rings. You will have no problem doubling or halving the recipe.

2 baking sheets

6 oz almond flour (150 g)
1½ cups confectioners' sugar (150 g)
3 1/2 oz, or about 2, eggs (100 g)
5 1/2 oz, or about 8, egg yolks (160 g)
¾ cup sugar (150 g)
8 oz, or about 8, egg whites (240 g)
5 g lemon juice (1 tsp)
½ cup sugar (100 g)
1¼ cup corn starch (145 g)
1¼ oz cocoa powder (35 g), preferably Valrhona 20/22

1. Preheat oven to 425° F (220° C).
2. Blend a tpt, that is, almond flour and confectioners' sugar, in a food processor or blender.
3. Beat the tpt with an electric mixer along with the eggs, egg yolks and ¾ cup sugar for 10 minutes to a firm foam.
4. Beat the egg whites, lemon juice and ½ cup sugar to a firm meringue.
5. Fold the egg mixture into the meringue with a rubber spatula. Pour 2 1/3 cups of the batter (550 g) into a second mixing bowl.
6. Sift ¾ cup of the corn starch (90 g) and fold into the first bowl with a rubber spatula.
7. Sift ½ cup of the corn starch (55 g) and the cocoa powder, and fold into the second bowl with a rubber spatula.
8. Pour the batters into separate pastry bags, and pipe them diagonally next to each other, alternating white and brown, until the sheet is covered. Do likewise on the second sheet with the rest of the batter.
9. Bake both sheets for 7–8 minutes. Cool on an oven

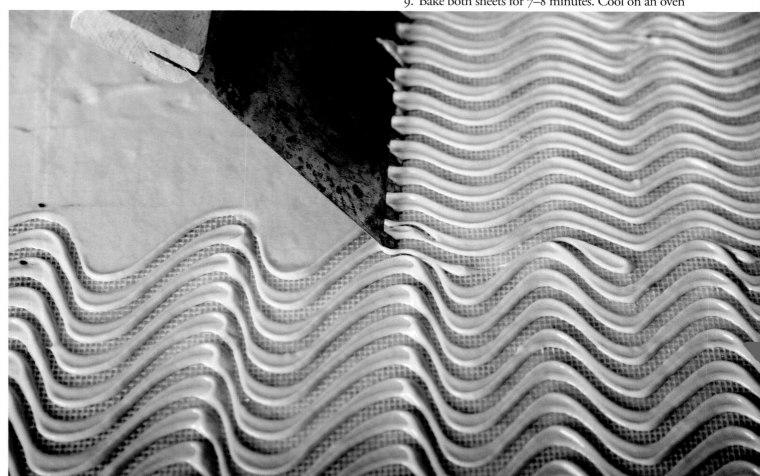

rack.

Chocolate almond bottom

This delicious and moist bottom is suitable for a filling of orange fromage or chocolate mousse, see the Messina cake on page 174.

1 baking sheet

4 oz almond paste (100 g) 50/50
3 1/2 oz, or about 5, egg yolks (100 g)
½ cup sugar (100 g)
6 oz dark chocolate (150 g), preferably
    Valrhona Grand cru
Guanaja 70 %
2/3 cup butter (150 g)
6 oz, or about 6, egg whites (175 g)
¼ cup sugar (50 g)
1 tsp lemon juice (5 g)
barely 2/3 cup flour (75 g)

1. Preheat oven to 450° F (230° C).
2. Warm the almond paste in a microwave oven and, with your hand, mix in the egg yolks until smooth.
3. With an electric mixer, beat the batter along with ½ cup sugar until stiff.
4. Sift the flour onto a sheet of paper. Melt the butter and chocolate together to a temperature of 125° F (50° C).
5. Beat the egg white along with the lemon juice and ¼ cup sugar to a stiff meringue.
6. Fold the yolk foam into the meringue along with the melted butter and chocolate, followed by the flour, with a rubber spatula until smooth.
7. Spread the batter evenly with a palette knife onto a baking mat or linen, and bake until golden brown for 7–8 minutes.
8. Sprinkle some sugar on top and immediately transfer the bottoms to a cold sheet.

Plain or chocolate almond bottom

1 baking sheet

1/3 cup unsalted butter (80 g)
3/4 cup + 1 tbsp flour (100 g)
1½ tsp baking powder (8 g)
6 oz almond paste (160 g) 50/50,
    see the recipe on page 37
1 3/4 oz, or about 1, egg (50 g)
4 oz, or about 6, egg yolks (120 g)
6 tbsp sugar (80 g)
6 oz, or about 6, egg whites (175 g)
1 tsp lemon juice (5 g)
a bare 1/3 cup sugar (60 g)

For the chocolate variant, replace ¼ cup of the flour (25 g) with an equal amount of cocoa powder, preferably Valrhona 20/22.

1. Preheat oven to 450° F (230° C).
2. Melt the butter and set aside.
3. Sift the flour and baking powder (optionally, along with the cocoa for a chocolate bottom) onto a sheet of paper.
4. Heat the almond paste in the oven until warm and soft.
5. Using your hand, mix in the whole egg until smooth.
6. Add the egg yolks and 6 tbsp sugar and beat for 10 minutes to a firm foam.
7. Beat the egg whites, lemon juice and one-third of the bare 1/3 sugar to a meringue in a perfectly clean metal mixing bowl. Increase the speed and add another one-third of the sugar, and finally the last one-third.
8. Beat to a firm meringue.
9. With a large rubber spatula, carefully fold the almond/egg mixture into the meringue, followed by the flour and baking powder (and, optionally, the cocoa for a chocolate bottom), so that the batter does not lose volume.
10. Stir the melted butter with a large spoonful of the batter, and fold into the rest.
11. Spread the batter evenly with a palette knife onto a baking mat or sheet of parchment paper.
12. Bake until golden brown, about 8–9 minutes and turn them out skin side down onto a sheet of parchment paper sprinkled with sugar.
13. Cool for one hour and carefully remove the parchment paper.

Meringue

The recipe for a classic meringue comes originally from Mehringen in Switzerland, where meringue cookies topped with chocolate sauce are very popular. The royal chef Werner Vögeli loved Swiss meringue as much as his compatriots did.

Many different types of meringue are used in cakes. Classic, so-called French, meringue should contain twice as much sugar as egg white by weight.

When beating meringues, always use clean bowls. Always wash your mixing bowls with 2 tbsp acetic acid mixed with 1 tsp salt, and rinse in cold water. Always use bowls of stainless steel or copper not lined with tin, but never plastic bowls.

Make sure that the eggs are completely separated, and that the egg whites have no trace of yolk (we call these goldfish). Egg yolks contain the fat that hinders foaming.

The best results are obtained with egg whites that have been airing in the refrigerator for a few days.

Egg whites may be frozen, but they keep in the refrigerator at least a week. Before freezing egg yolks, however, add 10 % sugar and beat gently. Without sugar, yolks become grainy and useless for baking.

Egg whites can be whisked to as much as eight times their volume, especially if you use a copper mixing bowl and a balloon whisk (see the illustration).

Copper produces a creamy, stable foam of maximum volume that is less likely to unfold.

Adding something sour, such as lemon juice, acetic acid, or vinegar, will affect the pH of the egg white and firm it up during beating. Pastry chefs often add a pinch of cream of tartar or citric acid. Expect to use ½ tsp lemon juice (2 ml) or 1/8 tsp cream of tartar (½ g) per egg white. Add the acid just before beating. Traditionally, chefs would add salt when the eggs were fresh, in order to obtain a frothy meringue; but salt, in fact, breaks down the albumin and extends the beating time.

Cold egg whites result in greater volume than those at room temperature.

Troubleshooting meringue

- If the meringue does not swell to foam, either there was a trace of yolk in the egg whites or the mixing bowl was not sufficiently clean. Or, the sugar might have been added too quickly. Beat at medium speed and increase towards the end.

Cold-beaten meringue (French meringue)

5 oz, or about 5, egg whites (150 g)
1½ tsp lemon juice (7 g)
6 + 6 tbsp sugar (75 + 75 g)
1½ cups confectioners' sugar (150 g)
sugar for sprinkling, for a crunchy surface

1. Preheat oven to 212° F (100° C) and trace three circles, 9 inches in diameter, onto sheets of parchment paper.
2. Beat the egg whites and lemon juice until the foam starts to rise.
3. Gradually add 6 tbsp sugar and beat by hand with large strokes or with an electric beater at medium speed. Sprinkle in the remaining sugar while beating and increase to high speed. Beat to a firm meringue foam.
4. Sift the confectioners' sugar and fold it into the foam with a rubber spatula.
5. Pour the meringue into a pastry bag. Pipe the meringue from the center and outwards until the tracings are full, and sprinkle sugar on top.
6. Bake the meringues for 90 minutes until they feel dry, light and airy. If they do not feel done, leave them in the oven until they are dry.

Store the bottoms in a sealed tin to keep them from going soft.

For a Swedish mocha cake, the meringue bottoms are baked at 265° F (130° C) until light brown and without a chalky consistency. Caramelization of the sugar in the meringue gives the cake its character.

Folding the sifted confectioners' sugar for a French meringue..

Warm-beaten meringue (Swiss meringue)

This meringue is usually used for flaming fruit parfaits, and certain chocolate mousses. A Swiss meringue will not run at room temperature when piped onto a cake, as a French meringue will.

Meringue mixture for one tart

7 oz, or about 6–7, egg whites (200 g)
5 cups confectioners' sugar (480 g)
2 tsp lemon juice (10 g)

1. Pour the egg whites, confectioners' sugar and le-mon juice into a metal bowl, or the top of a double boiler.
2. Beat until smooth.
3. Set the bowl over a pot of simmering water, or a double boiler.
4. Beat thoroughly until the batter reaches a tempera-ture of 125–140°F (50–s60°C).
5. Beat the meringue cold with an electric beater at low speed or gently by hand. The meringue should turn very stiff.
6. Pipe or spread onto the pastry, which is then flamed in a hot oven, 450–475°F (230–250°C). Alternatively, bake as for a cold-beaten meringue.

This meringue can be frozen unbaked.

Italian meringue

Mostly used for fruit mousses to make them light and fluffy.

5 oz, or about 5, egg whites (150 g)
1 tsp lemon juice (5 g)
1 ¼ cup sugar (250 g)
1/3 cup water (75 g)
¼ cup sugar (50 g)

1. Beat the chilled egg whites with the lemon juice and half of the 1 ¼ cup sugar at low speed until the foam starts to rise, add the other half of the sugar in sprinkles, and beat to a firm foam.
2. Dissolve ¼ cup sugar in boiling water in a saucepan while constantly wiping the inside edges with a brush and water. Heat to 250°F (122°C), or perform the cold-water candy test, see the illustration on page 35.
3. Pour the boiling syrup gradually into the egg white foam, while beating constantly, then reduce speed and beat until the meringue is cool.

Try mixing in mousses of mashed fruit, cream, and gelatin. Italian meringue freezes well and can be thawed when needed.

Almond meringue or nut meringue (Japonaise bottoms)

Unblanched almonds and raw hazelnuts will leave a powerful flavor. For a milder flavor of almond, blanch the almonds first. Personally, I prefer raw almonds and hazelnuts.

For a stabler bottom, you could add some flour, but you may lose some of the delicacy of texture. They should always be baked through and stored dry to maintain their brittleness.

Pastry chefs often store them in heating cupboards.

The bottoms may be spread with a palette knife or piped through a pastry bag. For a stabler bottom, add 10 g flour to the tpt.

Three bottoms, 9 inches in diameter

¾ cup + 2 tbsp sugar (175 g)
4 oz finely ground almonds with skins
   or hazelnuts (100 g)
4 1/2 oz, or about 4, egg whites (125 g)
1 tsp lemon juice (5 g)

1. Preheat oven to 340°F (170°C).
2. Trace three rings, 9 inches in diameter, onto sheets of parchment paper.

Cold-water candy test for Italian meringue: Dip your fingers in cold water. Grab a lump and chill it in the cold water until you can form a soft ball out of the syrup.

3. Prepare a tpt by blending ½ cup of the sugar and almonds (or other nuts) in a blender or food processor.
4. Beat the egg whites, lemon juice, and the remaining sugar to foam at medium speed, then increase the speed until the meringue is firm.
5. Fold the tpt into the meringue with a rubber spatula, and spoon or pipe out the bottoms.
6. Bake until golden brown and slightly brittle for 30 minutes. Air the oven occasionally during baking.
7. Turn onto a new sheet of parchment paper to even out the tops and to remove the bottom sheet.

Store in a dry place.

Walnut dacquoise bottom
This makes a softer meringue than the japonaise, which is brittler.

You can vary this recipe simply by replacing the walnuts with pistachios, pecans, etc., or by using almonds without skins.

Three bottoms, 9 inches in diameter

4½ oz shelled walnuts (120 g)
2 oz almonds with skins (50 g)
¾ cup + 2 tbsp sugar (170 g)
4 1/2 oz, or about 4, egg whites (125 g)
1 tsp lemon juice (5g)
6 tbsp sugar (80 g)

1. Preheat oven to 350° F (175° C).
2. Trace three rings, 9 inches in diameter, onto sheets of parchment paper.
3. Prepare a tpt by finely blending ¾ cup + 2 tbsp sugar, almonds, and walnuts in a blender or food processor.
4. Beat the egg whites, lemon juice and 6 tbsp sugar to foam at medium speed, then increase the speed until the meringue is firm.
5. Fold the tpt into the meringue with a rubber spatula.
6. Pour the mixture into a pastry bag.
7. Pipe three bottoms from the center of the circle and outwards.
8. Bake until golden brown, or for 15–20 minutes. The bottoms should be delicate, but elastic.

To prevent them from drying out, always use (or freeze) the bottoms straight from the oven.

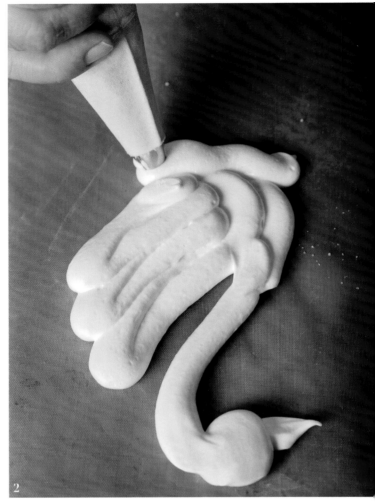

1 Pipe the French meringue cake bottoms.
2 Pipe a meringue swan, see *Spanische Windtorte* on page 206.
3 A flat nozzle is used for piping small meringues.

BASIC RECIPES

Sugar syrup

Soaking bottoms in a sugar syrup flavored with spirits, fruit juice, or coffee makes a cake that will stay succulent. A full recipe will weigh 22 oz (640 g), a half recipe 11 oz (320 g). Measured with a hydrometer, this syrup will have a density of 32° Baumé.

1 cup water (250 g)
1 2/3 cup sugar (340 g)
¼ cup corn syrup (60 g)

1. Bring the water and sugar to a boil in a saucepan, about 220°F (105°C). Dip a brush in cold water and brush down the crystals that are sticking to the inside of the saucepan. Covering with the lid ajar will achieve the same effect. Skim with a tea strainer.
2. Add the syrup and bring once more to a boil.
3. Pour into a very clean glass jar with a lid.

Storage: Sugar syrup will keep refrigerated for two weeks.

Brushing the inside of the pot with water.

Almond paste

Store-bought almond paste contains preservatives, corn syrup, and the occasional apricot pit – to keep the price down – along with Californian almonds.

Genuine almond paste should consist of 50 % almonds and 50 % sugar, and nothing else.

Most pastry chefs today buy industrially produced almond paste, which usually contains 10–11 % water. The better alternative is, of course, to make your own.

Using an aromatic almond is important, such as a Spanish macarona almond or an Italian almond from Bari. California almonds are, unfortunately, less aromatic. Bitter almonds may also be used as spice to enhance the nutty flavor.

The first almond paste I ever made consisted of two pounds of Spanish sweet almonds and two ounces of bitter almonds. The nuts were blanched and blended with 2 ¼ pounds of sugar, then milled to a fragrant almond paste.

9 oz sweet almonds (250 g), preferably Spanish
1 ¼ cup sugar (250 g)
Optionally, replace 1/3 oz (10 g) of the sweet almonds with an equal amount of bitter almonds

1. Blanch the almonds in plenty of water for a few minutes.
2. Rinse them in cold water and drain.
3. Remove the skins.
4. Blend the almonds and sugar for a few minutes to a fine almond paste.
5. Wrap the paste in plastic and let it stand overnight. Store in the refrigerator.

Tant pour tant (tpt)

Tant pour tant means "equal amounts", 50 % nuts and 50 % sugar, the identical proportions for almond paste. The difference is that here the almonds are not blanched, and are therefore less moist than those used in almond paste. If you prefer to make a tpt with blanched almonds, dry them in the oven after blanching. Tpt can be made from various kinds of nuts: walnuts, pistachios, hazelnuts, pecans, etc.

Almond flour

Pastry chefs usually purchase commercially available almond flour, which is as good as home-made. But for those who wish to make their own, it is not difficult.

1. Preheat the oven to 212°F (100°C).
2. Blanch the almonds and let them dry for one hour on a sheet in the oven.
3. Blend the almonds to a fine powder in a blender. Sift the powder to break down any lumps. Store in a can with a lid. It is simpler to make a tpt with sugar and almonds, since the sugar prevents the almond oils from creeping.

Rolled marzipan

The word marzipan is derived from the Italian *marzapane*. It is used in various cakes, but most famously the princess cake. These days most confectioners purchase rolled marzipan commercially. The downside is that no matter where you buy your pastries, it all tastes alike. Naturally, you may choose to buy marzipan at the store, but the difference lies in the fact that home-made marzipan contains no preservatives or additives.

This is how we made rolled marzipan when I was an apprentice in Malmö:

2½ cups confectioners' sugar (250 g)
1 lb almond paste 50/50 (500 g)
½ cup corn syrup (100–150 g)
optionally, food coloring, preferably natural

1. Sift the confectioners' sugar and warm the almond paste in a microwave oven to a temperature of 30° C (there were obviously no microwave ovens back then; we warmed it in a baking oven). The heat inhibits the almond oil from creeping out into the mixture, which would occur if it were cold.
2. Blend everything in a food processor to a smooth paste and, optionally, add food coloring.
3. Cover with plastic wrap and let stand for a few hours.
4. Roll out the marzipan with some sifted confectioners' sugar to 1/8 inch thick, after which it is suitable for cake covers or bottoms. Never use wheat flour when rolling the marzipan, since it might start to rise.

IMPORTANT!

If the marzipan feels dry, moisten it with a little corn syrup or sugar syrup.
Storage: Marzipan may be stored well wrapped in the refrigerator. But always bring it to room temperature before rolling out to avoid cracking.

Figure marzipan

For marzipan roses and figures:

1/3 oz bitter almonds (10 g)
11 oz sweet almonds (300 g)
4 cups confectioners' sugar (400 g)
7 tbsp corn syrup (100 g)

DAY 1

1. Preheat oven to 212° F (100° C).
2. Blanch the almonds and let them dry for one hour on a sheet in the oven.
3. Blend the almonds to a fine powder in a food processor or blender.
4. Stir in the confectioners' sugar, add the corn syrup, and blend the marzipan in a food processor (preferably with serrated knives) to an almond paste. The paste should feel warm, about 120° F (50° C).
5. Immediately enclose in a plastic bag and let it stand for 24 hours.

DAY 2

6. Knead the marzipan until smooth and, optionally, add food coloring. If it feels dry, moisten it with a little corn syrup or sugar syrup; if it is too soft, add some sifted confectioners' sugar.

Rolling out the marzipan with confectioners' sugar, not flour.

Praline Paste

This basic paste that is mainly used for praline production is also suitable for cake fillings.

2 cups sugar (400 g)
4/5 cup water (200 g)
1/2 vanilla bean
1 1/3 cup roasted and unpeeled almonds or roasted and peeled hazelnuts (500 g)

1. Bring sugar, water and the halved vanilla bean to a boil at 240° F (115° C).
2. Add the roasted nuts and boil until they begin to make cracking noise.
3. Stir using a spatula until the sugar begins to whiten, that is to crystallize, and "die".
4. Caramelize the mixture until it's golden brown.
5. Pour onto parchment paper and let cool.
6. Crush the solidified mixture and run it in a food processor or a blender, until it's a loose and oily substance with a temperature of 160° F (70° C).
7. Store the mixture in a jar in the fridge.

Nut Paste

For flavoring mousse.

1 1/3 cups hazelnuts, preferably Italian from Piemonte or Spanish (200 g)

1. Roast the hazelnuts in the oven at 390° F (200° C), until they are quite dark and remove the shells.
2. Run them in a food processor or a blender at a temperature of 160° F (70° C) into an oily paste.
3. Store the paste in a jar in the fridge.

Pistachio Paste

Try to get hold of pistachios from Italy; the Sicilian ones are the best, with a nice green color.

1 1/3 cups pistachios, preferably from Sicily (200 g)

1. Run the pistachios in a food processor or a blender into a paste that has a temperature of 160° F (70° C).
2. Store the paste in a jar in the fridge.

Quick Puff Pastry (Pate feuilleté rapide)

You don't have to make traditional pastry dough for cakes and pastries, as it usually rises too much and the cake becomes too flaky. Quick puff pastry is smaller in the bite and crisper for cakes and pastries. This dough doesn't shrink as much as classic puff pastry either.

3 1/2 cup bread flour (500 g)
2 tsp salt, preferably fleur de sel (10 g)
2 1/5 cups unsalted butter (500 g)
1 1/2 oz, or about 2, eggs (40 g)
4/5 cup water (200 g/about 2 dl)
2 tsp lemon juice or white wine vinegar (10 g)

1. Sift flour and salt on a pastry table or a bench. Make a circle out of the flour (or pour it into a food processor).
2. Cut the cold butter into sugar cube-sized pieces and place them in the middle.
3. Mix butter, flour and salt using your fingertips or in a food processor, until the butter begins to crumble. Add egg yolks, water and lemon juice or vinegar.
4. Work the mixture into a concoction, but note that there should still be lumps of butter in the dough.
5. Wrap the dough in plastic film and leave for at least 30 minutes in the refrigerator.
6. Roll out two three-folds, the same way you would when making traditional puff pastry.
7. Leave in the refrigerator for another 30 minutes.
8. Roll out another two three-folds and leave for at least 30 minutes in the refrigerator.

Storage: You can store the dough in the fridge for a few days. It can last for weeks in the freezer.

Fold a traditional three-fold.

It's important that there are some lumps of butter left in order for the dough to be laminated in the right way and for it to become crunchy the way puff pastry should be. This method is widely used in America, and this is why the dough often is called American puff pastry.

The lemon juice or the vinegar and the cold water delays the development of gluten and it helps to avoid a dough that is too elastic. Steam is formed between the layers of butter and dough when cooked. The steam melts the butter, which consequently prevents the layers of dough from sticking together. The protein (the gluten) coagulates and the starch gelatinizes (solidifies). The encapsulated water that vaporizes causes the dough to expand and rise.

Traditional Shortcrust Pastry 1-2-3
This dough is well suited as a basis for cake bottoms and to line molds with. Remember not to overwork the pastry, the ingredients should only be mixed together. One can certainly make the dough in a food processor with good results as well, but I prefer the old method that I learned when I was an apprentice. If you want to refine the pastry, you can replace the 2 teaspoons of sugar with pure vanilla extract and add zest from half a lemon for more flavor, but I think it's perfectly fine the way it is.

1/2 cup sugar (100 g)
3/4 cup butter (200 g)
2 1/2 cups all purpose flour (300 g)
1 3/4 oz, or about 1, egg (50 g)

1. Sift flour over the pastry table and shape a circle of flour.
2. Add the soft butter and sugar in the middle and work the ingredients together using your hands. Add the egg.
3. Work the flour in from the sides and knead it all into a dough. Don't overwork the dough or it will become tough.
4. Wrap the dough in plastic film and let it solidify in the refrigerator.

Mazarin Bottom
This cake filling was named after French Cardinal Mazarin, although mazarin does not exist in France. The French however use *crème d'amande,* a similar filling that's made with almond meal instead of almond paste.

Use room temperature ingredients to prevent the paste from curdling. If it does curdle however, let stand at room temperature and wait a while before stirring it back together and the problem is solved.

If you want you can add a thin uncooked shortcrust pastry in the bottom of the ring, to make the cake sturdier.

This moist bottom is ideal for wedding cakes that need to be durable.

Two 2x9-inch cake ring or one springform pan

17 2/3 oz almond paste 50/50 (500 g)
1 cup butter (250 g)
9 oz, or about 5, eggs (250 g)
1/4 cup corn starch or all-purpose flour (25 g)

1. Preheat the oven to 375° F (190° C).
2. Gradually dissolve the almond paste with one third of the butter into a lump-free substance using a blender or your hands.
3. Add the eggs one by one to form a smooth paste. Finally knead in the flour.
4. Add it to two cake rings or one springform pan. Bake bottoms until golden brown for about 35 minutes. Make sure they are thoroughly baked by using the tip of a knife or a thermometer. They are done when they have reached a temperature of 185–195° F (85–90° C).
5. Let cool in the cake ring placed on a baking grid.

Petits-choux
The French name for this dough is *Pâte à choux,* which means head cabbage dough. That stems from the dough swelling when baked, which makes it resemble a head cabbage. Marie Antoine Careme, who was the greatest pastry chef and kitchen manager of that era, originally published the recipe in 1815 in the book *Le Pâtissiér Royal.*

The dough is distinctive, as you cook it to make the flour swell. The baked goods are consequently used as vessels for fillings, which are useful for both sweet and savory pastries.

Whenever the dough is roasted during cooking, the starch in the flour swells and part of the protein coagulates, which prevents the steam from escaping while subsequently baking it. The steam that is generated during baking is instead contributing to the increase in volume – the pastry will rise. Make sure that the oven ventilator is open at the end to allow steam to evaporate.

The ideal temperature of the roasted concoction is 175° F (80° C), so use a thermometer to check the temperature of the dough.

1 cup + 2 1/2 tbsp all-purpose flour (140 g)
1/2 cup water (125 g)
1/2 cup milk, 3% (125 g)
1 tsp salt (5 g), preferably fleur de sel
1 tsp sugar (5 g)

1/2 cup unsalted butter (110 g)
9 oz, or about 5, eggs (250 g)

1. Sift the flour onto a sheet of paper.
2. Heat the water, milk, salt, sugar and butter in a large, heavy-bottomed saucepan. Bring the mixture to a boil while stirring and remove pan from stove.
3. Add all of the flour at once and stir vigorously using a wooden spoon.
4. Place the saucepan back on the stove and roast the mixture while constantly stirring, until the batter is released from the edges of the pan and forms into the shape of a ball.
5. Let the dough cool for 5 minutes.
6. Preheat the oven to 435° F (225° C). Place a baking sheet in the oven to warm up.
7. Stir in eggs one at a time. Stir well between each egg. Once the eggs are added, the dough should have a smooth and creamy consistency.
8. Pipe pastry with a flat or a fluted nozzle on parchment paper or a pastry cloth with ample spacing.
9. Bake the cakes and keep the ventilation closed until the pastries start to get color, have risen and are firm.
10. Open the oven ventilation and bake until pastries start to develop a nice color and feel porous and light when you lift them, a total of about 20–35 minutes depending on size. If you take out the pastries too soon, they will collapse.
11. Let cool on a rack.

Petits-choux can be frozen baked or unbaked.

1 Add the sifted flour.
2 Toast the mixture.
3 Add the eggs one at a time while stirring.

1 Pipe walnut-sized balls for the Rubinstein cake.
2 Pipe circles for Paris-Brest.
3 Finished rings.

Fondant

Fondant means melting in French. The sugar crystals become smaller when tablering. The glucose allows the maltose and sucrose to sprout, the fondant gets a smooth texture and small crystals are shaped. Some recipes also add cream of tartar, which keeps the fondant fluid for making chocolates. It is heated to 165°F (74°C) for pralines, such as peppermint patties, and to 95–105°F (35–40°C) for glazing of cakes, pastries and petit fours.

If you heat the fondant too much when glazing it, it will lose its shine.

Fondant is used to glaze mazarines, petit-fours and cakes. It has a nicer shine than the so-called water glaze, which only consists of water and confectioners' sugar.

It's important to first brush the pastry with a thin layer of apricot preserve before glazing it, see page 45. This will prevent the pastry from absorbing the water from the fondant and dying, that is, losing its luster.

about 3 cups

4/5 cup water (200 g/2 dl)
2 1/2 cup sugar (500 g)
2/5 cups glucose (100 g)

1. Bring water and sugar to a boil in a saucepan while constantly covering the inside of the pan with cold water. Remove any foam with a tea strainer.
2. Add the glucose and boil on high heat to 245° F (118°C).
3. Immediately cool saucepan in a bowl filled with cold water to stop the ebullition.
4. Pour the syrup onto a water-drenched surface, preferably a marble slab or a clean kitchen sink. Splash the syrup with cold water to prevent a crust from forming on the surface.
5. After about 5 minutes, when the mixture has cooled down, work it by using a painting spatula until the frosting turns white.

Storage: Place the frosting in a glass jar and splash the surface with water to prevent it from drying out. Cover it with a tight-fitting lid and store in refrigerator. It will keep in the fridge for several weeks. If the fondant is going to be used for glazing, heat it to 95–105°F (35–40°C) and dilute with simple syrup if needed, see page 37.

Neutral Gelatin Glaze for Cakes

This jelly is tasty and natural in its flavor and easy to work with. You can also make a so-called pandan jelly with pectin or agar-agar. The possibilities are endless.

If you want to make a smaller amount, the recipe can be halved, although you can store jelly in the freezer. The recipe makes about about 1 quart.

Apple Jelly

4 cups water (1 kg)
2 pounds of green apples (1 kg), tangy and immature
1 large lemon
4/5 oz gelatin leaves (24 g/about 12 leaves)
2 cup sugar (400 g)
1/2 cup glucose (120 g)

1. Bring the water to a boil with squeezed lemon juice and add the rinsed and halved apples.
2. Bring to a boil and let the apples simmer for about 30 minutes leaving the lid on, until they disintegrate.
3. Pour the fruit mixture into a fine sieve lined with a thin, water-soaked cloth and leave the fruit mixture to drain, to ensure that the juice is completely clear.
4. Soak the gelatin leaves in plenty of cold water for at least 10 minutes.
5. Bring the apple juice to a boil with the sugar and glucose and remove any foam. Take the saucepan off the stove.
6. Remove the gelatin from the water and add to saucepan including any water remaining on the leaves.
7. Stir until the gelatin is melted, pour the jelly into a bowl and cover with plastic film.

Storage: One week in the refrigerator, freeze if possible.

Usage: Melt the jelly to about 120°F (50°C), then cool until it nearly starts to solidify. Spread it over the berries on top of a frozen cake and smooth using a palette knife.

Fruit Jelly

Can be made with all kinds of fruit purées.

1/5 oz gelatin leaves (6 g/about 3 leaves), 1/3 oz for passion fruit (10 g/about 5 leaves)
4/5 cups fruit puree (200 g), e.g. raspberries, with 10% sugar
1/2 cup sugar (100 g)
3 tbsp glucose (40 g)

1. Soak the gelatin in plenty of cold water for at least 10 minutes.
2. Bring the purée and sugar to a boil and remove any foam.
3. Add the glucose and bring to boil once more. Remove the saucepan from the stove.
4. Remove the gelatin from the water and add to saucepan. Let any water remaining on the leaves follow.
5. Stir until gelatin is melted, pour the jelly in a bowl and cover with plastic film.

Storage: about one week in the fridge, but it can also be frozen. Usage: Heat the jelly to 95°F (35°C) before glazing.

Jam

If you want to add other jams and marmalades to your cakes than those found in this book, then check out my book, *Jam and Marmalade*. You will find lots of recipes in that one.

Raspberry Jam for Cakes

Clean the raspberries without rinsing them, to avoid losing too much juice. I don't want my jam filling to contain whole raspberries, because the cake bottoms would be ruined when applying the jam. Mix the berries first to avoid this scenario.

If you want to make strawberry jam for cakes, make it in the same manner, but replace the raspberries with sun-ripened strawberries.

Approximately 53 oz jam (1 1/2 kg)

36 oz raspberries (1 kg)
4 cups sugar (800 g)
5 1/4 tbsp lemon juice (75 g)

DAY 1
1. In a food processor or a blender, mix the raspberries with sugar and lemon juice for about 5 minutes. Cover with plastic film and marinate overnight.

DAY 2
2. Pour the mixture into a jam pan and bring to a boil, stirring constantly and brushing the inside of the pan with cold water to prevent sugar crystals. Occasionally stir with a spoon, until the jam is completely clear.
3. Boil to 221–223°F (105–106°C). At that point, the surface is usually a little wrinkled and the jam starts to become transparent. You can also do a jam test by dripping a small amount of jam on a cold plate. If it has hardened after about 1 minute it's ready, if not, continue to boil.
4. Immediately pour the jam into sterilized jars. Screw the lids on right away and turn the jars upside down.

DAY 3
Wash and label the jars.

Strained Apricot Jam

Strained apricot jam is suitable as a cake filling and for pastries. Add a little bitter almond to enhance the apricot flavor.

You can also use dried apricots; let them soak in lukewarm water overnight and drain. The rest of the recipe is made the same way as with fresh apricots. You will have approximately 1500 g of finished jam.

6 bitter almonds
2 2/3 pounds fresh apricots, ripe (2 1/5 pounds net)
1 1/4 cup water (300 g)
1 lemon, juice from the fruit
1 vanilla bean, preferably Bourbon
4 cups sugar (800 g)

DAY 1

1. Bring a little water to a boil and scald the almonds. Immediately place them in cold water and remove the shell.
2. Pound them into a paste in a mortar.
3. Bring 2 quarts of water to a boil and scald the apricots for about 1 minute. Immediately place them in cold water and remove the shell using a sharp knife. Cut them in half and remove the core.
4. Bring one and a quarter cups of water to a boil and add the blanched and peeled apricots, together with the lemon juice and bitter almond. Cover with a lid and cook for about 10 minutes, until the apricots are very soft.
5. Pour them into a blender and blend the fruit mixture in portions. Pass it through a sieve to yield a smooth purée.
6. Pour the purée back into the jam pan. Cut the vanilla bean lengthwise, scrape out the seeds with a small knife and put into the pan.
7. Add the sugar and boil while constantly stirring, remove any foam using a spoon. Brush the inside of the pot with cold water, to prevent sugar crystals.
8. Boil to 220° F (105°C), or perform the so-called spoon test. Drizzle some jam on a cold plate and let stand for 1 minute and if it has hardened, the jam is ready.
9. Immediately pour the mixture into sterilized jars and put the lids on at once. Turn the jars upside down.

DAY 2

Wash and dry the jars and label with the date.

Apricot Preserve

7 oz strained apricot jam (200 g), see page 44
1/5 cup lemon juice (50 g)
1/4 cup sugar (50 g)
1/5 cup water (50 g)

1. Bring all the ingredients to a boil. Simmer on low heat until the mixture turns into a thick jelly.
2. Do a jelly test by drizzling a droplet on a plate. Touch it after 1 minute; it should be firm and not stick to your skin.

Coffee Essence

When I started working in the pastry profession, coffee essence was something you always made from scratch. It was used for flavoring buttercream, cream, ice cream and parfait.

Above all, the filling provided the pastries with a lovely color. Use a large pot, because the caramel will rise in the pan as the sugar swells. The essence keeps for several years.

5 cups sugar (1 kg)
1/2 cup water (100 g)
2 cups extra strong coffee (500 g)

1. Bring sugar and water to a boil until it becomes black and it starts rising in the saucepan.
2. Stir in the strong hot coffee and boil it all until the sugar is dissolved.
3. Strain the essence and pour into a bottle.

When a droplet starts to form on the thermometer it's a sign of the jam being nearly ready.

French Buttercream for Cakes

1 1/4 cup sugar (250 g)
2/5 cup water (473 g)
1 vanilla pod (Tahiti or Bourbon)
5 1/2 oz, or about 8, egg yolks (160 g)
2 cups unsalted butter (500 g)

1. Bring sugar and water to a boil together with the vanilla seeds to 243° F (117° C).
2. Brush the inside edges of the pan using a brush dipped in cold water, to avoid sugar crystals. If you do not have a sugar thermometer you can perform the cold-water candy test, see page 35.
3. In the meantime, whisk the egg yolks to a foam in a food processor or with an electric hand mixer.
4. Add the syrup in a steady stream and whisk the egg foam until cold.
5. Add the butter and beat on low speed until you have a light and porous cream.

Lemon Curd (Lemon Cream)

This cream can be varied with passion fruit juice, orange, lime, elderflower, sea buckthorn, raspberries and cloudberries, the choices are endless. It's a classic pastry cream, as it makes a tasty filling, but you can also serve it on toast. My dear mother always made lemon curd for breakfast and afternoon tea.

1/6 oz gelatin leaves (4 g/about 2)
10 1/2 oz, or about 6, eggs (300 g)
3/4 cup sugar (150 g)
2/3 cup lemon juice (150 g)
3 lemons
3/4 cup sugar (150 g)
3/4 cup unsalted butter (200 g)

1. Soak the gelatin in plenty of cold water for at least 10 minutes.
2. Beat the eggs and three quarters of a cup of sugar until fluffy.
3. Wash and grate the lemon zest but only the outermost yellow parts. Squeeze out the juice from the lemons.
4. Bring the lemon juice, zest, three quarters of a cup of sugar and butter to boil in a saucepan. Add the egg foam and mix well.
5. Gently heat the cream while whisking, until it thickens and is brought to a boil. Remove the saucepan from the heat and whisk it until smooth.
6. Remove the gelatin from the water and add the cream. Let any water that remains on the leaves follow. Beat until melted.

7. Strain cream through a sieve.
8. Pout the mixture into jars and quickly cool them in a water bath. Store in refrigerator.

Caramel

2 1/2 cup sugar (500 g)
1 cup glucose (glucose syrup) (250 g)
4/5 cup water (200 g)

1. Boil to 310° F (155° C) while constantly drenching the inside of the pot using a brush.
2. Dip the pot in cold water before using the mixture, to stop the boiling.
3. Optionally embellish with color, preferably a natural vegetable color.

Vanilla Cream

Crème pâtissérie is the French term for vanilla cream, we call it pastry cream in Sweden. The first time the cream was mentioned in the history of confectioners was in the 1600s, in the book La Cuisine La Pâtissèrie Varenne.

This is one of the key creams that a confectioner should know how to make. It's often the last thing you make in the day, as it will be cold and ready to use the next day.

The cold vanilla cream should be pressed through a sieve before usage.

It is important to use a good, thick vanilla bean of the highest quality, preferably from Tahiti, which is my favorite.

You can also get a nice Bourbon Vanilla from Madagascar or Mexican vanilla. I usually use two vanilla beans per quart of vanilla cream.

Remember that a vanilla cream should be properly boiled, or the starch won't swell out and the cream will become loose. Vanilla cream doesn't keep for very long. When I was a boy, we used to pour it directly on to a cleaned marble top so that it would quickly cool and then we would spread it out until it cooled down.

2 cups milk (500 g) 3%
1 vanilla bean, preferably Tahiti
4 oz, or about 6, egg yolks (120 g)
2/3 cup sugar (125 g)
1/3 cup corn starch (40 g)
2 tbsp unsalted butter (25 g)

1. Pour the milk into a heavy-bottomed saucepan.
2. Cut the vanilla bean lengthwise. Scrape the seeds into the milk and also add the vanilla bean.
3. Bring the milk to a boil. Remove the saucepan from the heat and let stand for 10–15 minutes. Remove the vanilla bean.
4. Whisk egg yolks, sugar and cornstarch until light and fluffy in a bowl.
5. Pour the milk into the egg mixture while whipping. Whisk until mixture is completely smooth.
6. Pour the mixture back into the saucepan. Heat while carefully stirring with a whisk until the cream is properly boiling.
7. Add the butter. Remove the cream from heat and whisk it until smooth.
8. Pass the freshly boiled cream through a sieve into a shallow pan. Immediately cool the cream, preferably in an ice-cold water bath. The more rapid the cooling is, the longer it will keep. Cover the pan with plastic film and store in refrigerator until it's ready to use.

Storage: 1–2 days in refrigerator.

Whipping Cream

The requirements for whipped cream is that it should be easy to beat, it should double in volume and have a firm and balanced foam-like texture that doesn't turn into liquid. The fat content should be 40%, but many advocate that it should be 35%. Fat globules appear on the surface of the air bubbles during the whipping process, and the result of the whipping is that some of the flowing fat is pushed aside and the fat globules connect. If the temperature is too high, the fat will melt and the cream will become unwhippable.

The result of the whipping is entirely dependent on the cream being refrigerated, it should be below 46°F (8°C), but preferably 37–39°F (3–4°C).

The vessel that you use to whisk the cream in should be chilled and the whipping should be rapid so that the friction doesn't cause the temperature to rise.

The vessel should be at least twice the size of the amount of cream, as the air that is going into it causes the cream to increase in volume.

The flavoring of the cream should happen at the end of the whipping process. One third of a cup of sugar per quart of cream is ideal and you can also add a little pure vanilla extract or vanilla essence.

If you overwhip the cream, you can bring it to a boil and make ice cream or ganache out of it. Always store the cream in a cool place covered with plastic film, as it easily absorbs other flavors.

Gelatin

To ensure that your gelatin is a success, it should always be melted in a water bath so that it doesn't exceed 120°F (50°C), as a bad taste can arise and its ability to harden deteriorates. Jelly melts at about 86°F (30°C) and provides a comfortable mouthfeel at that temperature. I always melt gelatin in the microwave.

Gelatin sheets absorb 6 times their weight in water. Their binding capacity is measured in Bloom. Gold leaf gelatin weighs one twelfth of an ounce (2 g) (180/200 Bloom), silver gelatin weighs one tenth to one sixth of an ounce (3–5 g) and Bronze gelatin varies in weight. Try to get a hold of gold gelatin leaves to guarantee successful results. The gelatin that is sold in stores generally is gold gelatin.

Gelatin has many advantages when it comes to making mousse, fromage and cream, compared to other stabilizers such as agar-agar, locust vanilla bean gum etc.

In order for the gelatin to dissolve without lumping, it must first swell in cold water for about 10 minutes. Soak it in plenty of cold water for at least 10 minutes, preferably running water for a better taste. Remove the gelatin from the water and let any water remaining on the leaves follow into the mixture. Mix the melted gelatin rapidly, to prevent lumps.

The firmness may depend on what kind of gelatin you're using, but one leaf should make less than three and a half ounces of tasteless jelly. The acid may affect the firmness of it. Since gelatin is a protein, it can be split by proteases, which are protein-digesting enzymes. They exist in pineapple and kiwifruit, so if the mentioned fruits are raw, they should not be used in combination with gelatin. Even buckthorn and passion fruit purée can be difficult.

Fruit purée and whipped cream.

Finished mousse mixture.

It takes 6 hours before the gelatin in a mousse or a fromage sets properly.

You can stabilize mousse, cream and bavaroise with cocoa butter instead of gelatin. This makes the food more widely appealing, as gelatin is perceived as less appealing to vegetarians and certain religions. Cocoa butter gives the mousse a velvet-like texture, but with a shorter bite than the gelatin.

Fruit Mousse

These are general instructions for the preparation of fruit mousse. The ingredients are listed in each recipe.

1. If the fruit purée is frozen, slowly thaw it in the fridge.
2. Weigh all the ingredients according to the exact measurements.
3. Soak the gelatin leaves in plenty of cold water for at least 10 minutes, preferably use gold gelatin sheets.

4. In a chilled bowl, whip the cream on low speed to a foam that isn't too firm.
5. Make an Italian meringue, see page 34, or a Pâte à bombe, see page 51, depending on the recipe.
6. Allow the gelatin to drain and melt it in the microwave or on the stove to 110-120° F (45-50° C).
7. Mix the gelatin into the thawed fruit purée and optionally add lemon juice or liquor, depending on the recipe.
8. Add the whipped cream to the meringue or the Pâte à bomb and mix into a light and porous mousse.
9. Add one quarter of the cream mixture to the gelatin/fruit purée and mix until a smooth paste is formed. Turn it into the remaining cream mixture using a spatula.

Use the mousse as a cake filling right away, before the gelatin solidifies. Freeze it as quickly as possible.

Opéra Glaze

This is a classic glossy glaze that is used for the fantastic Opéra cake. You can find the recipe in my book Chocolate Passion.

This glaze should be cooked the day before, as the gloss will turn out better. If you need to use the glaze on the same day, add one soaked gelatin leaf to the cream before mixing it with the chocolate and the shine will last longer.

7 oz dark chocolate, preferably Valrhona Grand Cru
    Guanaja 70% (200 g)
1/3 cup milk 3% (75 g)
1 fl oz whipping cream 40% (35 g)
2 tbsp sugar (25 g)
3 1/2 tsp honey (25 g)
2 tbsp butter (25 g)
one gelatin leaf (optional)

1. Chop the chocolate finely and pour it into a bowl.
2. Bring the milk, whipped cream, sugar and honey to a boil and turn the boiling mixture over the chocolate. Stir the chocolate with a spoon until melted and use a hand blender to form an emulsion.
3. Add the room temperature butter and blend until melted.
4. Cover the bowl with plastic film. Leave at room temperature until the next day.
5. When ready to use, heat the glaze in a microwave or in a water bath to about 113°F (45°C).

Opéra Glaze with Milk Chocolate

For the Diplomat Cake on page 171.

This is the same recipe as above, but it consists of 8 3/4 oz of milk chocolate instead of the dark chocolate, preferably Valrhona Jivara Lactée 40%.

Opéra Glaze with White Chocolate

For the Champagne Cake on page 203.

This is the same recipe as above but it consists of 8 3/4 oz of white chocolate instead of the dark chocolate, preferably Valrhona Ivoire.

Fromage

Fromage is a light and porous filling and it is based on a warm whipped egg yolk and sugar foam, as well as a flavoring and gelatin for a firm filling. Some pastry chefs use vanilla cream as a base for the fromage, but in that case it's called a diplomat cream.

Zola cake and Zola pastries were popular when I was an apprentice. You applied a layer of apple jam on a pastry base, put a ring around it and filled it with fromage.

Once it was solidified, you added another pastry base and glazed it with arrack fondant.

Orange Fromage

Makes a dessert or a cake filling

1/3 oz gelatin leaves (10 g/about 5)
2 ripe oranges
1/2 lemon, yellow and ripe
1/2 cup orange juice (140 g)
2 tbsp lemon juice (30 g)
3 1/2 oz sugar cubes (100 g)
1/2 cup sugar (100 g)
3 oz, or about 4, egg yolks (80 g)
1/5 cup dry white wine (50 g)
16 4/5 fl oz whipping cream (500 g) 40%

1. Soak the gelatin in plenty of cold water for at least 10 minutes.
2. Wash and grate the peel of the oranges using the sugar cubes until the entire surface has been grated.
3. Squeeze the juice from the oranges and measure the correct amount. Squeeze the lemon as well.
4. Beat the egg yolks until foamy, bring the wine, orange sugar and orange juice to a boil and beat the boiling mixture over the egg yolks. Whisk into a cold foam.
5. Dissolve the drained gelatin leaves in lemon juice and heat to 110–120°F (45–50°C).
6. Fold the gelatin mixture into the egg foam and fold the whipped cream into a light and fluffy fromage.
7. Fill a wreath pan with the batter and set in freezer for 1 hour (serve it in the same manner as the lemon fromage on page 185).

Basic Recipe for Liqour Fromage

The so-called Zola fromage.
1/6 oz gelatin leaves (4 g/about 2)
16 4/5 fl oz whipping cream (500 g)
1 vanilla bean, preferably Tahiti
3 tbsp egg yolks (40 g)
1/3 cup confectioners' sugar (40 g)
1/8 cup arrack or punch (25 g)

1. Soak the gelatin in plenty of cold water for at least 10 minutes.
2. In a chilled bowl, whip the cream into a solid foam.
3. Cut the vanilla bean lengthwise, scrape out the seeds using a knife and place them in a bowl.
4. Add the egg yolks and sugar and whisk together.
5. Place the bowl in a simmering water bath and heat while whipping, until the egg mixture is 110–120°F (70°C).

6. Whisk the egg mixture for 10 minutes into a firm foam.
7. Remove the gelatin from the water and let the remaining water on the leaves follow. Melt the leaves to 110–120°F (45–50°C).
8. Add the liquor to the gelatin and stir. Mix it into the egg foam and fold in the whipped cream until it's a light and fluffy fromage.
9. Add the fromage to a ring and leave to solidify in the fridge.

Diplomat Cream

This tasty filling consists of equal parts of boiled vanilla cream and whipped cream, most commonly stabilized with gelatin and sometimes flavored with liquor, chocolate or nut paste etc., and is perfect for Napoleon Pastries with a rich and smooth mouthfeel. Each morning during my internship, I strained at least 55 pounds of vanilla cream that were going to be used for cakes and pastries. It was to be mixed into a crème diplomat.

1/6 oz gelatin leaves (6 g/about 3)
2 cups vanilla cream (500 g), see recipe on page 46
8 1/3 cups whipped cream 40% (500 g)

1. Soak the gelatin in plenty of cold water for at least 10 minutes.
2. Pass the vanilla cream through a sieve and whip the cream into a solid foam in a chilled bowl.
3. Remove the gelatin from the water and drain. Melt the gelatin to 110–120°F (45–50°C).
4. Mix a little vanilla cream into the gelatin and then whip it into the vanilla cream using a whisk. Fold in the whipped cream using a spatula.

Chocolate Diplomat Cream

We used this tasty smooth chocolate filling at the Honold Confiserie in Zurich for the Schwarzwälder kirschtorte, which we made hundreds of every week.

1/6 oz gelatin leaves (5 g/about 2 1/2)
1/2 cups vanilla cream (125 g)
7 oz dark chocolate, preferably Valrhona Grand Cru Pur Caribe 66% (200 g)
10 1/2 cup whipped cream 40% (625 g)

1. Soak the gelatin in plenty of cold water for at least 10 minutes.
2. Pass the vanilla cream through a sieve.
3. Finely chop and melt the chocolate in a plastic bowl in the microwave oven or in a 130°F (55°C) water bath.
4. In a chilled bowl, whip the cream into a firm foam.

5. Remove the gelatin from the water and let the remaining water in the leaves follow. Melt the gelatin to a temperature of 110–120°F (45–50°C) and mix it into the vanilla cream.

Add the chocolate and fold in the whipped cream.

Bavaroise

This soft tasty filling consists of a so-called Crème Anglaise, with vanilla and egg yolk as a thickener. The cream is stabilized with gelatin, mixed with whipped cream and flavored in various ways, with alcohol, chocolate, gianduja, praline paste, or with berries and fruits.

This is how we made the basic cream at the cake station at Honold Confiserie in Zurich. It has a little more egg yolk than most recipes. We used it as a basic cream for various Charlotte Cakes and measured one part of basic cream with two parts of whipped cream. We also often used it for the Saint Honore Cake on Fridays and Saturdays. We usually flavored it with Kirschwasser.

1/3 oz gelatin leaves (8 g/about 4)
1 vanilla bean, preferably Tahiti
1 cup milk, 3% (250 g)
1/3 cup sugar (75 g)
4 oz, or about 6, egg yolks (120 g)
15 fl oz whipping cream, 40% (450 g)

1. Soak the gelatin in plenty of cold water for at least 10 minutes.
2. Cut the vanilla bean lengthwise and scrape out the seeds using a knife. Add the vanilla bean and seeds into the milk, bring to a boil and let it steep for about 10 minutes to absorb the vanilla flavor.
3. Beat the egg yolks and sugar and pour it over the vanilla milk. Mix well.
4. Heat all the ingredients to 185°F (85°C), while constantly stirring, or perform a spoon test.
5. Remove the gelatin from the water and add it to the mixture. Let the remaining water on the leaves follow. Stir until the gelatin is melted.
6. Pass through a sieve and cool to 70°F (20°C) in a water bath.
7. Fold the cream into the whipped cream in two rounds until you have a light and porous bavaroise.
8. If you are going to pipe the mixture, leave it to settle before piping.

Fruit Bavaroise

1/5 oz gelatin leaves (6 g/about 3)
1/2 cup milk 3% (125 g)
1/2 vanilla bean, preferably Tahiti
1/3 cup sugar (75 g)
2 oz, or about 3, egg yolks (60 g)

1/2 cup fruit puree with 10% sugar (125 g)
8 1/3 fl oz whipping cream, 40% (250 g)

Prepare it in the same manner as above, but mix the fruit purée into the basic cream before it's added to the whipped cream.

Ganache for Pastries and Cakes

An unknown person invented this delicious chocolate cream in France in the late 1800s.

Cake and pastry ganache should be soft and smooth, easy to spread, yet have a firm texture.

Valrhona Grand Cru Guanaja 70%, 4 2/5 oz (125 g)
Valrhona Grand Cru Araguani 72%, 4 1/4 oz (120 g)
Valrhona Grand Cru Manjari 64%, 4 1/2 oz (130 g)
Valrhona Grand Cru Pur Caribe 66%, 4 1/2 oz (130 g)
Valrhona Grand Cru Jivara Lactée milk chocolate 40%, 8 oz (225 g)
Valrhona Grand Cru Ivoire white chocolate, 10 1/3 oz (290 g)
chocolate (amount depends on the cocoa content, see above)
5 fl oz whipping cream 40% (150 g)
3 1/2 tsp glucose or honey (25 g) (or inverted sugar syrup, such as trimoline)

Chocolate Mousse

I think Valrhona is the best chocolate, which is why my recipes are based on it. You can certainly use other types of chocolate, but it won't be the same.

You want to be able to cut the mousse cake into pretty cake pieces using a knife dipped in warm water. The mousse should be firm and it shouldn't smear onto the knife. If it does, it contains too little chocolate. Add more chocolate, or more gelatin if it's milk chocolate mousse or white chocolate mousse.

Chocolate mousse with pâté à bombe is great as a pie filling, since it is light and porous. I also have a method of making chocolate mousse with crème anglais. It's smoother and softer in texture. I use these two methods mostly for cakes and pastries and also for a so-called steamed chocolate mousse, which is creamy and similar to ice cream in its consistency, see Irish Coffee Cake on page 157.

You usually use twice as much as simple syrup as egg yolk and it is heated to 185° F (85° C), and then whipped until cold in a food processor. That's the way almost every confectioner used to make it, and it was also used for parfait, ice cream soufflé, mousse, etc.

You can also make a so-called quick pâté à bombe, which is the most common version, as it's faster to make. The syrup is cooked to 250–257° F (121–125° C) and is poured over the beaten egg yolks while still boiling –whole eggs are sometimes used to achieve a more porous mixture.

1 Melt the chocolate while stirring occasionally.
2 Mix the chocolate and cream.

Chocolate mousse can be varied in several different ways, and the amount of chocolate that is added depends on the cocoa content:

Valrhona Grand Cru Guanaja 70%: 10 1/2 oz (300 g)
Valrhona Grand Cru Araguani 72%: 10 1/3 oz (290 g)
Valrhona Grand Cru Manjari 64%: 11 1/2 oz (325 g)
Valrhona Grand Cru Pur Caribe 66%: 11 oz (315 g)
Valrhona Grand Cru Jivara lactée milk chocolate 40%: 16 1/4 oz (460 g)
Grand Cru Valrhona Ivoire white chocolate: 17 oz (480 g)

4 oz, or about 6, egg yolks (120 g)
1 3/4 oz, or about 1, egg (50 g)
1/2 cup sugar (90 g)
1/4 cup water (60 g)
13 1/2 fl oz whipping cream 40% (400 g)
chocolate (the amount depends on the cocoa content, see above)

For white chocolate and milk chocolate mousse, you will need one fifth to one third ounces of gelatin in order for the mousse to be firm enough to cut into pieces without sticking to the knife.

METHOD 1

1. Mix egg, sugar and water in a metal bowl and heat in a 185° F (85° C) water bath under continuous whipping, or perform a so-called spoon test.
2. Whisk the egg mixture until cold and use immediately.

METHOD 2

1. Whisk egg yolks and eggs until fluffy using an electric hand blender.
2. Bring sugar and water to a boil to 257° F (125° C) while constantly soaking, using a brush dipped in water. If you don't have a thermometer, perform the so-called cold-water candy test, see page 35. Pour the boiling syrup in a stream while constantly whipping until it is cold.
3. (Method 1 and 2) Melt the chocolate to 120–130° F (50–55° C), depending on what kind of chocolate you are using (max 122° F (50° C) for milk chocolate and white chocolate).
4. In a chilled bowl, whip the cream into a light foam and fold in approximately one third of the chocolate to form a ganache-like batter.
5. Add the remaining whipped cream using a spatula and finally the egg mixture until you have a light and fluffy mousse.
6. Immediately add to the rings before the mousse stiffens.

Chocolate Mousse with Crème Anglaise

Chocolate mousse with crème anglaise has a smooth and melting texture.

Basic recipe for Crème Anglaise

1/2 cup milk 3% (120 g)
7 1/2 cups whipped cream 40% (120 g)
1 3/4 oz, or about 3, egg yolks (50 g)
2 tsp sugar (10 g)

1. Bring the milk and whipped cream to a boil.
2. Gently beat the egg yolks with the sugar. Pour the hot mixture over the egg yolks and mix well.
3. Pour it back into the saucepan. Heat to 185° F (85° C) while constantly stirring, or perform a spoon test.
4. Pass through a fine sieve, a so-called chinoise.

Crème Anglaise Chocolate Mousse

1 1/4 cups Crème Anglaise (300 g)
7 1/2 cups whipped cream 40% (450 g)
chocolate, optional according to table below
1/3 oz gelatin (6–10 g) if using milk chocolate or white chocolate

Valrhona Grand Cru Araguani 72%: 11 2/3 oz (330 g)
Valrhona Grand Cru Guanaja 70%: 11 1/2 oz (325 g)
Valrhona Grand Cru Manjari 64%: 11 1/2 oz (325 g)
Valrhona Grand Cru Pur Caribe 66%: 12 oz (340 g)
Valrhona Grand Cru Jivara Lactée 40% milk chocolate: 19 1/2 oz (550 g)
Grand Cru Valrhona Ivoire white chocolate: 17 2/3 oz (500 g)

Chop the chocolate finely and beat the hot crème anglaise over it. Stir with a plastic scoop in the same manner as when making a ganache, see page 51. When the mixture has a temperature between 95° F and 105° F (34–40° C), mix it in with the whipped cream into a mousse.

Add one fifth to one third ounce of gelatin to the white chocolate and milk chocolate mousse, or it will be difficult to cut.

CHOCOLATE DECOR

Tempering

There aren't very many achievements in gastronomy that are attributable to England, but in 1847 the first chocolate cake was cast in Bristol, by chemist Joseph Fry. One may say that the problem of tempering of chocolate was solved there.

In order to immerse cakes and biscuits in chocolate, one must learn how to temper chocolate, or the cocoa butter that is in the chocolate. It's only the cocoa butter that is affected by tempering. If you don't temper the chocolate, it becomes gray and dull and it won't solidify properly.

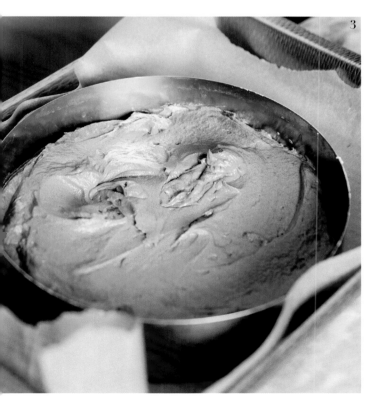

1 Mix the chocolate with crème anglaise.
2 Turn the mixture into the whipped cream.
3 Place the chocolate mousse in a ring lined with plastic cake wrap.

Reasons to temper chocolate

The chocolate will
• have a beautiful color
• have a sharp snap, hardness
• have a soft, melting texture
• have the ability to shrink, which makes it easy to loosen from molds.

These desirable qualities are dependent on the cocoa butter being cooked correctly. If the tempering is incorrectly performed, there is a risk of
• dapple-grey chocolate
• a grainy and short texture
• rapid melting when touching
• chocolate that doesn't pull together, and sticks to molds.

Cakes and pastries that are going to be dipped in chocolate should have a temperature of 68° F (20° C) to obtain a glossy and nice-looking finish. Never dip cold pastry into chocolate, as it becomes dull and gray and starts to solidify from the inside instead of the outside. Biscuits with buttercream should be chilled and then placed at room temperature for 30 minutes before dipping.

Various types of chocolate are tempered to different temperatures. White chocolate and milk chocolate have lower melting points than dark, and the tempering is carried out at a lower temperature. They should not be heated above 118° F (48° C), as they contain the milk protein casein that will spoil the distillation at 129° F (54° C), which will ruin the chocolate.

Equipment

When tempering the chocolate, you have to keep track of the temperature. That's why you want to use a thermometer that can measure up to 122° F (50° C) (a regular digital oven thermometer works fine).

You also need a small marble slab, and you should ideally have a microwave and a spatula or a palette knife and a plastic bowl, a microwave bowl, to melt the chocolate in.

Melt in the microwave with great care, to prevent the chocolate from burning. Never melt directly on the stove. Stir frequently and do not use metal objects. You can also melt the chocolate in a water bath, the way they did it in the old days.

Avoid the moisture from the steam and stir frequently, as the water quickly can reach temperatures between 175° and 195° F (80–90° C).

Method 1

This is a good method if you don't have a marble top, although the shine always turns out better from a traditional tempering on a marble slab, a so-called called tablering. This is because air is incorporated while stirring, and the less air in the chocolate, the glossier it will turn out.

1. Chop the chocolate finely.
2. Heat half the amount to 118–122° F (48–50° C) degrees for dark chocolate, 113° F (40° C) for milk chocolate and 104° F (40° C) for white chocolate.
3. Mix in the rest of the chocolate.
4. Stir until the temperature is 80–82° F (27–28° C) for dark chocolate, 79–81° F (26–27° C) for milk chocolate and 77–79° F (25–26° C) for white chocolate.
5. Next, heat to 88–90° F (31–32° C) for dark chocolate, 84–86° F (29–30° C) for milk chocolate and 82–84° F (28–29° C) for white chocolate. The simplest and best way to heat the chocolate is in the microwave. Heat for 30 seconds at a time, check the temperature and stir in between.

Method 2 - traditional tablering

This is the most common method among experts.
1. Heat the chocolate to the correct temperature depending on what type you are using, see below.
2. Pour three quarters of the chocolate onto a marble table.
3. Spread it back and forth until the chocolate begins to harden.
4. Scrape the chocolate into the bowl with the remaining chocolate and mix thoroughly.
5. Heat while stirring to the correct temperature.

Dark Chocolate
Heat to 118–122° F (48–50° C), cool to 80–82° F (27–28° C) and heat to 88–90° F (31–32° C).

Milk Chocolate
Heat to 113° F (45° C), cool to 79–81° F (26–27° C) and heat to 84–86° F (29–30° C).

White Chocolate
Heat to 104° F (40° C), cool to 77–79° F (25–26° C) and heat to 82–84° F (28–29° C)

Time - stirring - temperature

It is of utmost importance to be aware of these three factors. If you are careless, the chocolate will be impossible to temper.

There are three fat crystals in cocoa butter: alpha, beta and gamma. The purpose of tempering is to create crystals that are as small as possible. The beta form is the only stable one. The others are unstable and have a lower melting point, as well as a tendency to transcend into stable crystals for a period of time, resulting in gray stains. It is therefore important be in control of the process, so that the chocolate is left with stable beta crystals only. This is accomplished during the tempering process.

The gloss is entirely dependent on the position of the crystal - the flatter the crystals are lying against one another, the better the shine.

Tempering Chocolate

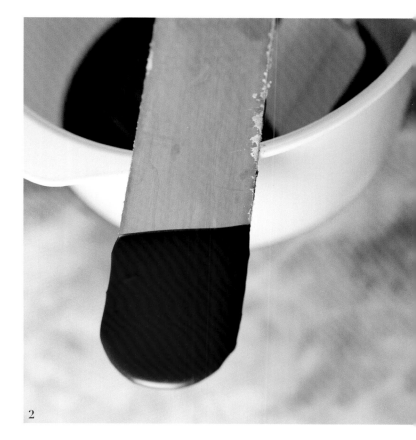

Spreading of chocolate discs.

1 *The marble table and the palette knife effort lowers the temperature of the chocolate.*
2 *Make sure that the chocolate hardens after tempering.*
3–4 *Spread the chocolate onto an acetate sheet, preferably with a cocoa butter pattern*

Chocolate Shavings

Chocolate spiral.

1 Spread the chocolate thinly on a marble slab until it starts to harden.

2 Scrape the chocolate into chocolate shavings using a sharp knife.

3 Pour the chocolate onto a 6 inch wide plastic sheet strip with a cocoa butter pattern.

4 Spread the chocolate thinly using a palette knife. Create stripes in the chocolate by using a glue scraper.

5 Place the striped strip in a glass to solidify.

Marbling a Chocolate disc

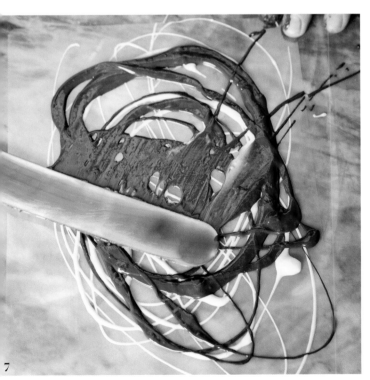

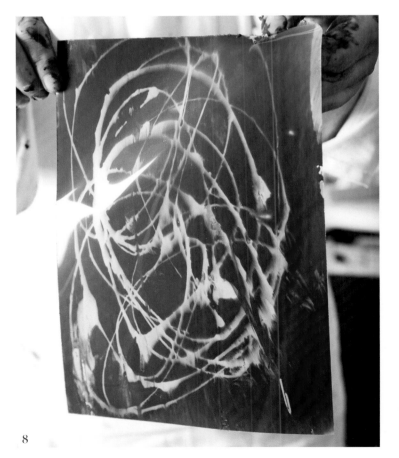

6 Drizzle white chocolate onto a plastic sheet and leave to
  solidify.
7 Spread a thin layer of dark chocolate onto the plastic sheet.
8 The marbled sheet.

Wave Patterned Chocolate disc

1 Spread white tempered chocolate thinly on a plastic sheet and use a glue scraper to form pattern.
2 Spread the dark tempered chocolate thinly on top of the solidified white chocolate.
3 Completed sheet with white and dark chocolate streaks.

Striped Chocolate Cigarettes

1 Spread a thin layer of white chocolate on a marble top
  and create stripes using a glue scraper. Leave to harden.
2 Spread a thin layer of dark chocolate on top.
3 Scrape rolls using a paint scraper, as the chocolate starts
  to harden.

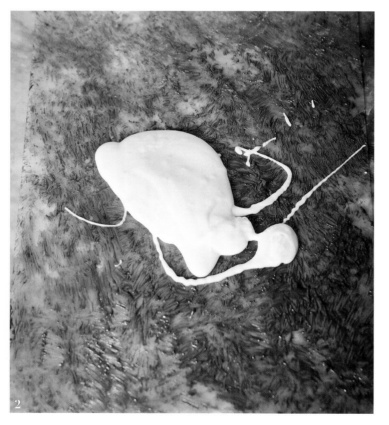

Marbling using a brush

1 Create streaks out of the tempered dark chocolate using a brush on a plastic sheet.
2 Apply a thin layer of tempered white chocolate on top.
3 Leave the finished marbled plastic sheet to solidify in the refrigerator under pressure, to ensure that the chocolate doesn't warp.

1

3

2

Feathers

1–2 Thinly spread tempered chocolate on a marble top. Scrape the feathers so that they stick around the finger.
3 Completed feathers.

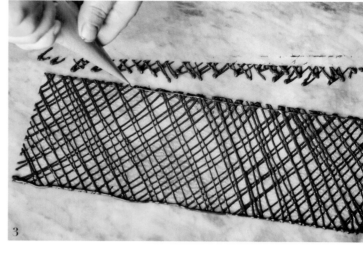

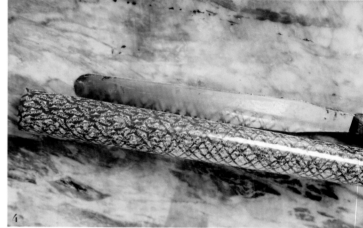

Chocolate Roll

1 Pipe the tempered chocolate onto a plastic sheet with
  a cocoa butter pattern.
2 Pipe back and forth like a net.

3 Strengthen the edges with a chocolate border.
4 Roll up into rolls.
5 Let harden in fridge and carefully remove the plastic.
6 The finished rolls.

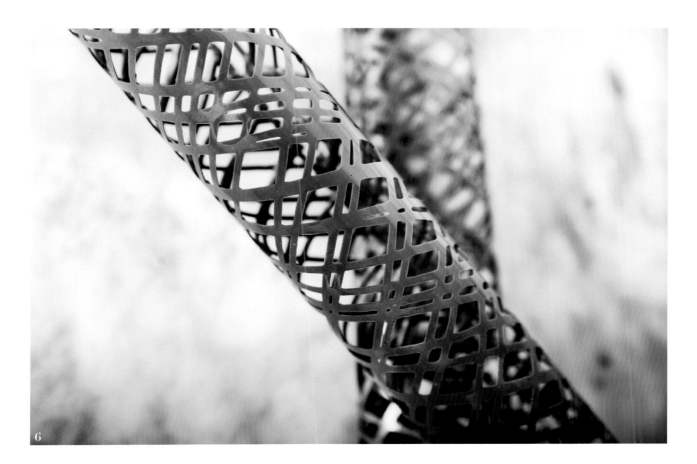

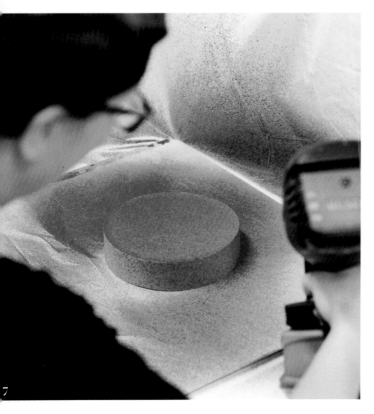

Spraying the frozen mousse cake

7 *Jessica sprays the frozen mousse cakes with dark chocolate and cocoa butter by using a pneumatic gun.*
8 *The finished mousse cake.*

Back in the old days, cream cake was Sweden's most common cake. These days it's rare to find the cake at pastry shops and no one would order it either.

A classic cake bottom was divided into three layers using a serrated knife. A layer of raspberry jam was spread on the first bottom, the next bottom was placed on top, as well as equal parts of vanilla cream and whipped cream (the so-called creamy cream). The last bottom was placed on top and covered with whipped cream. The sides of the cake were piped with whipped cream and the top was sometimes decorated with fruits or berries.

Shortcrust pastry cakes were also popular back in the old days, but you would never see the cake these days. Thin tasty pastry bottoms, four for each cake, were filled with jam and were left until the next day, when they were to be decorated with whipped cream. It's very sweet, yet tasty.

English Wedding Cake

This tasty cake can be prepared and beautifully decorated a whole week in advance and can be stored at room temperature until it's ready to serve. A properly baked English wedding cake is very tasty and durable.

It is a hallmark for a pastry chef to be able to bake pretty English wedding cakes without the fruit sinking to the bottom. When you mix the fruit with half of the flour it prevents it from sinking to the bottom of the baking pans. Also note that all ingredients must be at room temperature. If the egg and egg yolks are cold, the water from the butter will be pushed out, the mixture will curdle and the fruit will sink to the bottom of the pan.

I was 20 years old the first time that I baked an English wedding cake, and we piped ornaments and doves and horses and carriages, before assembling the cake. I shaped a heart made out of caramel and put it on top of the cake next to two doves. The pictures still exist, and I remember how proud I was when it was sitting in the dining room at the Savoy Hotel in Malmö.

APRROX. 30 PIECES

Plum Cake
Three springform pans, about 9.5 inches (24 cm),
   9 inches (20 cm) and 6 inches (16 cm) in diameter

4 cups California raisins (925 g)
2 1/2 cups chopped candied orange peel (575 g)
2 cups chopped succade (500 g)
12 1/2 fl oz dark rum (37 cl)

1 vanilla bean, preferably Tahiti
3 lemons
3 2/5 cups butter (900 g)
1 3/4 cups sugar (375 g)
2 cups crude sugar or cassonade sugar (375 g)
10 1/2 oz, or about 15, egg yolks (300 g)
13 oz, or about 7, eggs (375 g)
4 2/3 cups all-purpose flour (565 g) to coat the soaked
   fruit
4 2/3 cups all-purpose flour (565 g)

Assembling the cake
1 1/4 cup dark rum (300 g)
3 recipes of apricot preserve, see page 45
2 recipes of pastillage, see below confectioners' sugar

Pastillage
4/5 oz gelatin leaves (20 g/about 5)
1/4 cup white wine vinegar (60 g)
20 cups confectioners' sugar (2 kg)

Glaze (Glace Royale)
2 3/4 cups confectioners' sugar (275 g)
2 oz, or about 2, egg whites (60 g)
1 tsp white wine vinegar, vinegar or lemon juice (5 g)

(Confectioners usually use one part egg white and five parts confectioners' sugar when they beat a glaze. When piping ornaments made out of glaze, there is no acid added, to prevent the ornaments from falling apart and for the consistency not to be too loose. Glaze is used in English wedding cakes both with and without acid.)

DAY 1

1. Marinate the fruit in the liqour overnight, turn it a couple of times.

DAY 2

2. Cut the vanilla bean lengthwise and scrape out the marrow with a knife. Wash and tear off the outermost rind of the lemons.
3. Mix the room temperature butter with the sugars, lemon zest and vanilla marrow to a porous foam.
4. Add the room temperature eggs and egg yolks one by one while stirring.
5. Gently add four and two thirds of a cup (565 g) of all-purpose flour without over-working the substance.
6. Gently mix the marinated fruits with the remaining four and two thirds of a cup (565 g) of all-purpose flour, to form a thin rind around the fruit. Gently add them to the substance.

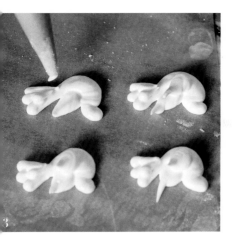

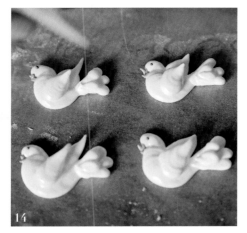

7. Preheat the oven to 340°F (170°C).
8. Add the mixture to the lubricated and floured springform pans.
9. Place pans on a baking sheet and bake them for about 55–60 minutes, until bottoms are golden brown. Make sure they are baked through using a knife point, or a thermometer. They should be 185–195°F (85–90°C) on the inside when baked.
10. Place the bottoms on grids to cool off but leave them in the pans to prevent them from drying out.

Assembling the cake
11. Brush the cake bottoms with liqour.
12. Brush the edges of the bottoms and the top with boiling apricot preserve.
13. Roll out the pastillage and make it about one eighth of an inch (3 mm) thick using the confectioners' sugar and a roller.

Marzipan or Pastillage Rose
 1 Cut the marzipan into pieces.
 2 Flatten the pieces with a palette knife.
 3 Form a bud.
 4 Shape the leaves.
 5 Put the leaves together into a rose.
 6 Finished rose.

Marzipan or pastillage carnation
 7 Roll out the marzipan.
 8 Mark the edge with a fork.
9–10 Shape the carnation leaves.
 11 Sprinkle a little red food coloring. Use a brush and knife.
 12 Finished carnation.

 13 Pipe the pigeons made out of icing on parchment paper.
 14 Paint the eyes with melted chocolate and beak with red icing.
15–16 Pipe glaze.
17–18 Pipe the smooth icing on parchment paper with a pattern underneath, see page 237, and leave to solidify.

14. Roll it up on the rolling pin and cover the cakes with the pastillage. Shape it with your hand to ensure that there are no visible wrinkles. Whittle away pastillage by using a dough cutter or a knife.

15. Let stand, in order for the surface to dry.

Pastillage

16. Soak the gelatin in plenty of cold water for at least 10 minutes. They should absorb six times their own weight in water.

17. Boil the vinegar and add the drained gelatin leaves.

18. Pour it over the confectioners' sugar and knead it into a dough in a food processor.

19. Run on medium speed to make a smooth paste and store it in an airtight jar to prevent it from drying out. Store in fridge. The mixture should be at room temperature when using it. If it's too hard, add egg whites.

Glaze

20. Sift the confectioners' sugar twice and then add the egg white, making sure there is no egg yolk in it.

21. Whip until it becomes light and fluffy substance that easily can be shaped and piped. If the icing is too firm, add more egg white. If it's too loose, add more sieved confectioners' sugar.

22. Place parchment paper over the patterned sheets and attach with tape to prevent them from moving.

23. Add the icing to a small pastry bag and cut a small hole in the front with a pair of scissors. Pipe along the patterns once and then three more times, so that the grids and ornaments stick together.

24. Allow to dry until the next day.

25. Whisk a new icing with acid and carefully remove the ornaments using a knife.

26. Attach them to the cake using the new icing.

Piping of doves for decoration

27. Pipe as shown in the picture and color the icing with a little red food coloring. Pipe a little beak. Dip a thin brush in brown food coloring and make a dot for the eye.

Strawberry and Rhubarb Charlotte

I personally love this combination and the beautiful silk ribbon around the cake makes it extra special. I remember this fantastic cake from the terrace at the Pallas Hotel in Lucerne, and with the views of Rigi Lake and the mountains in the background, it became special to me. Maria Escalante has tied the bow around the cake; she's a world champion at it.

10–12 PIECES

One cake ring, 2x9-inch (5x22 cm) or a springform pan with the same diameter measurement

Rhubarb Compote
2 cups dilute rhubarb, (500 g) peeled and diced
2/3 cup sugar (125 g)
1 3/4 tbsp lemon juice (25 g)
Approx. 3 gelatin leaves

Bisquit à la Cuillère
4 oz, or about 6, egg yolks (120 g)
1/2 cup sugar (95 g)
4 oz, or about 6, egg whites (120 g)
1 tsp lemon juice (5 g)
1/2 cup sugar (95 g)
3/4 cup all-purpose flour (90 g)
3/4 cup corn starch (90 g)
1/3 cup confectioners' sugar (30 g) to sprinkle over the biscuits

Strawberry Mousse with Italian meringue
Approx. 4 gelatin leaves
10 1/2 oz strawberry puree (250 g) with 10% sugar
5 1/4 oz Italian meringue (150 g), see page 34
4 cups whipped cream (250 g)

Strawberry Syrup for Drenching
4 oz strawberry puree (125 g) with 10% sugar
1 tsp lemon juice (5 g)
1 3/4 tbsp confectioners' sugar (25 g)

Whipped Cream
8 1/3 oz whipping cream (250 g) 40%
2 tsp sugar (10 g)
1 tsp pure vanilla extract (5 g)
17 1/2 oz strawberries (500 g) for decoration

1 neutral gelatin glaze recipe, see page 43
confectioners' sugar for decoration
One red silk ribbon, about 35 inches (90 cm) long (can be purchased in the flower shop)

Rhubarb Compote
1. Soak the gelatin in plenty of cold water for at least 10 minutes.
2. Cook the rhubarb with sugar and lemon until tender. Remove the gelatin leaves and leave the remaining water from the leaves, stir until melted.
3. Move the mixture into a round compote foil dish, nine inches (22 cm) in diameter, and freeze.

Bisquit à la Cuillère (Lady Fingers)
4. Preheat the oven to 430°F (220°C).
5. Draw two circles, eight inches (20 cm) in diameter, on parchment paper.
6. Sift flour and corn starch on a paper.
7. Beat the egg yolks and half a cup of sugar to a solid foam for about 5 minutes.
8. Beat the whites with the lemon juice into a solid foam in a clean metal bowl and add half a cup of sugar at a time. Whisk into a solid meringue.
9. Fold the egg yolk foam in the meringue with a spatula and fold all the flour into a light mixture.
10. Move the mixture into a plastic piping bag with a flat nozzle no. 12 or cut a hole and pipe two bottoms and dust them with powdered sugar.
11. Pipe 4 inch long biscuits with a flat nozzle no. 12 on parchment paper with the remaining mixture.
12. Sprinkle sugar on the top and let stand for 5 minutes so that the sugar melts a little bit. Sprinkle some more sugar before putting them in the oven.
13. Bake for about 15-18 minutes until golden brown. Let cool on baking grid.

Strawberry Mousse with Italian meringue
14. Soak the gelatin in plenty of cold water for at least 10 minutes.
15. Make the puree and Italian meringue. Beat meringue and strawberry puree together.
16. Remove the gelatin from the water and leave the remaining water on the leaf. Heat the gelatin to 110–120°F (45–50°C) and pour it into the meringue mixture while constantly stirring.
17. Fold the whipped cream in with a spatula and make a light and fluffy mousse.

Strawberry Syrup for soaking

18. Stir the strawberry puree, lemon juice and confectioners' sugar with a whisk until the sugar has melted.

Assembling the cake

19. Line a nine by two inch (22x5 cm) cake ring with plastic cake wrap.
20. Place a lady finger bottom in the cake ring and place it on a tray with parchment paper. Spread strawberry syrup on the bottom, but save half for the uppermost bottom.
21. Fill half of the ring with strawberry mousse.
22. Remove the rhubarb compote from the foil pan and press it into the mousse.
23. Evenly spread strawberry mousse over the ring.
24. Add the second bottom upside down on parchment paper. Spread strawberry syrup on the underside. Place it as you would a lid and set the cake in the refrigerator to solidify for 60 minutes.

Completing the cake

25. Whisk the cream, sugar and vanilla extract in a chilled bowl until it turns into a solid foam.
26. Loosen the cake from the ring, remove the plastic cake wrap and place it on a cake doily.
27. Loosen the lady fingers from the paper and cut them at one end to make them straight.

28. Nudge the lady fingers on the edges of the cake, as shown in the image.
29. Pipe bows out of whipped cream with a fluted nozzle no. 12 across the top of the cake, as shown.
30. Dip the rinsed strawberries, leaving the stems on, in the neutral gelatin glaze and arrange them neatly in the middle of the cake. Dust it with confectioners' sugar and wrap a red bow around the cake to make it look like a beautiful package.

Serve a strawberry coulis with it and it will taste even better.

Strawberry Coulis

17 1/2 oz rinsed and hulled ripe strawberries (500 g)
1 cup confectioners' sugar (90 g)
2 tsp lemon juice (10 g)

Mix all the ingredients into a puree and pass it through a sieve. Pour it into a sauce jug.

Princess Cake

Princess cake is Sweden's most common cake, and if it's made with real ingredients, it's a light and tasty cake. It is said that it first appeared in the Princesses Cookbook in the 1930s. Some people call it an Opera cake, some versions have jam in the bottom and others don't. But one thing most are sure of, is that there should be green marzipan on top. Kids as well as adults love this cake, including myself, as long as the cake bottoms aren't store-bought and the vanilla cream in the whipped cream is pure and tasty.

I learned to make this version of it when I was young, and I have no reason to change anything in the recipe.

10–12 PIECES

One traditional Swedish cake bottom, see page 16

3 1/2 oz raspberry jam (100 g), see page 44

Cream for the cake filling
Approx. 4 gelatin leaves

1 2/3 cups vanilla cream (400 g/about half a recipe of vanilla cream), see page 46

13 1/2 fl oz whipping cream (400 g) 40%

16 4/5 fl oz whipping cream (500 g) 40%

2 1/3 tsp pure vanilla extract (10 g)

1 3/4 tbsp sugar (25 g)

8 3/4 oz green marzipan (250 g), see page 38

confectioners' sugar

1 marzipan rose with green leaves for garnishing, see page 70

For garnishing
1 3/4 oz dark chocolate (50 g), preferably Valrhona Grand Cru Guanaja 70%

Cream
1. Soak the gelatin in plenty of cold water for at least 10 minutes.
2. Whip the cream into a solid foam in a chilled bowl.
3. Pass the vanilla cream through a fine sieve.
4. Gently mix the vanilla cream and the whipped cream with a spatula until the cream is light and fluffy, so that the air stays in the cream.
5. Remove the gelatin from the water and keep the remaining water on the leaves while melting to 110–120°F (45–50°C).
6. Add about half a cup of cream to the gelatin mixture and mix to a smooth cream. Gently fold it into the cream.

Assembling the cake
7. Whip the cream into a solid foam in a cooled bowl along with sugar and vanilla extract.
8. Cut the cake bottom out of the ring using a knife.
9. Divide the cake bottom into three equally thick bottoms using a serrated knife.
10. Place one cake base on a cake plate and spread a layer of raspberry jam using a palette knife and approximately a fifth cup of cream.
11. Add the second bottom and put the rest of the cream in the middle. Apply it in the shape of a dome.
12. Add the third bottom and shape the cake into a dome with your hands.
13. Add the whipped cream and shape the cake like a dome as smoothly and prettily as possible.
14. Place the cake in the fridge to set for about 30 minutes.
15. Roll out the marzipan about one twelfth of an inch thick by using a rolling pin and confectioners' sugar. If it feels hard, warm it a little in the microwave.
16. Roll the marzipan onto the rolling pin and roll it out on the cake.
17. Make sure that it fits evenly around it and even out any grooves. Whittle away any extra marzipan with a dough cutter or with a small, sharp knife.
18. Temper the chocolate, see page 52, and add it to a small pastry bag. Cut a small hole in the front using scissors.
19. Pipe a beautiful border around the cake as nicely as you can (see photo of border decorations on page 236).
20. Dust with a little confectioners' sugar and add a marzipan rose and a few green leaves. Transfer the cake to a cake doily.

French Nougat Cake

This is what I called the cake at Konditori Hollandia in Malmö in 1972. The combination of moist chocolate bottoms filled with a creamy milk chocolate mousse with caramel flavor was a success, and perhaps it still is. The entire cake is sprinkled with crushed nougat. This cake is delicious with its delicate texture of soft, smooth and crunchy.

10—12 PIECES

One cake ring, 2x9-inch (5x22 cm) or a springform pan with the same diameter measurement

Special Chocolate Bottom

6 1/2 oz, or about 4, eggs (190 g)
2 oz, or about 3, egg yolks (60 g)
3/4 cup sugar (145 g)
2 1/3 tsp pure vanilla extract (10 g)
3/4 cup all-purpose flour (80 g)
1/4 cup potato starch (30 g)
1/3 cup cocoa (30 g), preferably Valrhona 20/22
1/4 cup unsalted butter (60g)

Caramelized Milk Chocolate Mousse (boiled)

Approx. 1 1/2 gelatin leaves
6 oz chocolate (175 g), preferably Valrhona Jivara Lactée 40%
3 1/4 cup cream (750 g)
1/2 cup sugar (120 g)
1 tsp lemon juice (5 g)

Nougat

1 1/3 cup roasted and peeled hazelnuts (200 g)
3/4 cup sugar (160 g)
1/4 cup water (60 g)
2 tbsp unsalted butter (25g)
Approx. 1 tsp sodium bicarbonate (3 g)

DAY 1

1. Bake cake base in the same manner as chocolate génoise, see page 16.

Chocolate Mousse

2. Soak the gelatin in plenty of cold water for at least 10 minutes.
3. Finely chop the milk chocolate.
4. Boil half of the cream in a saucepan and set aside.
5. Melt the sugar with the lemon juice into a golden yellow caramel and add the hot cream. Cook without stirring until the sugar is dissolved.
6. Remove the saucepan from the stove. Remove the gelatin leaf from the water and leave the remaining water on the leaf. Add to the saucepan and stir until the gelatin is melted.
7. Add the chopped chocolate and stir until it melts too.
8. Mix the cream with a hand blender to an emulsion and add the remaining cold cream while constantly stirring.
9. Cover with plastic film and let stand to swell in the fridge for the next day.

Nougat

10. Bring sugar and water to a boil and 245°F (118°C), or perform a cold water test, see page 35.
11. Add nuts and boil until they start to crackle. Stir occasionally.
12. Increase the stirring when the sugar begins to whiten and crystallize. Stir vigorously until the nuts are covered with a golden yellow caramel.
13. Add butter and baking soda and stir.
14. Remove pan from the stove and pour the nougat on a baking sheet to cool.
15. Crush the nougat coarsely using a rolling pin. Store it in an airtight jar, or it will easily become moist and will lose its delightful texture.

DAY 2

Assembling the cake

16. Cut the cake base with a small knife, removing it from the ring.
17. Divide the cake base into three equally thick bottoms using a serrated knife.
18. Whisk the chocolate mousse in a chilled bowl using an electric mixer, until it's a light and airy mousse (don't whisk for too long, as it becomes heavy instead of light and airy).
19. Add a third of the mousse on the first bottom and even it out with a palette knife.
20. Add another bottom and even it out by using a baking sheet to push it down, add a third of the mousse and smooth it out the same way. Add the third bottom.
21. Use a baking sheet to even it out and place in the freezer for 30 minutes. Put the remainder of the mousse in the fridge.
22. Add the remaining mousse and spread it evenly on top of the cake and on the sides using a palette knife.
23. Use the crushed nougat and sprinkle it on top of the cake and around the edges.

Transfer the cake to a doily paper and enjoy it with a strong cup of coffee.

Sacher Cake

This cake was invented in 1832 by master confectioner Franz Sacher, to satisfy the sweet tooth of Prince Klemens Metternich. For many years there was a battle between the Sacher Hotel and Hofzuckerbäckerei Demel on Kohlmarksgasse about who had created the original, and Sacher won. The world's most famous cake is served at room temperature with Schlagobers (whipped cream), just like at the Hotel Sacher in Vienna. The Austrians consume whipped cream without thinking of their diets. They argue that an unknown Austrian pastry chef whipped the first cream about 350 years ago, while the French claim that chef Vatel at Chantilly Castle was the first to whip cream. I remember this legendary cake tasted at the Hotel Sacher, where my good friend Lennart Löfgren and I guided Swedish pastry chefs around the pastry shops of Vienna. Confectioner master Karl Kalmar gave me this recipe. He was a talented teacher in Vienna and his specialty was beautiful caramel pieces. He had worked at the cake department at the Hotel Sacher and at the Demels Hofzuckerbäckerei too. I couldn't tell you if it's the original, but I do know that it's moist and tasty.

10–12 PIECES

One cake ring, 2x9-inch (5x22 cm) or a springform pan with the same diameter measurement

Sacher Bottom
6 oz dark chocolate (180 g), preferably Valrhona Grand Cru Guanaja 70%
4 1/5 tbsp confectioners' sugar (60 g)
4 1/5 cups unsalted butter (120g)
4 oz, or about 6, egg yolks (110 g)
6 oz, or about 6, egg whites (170 g)
3/4 cup sugar (140 g)
1 tsp lemon juice (5 g)
1 cup all-purpose flour (120g)

Filling
7 oz strained apricot jam (200 g), see recipe on page 44

One recipe of apricot preserve, see page 45

Chocolate Glaze
1 1/2 cup sugar (300 g)
4 1/4 cup water (120 g)
8 3/4 oz dark chocolate (250 g), preferably Valrhona Grand Cru Guanaja 70%

DAY 1

Sacher Bottom
1. Preheat the oven to 350° F (180° C).
2. Chop the chocolate finely and melt it to 105° F (40° C).
3. Mix confectioners' sugar and room temperature butter.
4. Add the egg yolks one at a time and stir to a smooth substance. Fold in the melted chocolate.
5. Whisk egg white and lemon juice until fluffy with a third of the sugar at medium speed. Increase the speed and gradually add the remaining sugar. Whisk to a firm meringue.
6. Fold meringue into the chocolate mixture using a spatula. Sift the flour and gently fold it into the substance, to make it light rather than compact.
7. Add the mixture to a ring wrapped in parchment paper to prevent the batter from running out on the sides, or use a springform pan. Apply the batter to the edges to ensure that the cake is straight.
8. Bake the bottom for 50 minutes and raise the temperature to 390° F (200° C) for the last 10 minutes. Make sure that its thoroughly baked using a knife point.
9. Sprinkle sugar on top of the bottom and turn the cake upside down. Leave it with the ring on until the next day.

DAY 2

Assembling the cake

10. Remove the cake from the ring and cut the bottom in half using a serrated knife.
11. Spread the bottom with apricot jam using a palette knife.
12. Place the cake on a baking grid and spread the apricot preserve using a brush on the top and around the edges. Let stand and solidify for 30 minutes before glazing the cake.

Chocolate Glaze

13. Bring water and sugar to a boil and add the chopped chocolate. Boil until 230°F (110°C), stirring constantly and using a brush dipped in water to brush the inside of the pot, to prevent the syrup from crystallizing.

14. Pour a fifth of the icing on a marble table or kitchen sink and spread it back and forth using a palette knife, until it starts to harden. Meanwhile, use your other hand to stir the glaze to prevent it forming a skin on the surface.
15. Add the substance and stir until the glaze has slightly cooled off.
16. Place the cake on a pot and add the glaze. Spread it smooth, using a palette knife. Place the cake on a cake plate and let the glaze set, which will happen very quickly if the substance is rigid. (Glaze residues can be reheated with a little water and used again.)

Serve the cake in pieces with whipped cream flavored with a little real vanilla sugar, just like at the Sacher Hotel.

French Mocha Cake

This tasty cake has sadly disappeared from the line of cakes at most pastry shops. It consists of very brittle bottoms and is filled with a tasty mocha cream, which contrasts with a little arrack or punch (an essence or a flavor should never be used, only the real ingredient itself. There shouldn't be a strong taste of arrack, only a mild contrast of it.

The edges are sprinkled with freshly roasted and sliced almonds and the cake is garnished with mocha cream and coffee beans. In France this tasty cake is called Mascotte cake and it's a classic there as well.

Try a piece of it at Pâtisserie Ladurée on Rue Royale if you're visiting Paris, right next to the Place Madeleine, or the famous Pâtisserie Dalloyau on Rue Saint Honore. (If you make your own coffee essence, see page 45, the cream will be a very beautiful color).

10–12 PIECES

One recipe of fragile meringue, see Sans Rival cake on
　　page 92
2 tbsp sliced almonds (30 g)

Mocha Cream
2/5 cup milk, 3% (100 g)
1/4 cup brown sugar (45 g)
1/2 vanilla pod
1 tsp dark roasted instant coffee (5 g)
1 oz coffee beans, pure Arabica (30 g)
3 oz, or about 4, egg yolks (80 g)
1/4 cup sugar (45 g)
2/3 fl oz arrack or punch (2 cl)
1 1/2 cups unsalted butter (335 g)
2 tbsp egg whites (30 g/about 1)
1/3 cup sugar (60 g)
1/2 tsp lemon juice (2 g)

3 oz dark chocolate (80 g), preferably Valrhona Grand
　　Cru Guanaja 70%
1/3 cup toasted and sliced almonds (60 g) for decoration of the edges
12 marzipan coffee beans, see page 157

1. Preheat the oven to 265° F (130° C).
2. Draw three circles, nine inches (22 cm) in diameter on parchment paper.
3. Make a recipe of fragile meringue and add it to a plastic pastry bag with flat nozzle no. 12, or cut a hole on the tip of the cone.
4. Pipe meringue inside and out in the circles.

5. Sprinkle sliced almonds on top of the bottoms.
6. Bake the bottoms until golden brown and tender, for about 30 minutes.
7. Immediately turn the bottoms upside down when taking them out of the oven and remove the paper (if they are sticking it's a sign that they aren't baked and tender enough. If this is the case, put them back in the oven until ready).
8. Let the bottoms cool on a rack.

Mocha Cream
9. Heat the milk with the brown sugar, the marrow and vanilla rod to 120° F (50° C).
10. Add instant coffee and the coffee beans, after they have been roasted and ground, cover with plastic film and let stand for 10 minutes.
11. Beat the egg yolks with the sugar and add the coffee milk. Stir while heating to 185° F (85° C).
12. Pass the cream through a fine sieve and chill it in a 85° F (30° C) water bath.
13. Add the butter and stir the cream until frothy and light using an electric mixer on low speed.
14. Whisk the egg whites, lemon juice and confectioners' sugar in a metal bowl and place the bowl in simmering water. Heat the mixture to 120–140° F (50–60° C), while constantly whipping.
15. Beat the meringue until very chilled, about 70° F (20° C), and add it to the airy mocha cream. Add arrack or punch. (If you have your own coffee essence, add a little for a beautiful color.)

Assembling the cake

16. Chop and melt the chocolate in a microwave or in a 130° F (55° C) water bath.
17. Brush one of the bottoms with the melted chocolate and put it in the fridge to solidify.
18. Place the chocolate-covered side of the bottom face-down.
19. Spread a third of the mocha cream using a palette knife and add another bottom. Use a baking tray to push with, to ensure that its even. Add another third of the cream and spread it in the same manner.
20. Add the top bottom and make it even by using a baking sheet. Add half of the remaining cream and spread it evenly around the edges and on top using a palette knife.
21. Lift the cake using your hand and sprinkle the toasted sliced almonds.
22. Add the remaining cream to a plastic pastry bag with fluted nozzle no. 12. Pipe the cake on the top as shown and decorate with marzipan coffee beans. Place in the fridge to set for about 60 minutes.

Other variations of the mocha cake

Traditional Swedish Mocha Cake

Three meringue bottoms, nine inches (22 cm) in diameter, made from one meringue recipe, see page 32
One recipe of mocha cream, see above
12 marzipan coffee beans, see page 157
1/3 cup sliced and toasted almonds (60 g)

Fill the bottoms and garnish them in the same manner as French mocha cake.

Fragilité Cake

Same as French mocha cake, but the top bottom should have the sliced almonds facing upwards and be dusted with confectioner's sugar, and have no other decorations.

Truffle Cake

This tasty moist cake with raspberries and chocolate bottoms was a specialty at the Pâtisserie Dupont in Paris. The pastry shop has unfortunately closed down. The cake consists of a succulent chocolate bottom that is filled with ganache and a layer of real raspberry jam.

The top is crowned with milk chocolate folding fans dusted with cocoa. Wrapping a silk ribbon around it makes the cake look more exclusive and is typical of the continent. It's a delicious cake to pair with coffee and avec.

12 PIECES

One cake ring, 2x9-inch (5x22 cm) or a springform pan with the same diameter measurement

Heavy Chocolate Bottom
1/2 cup unsalted butter (120 g)
4 oz dark chocolate (120 g), Vahlrona Grand Cru Guanaja 70%
4 oz, or about 6, egg yolks (120 g)
1 cup all-purpose flour (120 g)
5 oz, or about 5, egg whites (150 g)
1 tsp lemon juice (5 g)
2/3 cup sugar (120 g)
1 tsp corn starch (3 g)

Filling 1
3 1/2 oz raspberry jam (100 g), see recipe on page 44

Filling 2
One recipe of ganache with chocolate Guanaja 70%, see page 51

Chocolate Folding Fans, see photo on page 61
5 2/3 oz chocolate (160 g), preferably Valhrona Grand Cru Jivara Lactée 40%

One silk ribbon to wrap around the cake

DAY 1
Chocolate Bottom
1. Preheat oven to 375° F (190° C).
2. Bring the butter to a boil in a pan and put aside.
3. Chop the chocolate and add it to the pan. Stir until it's melted.
4. Add the egg yolks and mix with a hand blender to an emulsion.
5. Sift flour on a paper.
6. Using an elecric mixer, beat the whites until fluffy together with the lemon juice and a third of the

sugar. Gradually add remaining sugar and corn-starch and mix to a firm meringue.
7. Fold the chocolate cream into the meringue using a rubber spatula and then fold in the flour.
8. Add the batter to the ring and spread it to the edges.
9. Bake the bottom for about 45–50 minutes. Use a stick to ensure that it's baked through.
10. Sprinkle with sugar on the top and place on a baking grid, leaving the ring on.

Ganache
11. Follow the recipe for ganache using Guanaja 70% chocolate.
12. Cover with plastic film and let stand at room temperature until the next day.

DAY 2
Assembling the cake
13. Divide the bottom into three equally thick bottoms using a serrated knife.
14. Apply a layer of raspberry jam on the first bottom using a palette knife.
15. Add the second bottom and use a baking sheet to even it out. Apply ganache using a palette knife.
16. Add the third bottom and smooth it out by pushing down with a baking tin.
17. Spread ganache around the sides and on top of the cake.
18. Heat the milk chocolate to 118–122° F (48–50° C) and spread it as thinly as possible using a palette knife on a marble top or a kitchen sink.
19. Shape folding fans out of the chocolate using a paint scraper and place on top of the cake as shown.
20. Dust some cocoa through a sieve. Let cake stand in the refrigerator for 1 hour.
21. Place the cake on a paper. Wrap a ribbon around it and secure with a paper clip.

Schwarzwald Cake

The Black Forest cake is made differently in Schwarzwald, but this is what we call a Schwarzwald cake in Sweden. The original cake can be found in my book *Jam and Marmalade*. Confectioner Master Oscar Barregård in Stockholm brought the recipe home after interning in Switzerland and launched the cake in Sweden in the 1930s. Later it was distributed to most other Swedish bakeries.

When I was an apprentice I always used to whip meringue, turn the almonds and coat the bottoms using a stencil on buttered baking sheets. They were baked at 340° F (170° C), until they were completely brittle. After that I brushed the bottoms with dark chocolate. During my first apprenticeship year I was just baking the bottoms, but in my second year I got to assemble the cake, too.

I remember how Kurt Lundgren used to joke around about other pastry shops that didn't use real chocolate on top of the cakes, because they didn't know how to temper the chocolate properly. Instead they used a non temp, a so-called fat glaze. If you make this cake the right way, it's delicious, but you have to use first-class chocolate and the bottoms must be fragile and brittle. The cake is suitable to freeze.

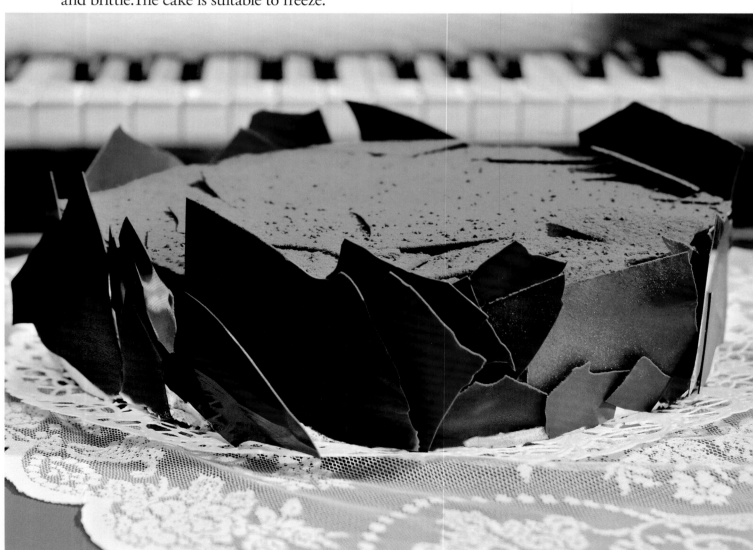

10–12 PIECES

Schwarzwald Bottoms

1 cup finely grated unpeeled almonds (125 g)
2/3 cup sugar (125 g)
2 tsp all-purpose flour (10 g)
4 1/2 oz, or about 4–5, egg whites (125 g)
1 tsp lemon juice (5 g)
1/4 cup sugar (50 g)

Decoration

1/3 cup cocoa (25 g), preferably Vahlrona 20/22
7 oz dark chocolate (200 g), preferably Valrhona
    Grand Cru Guanaja 70%

Filling

Approx. 2 gelatine leaves
16 4/5 fl oz whipping cream (500 g)
1 2/5 tbsp sugar (20 g)
2 1/3 tsp pure vanilla extract (10 g)
1 3/4 tbsp milk, 3% (25 g)

1. Cut a two-inch (5 cm) thick stencil from a cake box that is nine inches (22 cm) in diameter.
2. Preheat the oven to 340° F (170° C).
3. Mix the almonds with one and a quarter cups (135 g) of sugar and flour into a tpt in a food processor.
4. Beat the egg white and lemon juice into a foam. Add one quarter of a cup (50 g) of sugar bit by bit. Start to whip at low speed and increase the speed at the end until it's a firm meringue.
5. Fold the almond sugar into the meringue using a spatula.
6. Place the stencil on parchment paper and spread out the three bottoms using a palette knife.
7. Bake bottoms until golden brown, for about 30 minutes. Immediately put down the parchment paper, turn the bottoms on to the paper and roll them out evenly.
8. Pull off the paper and place the bottoms in an open oven door to dry, they'll be quite brittle.

Decoration

9. Temper the chocolate, see page 52, and brush one of bottoms with chocolate.
10. Spread the remaining chocolate thinly on two acetate sheets and allow to solidify under pressure in the fridge with a parchment paper on top to ensure that the chocolate does not warp.

Filling

11. Soak the gelatine in plenty of cold water for at least 10 minutes.
12. In a chilled metal bowl, whip the cream until fluffy.
13. Remove the gelatine from the water and drain the remaining water.
14. Melt gelatin to a temperature of 110–120° F (45–50° C).
15. Stir one fluid ounce of milk into the gelatine and whip a few tablespoons of cream into the mixture. Fold the mixture in the whipped cream using a spatula.

Assemblage

16. Add the chocolate covered schwarzwald layer on the bottom and apply one third of the cream using a palette knife. Apply the next layer and use your hand to press it evenly.
17. Apply another third of the cream and add the top layer.
18. Cover the entire cake as evenly and beautifully as possible using a pallete knife.
19. Set the cake in the refrigerator for one hour to solidify.
20. Decorate the borders with chocolate leaves from the acetate sheet. Dust with cocoa as shown in the image.

A variation of the schwarzwald cake that was very popular back in the day is the apollo cake. Place three chocolate covered schwarzwald layers together with cream. Sprinkle the edges with toasted and sliced almonds. Spread a thin layer of apricot jam on top and pipe cream bows around the edges. Dust with cocoa.

Raspberry Cake

This traditional cake is perfect – the jargon term for the cream inside is diplomat cream, which is a real delicacy with the succulent cake base.
Berries or fruit topped with a tasty tart jelly is what makes it a real summer cake.

10–12 PIECES

One traditional Swedish cake bottom, see page 16

Cream
Approx. 4 gelatine leaves
1 3/4 cups (half a recipe) vanilla cream, see page 46
13 1/2 fl oz whipping cream (400 g) 40%
21 oz raspberries, mixed fresh berries or fruit (600 g)

3 1/2 oz raspberry jam (100 g), see page 44
5 1/4 oz neutral gelatine glaze (150 g) see page 43
1/3 cup sliced and toasted almonds (60 g) for decoration of the edges

Cream
1. Soak the gelatine in plenty of cold water for at least 10 minutes.
2. Pass the vanilla cream through a fine sieve.
3. Whip the cream to a solid foam in a chilled bowl.
4. Mix the vanilla cream with the whipped cream to a light and airy cream using a spatula.
5. Remove the gelatine from the water and leave the remaining water on the leaves when melting the gelatin to a temperature of 110–120° F (45–50° C).
6. Add about two fifths of a cup (100 g) of cream to the gelatine solution and drop the gelatine mixture into the cream.

Assemblage
7. Cut the cake base out of the ring using a small knife.
8. Divide the cake into three equally thick parts using a serrated knife.
9. Apply a layer of raspberry jam on the first bottom using a palette knife.
10. Add the next bottom and apply three quarters of the cream.
11. Add the last bottom with the skin facing up and push it down evenly with the help of a baking tray.
12. Spread the cream along the edges of the cake, but not on top, as the fruit will slide off. Sprinkle the sides with sliced almonds.
13. Place cake on a cake plate and refrigerate for one hour to solidify.
14. Garnish with raspberries and brush with the neutral gelatine glaze.

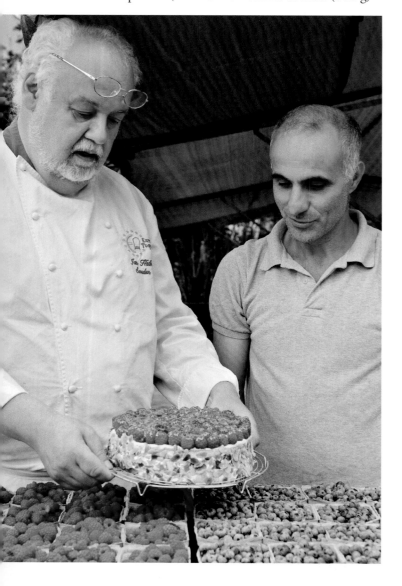

*Jan Hedh shows fruiterer
Ertan Sahin the final result.*

Sans Rival Cake

This traditional Swedish cake is seldom seen today, but I promise that it's worth a renaissance. The name means "without competition" and I can agree that it is tasty indeed. The chewy almond bottoms are filled with a really tasty ice cream and surrounded with lots of freshly roasted sliced almonds. The traditional bow of green marzipan must not be forgotten. Make a promise that you will try this tasty cake that is perfect for Christmas, Easter and Midsummer.

10–12 PIECES

Fragilité Bottoms
2 baking sheets

7 oz almond paste 50/50 (200 g)
1/5 cup milk, 3% (50 g)
7 oz, or about 6–7, egg whites (200 g)
1 tsp lemon juice (5 g)
1 1/4 cups sugar (240 g)
1/4 cup potato starch (25 g)
2 1/2 tbsp sliced almonds for garnish (30 g)

Nougat
1/2 cup sugar (100 g)
1 tsp lemon juice (5 g)
2/3 cup unpeeled toasted almonds (100 g)

Ice Cream, identical to the one used in Casablanca, see page 94
1/6 oz gelatine leaves (4 g/about 2)
1 vanilla pod, Tahiti
6 1/3 fl oz whipping cream (190 g) 40%
4/5 cup milk, 3% (190 g)
5 oz, or about 8, egg yolks (150 g)
3/4 cup sugar (150 g)
1 2/3 cups unsalted butter (375 g)

2/3 cup sliced and toasted almonds for decoration (90 g)
5 1/4 oz green marzipan for decoration (150 g)

1. Preheat oven to 265° F (130° C).
2. Heat the almond paste in the microwave to make it a little warm, then mix by hand to dissolve it in the milk.
3. In a clean metal bowl, beat the whites with the lemon juice and a third of the sugar. Start whipping at low speed, increase the speed and gradually add the remaining sugar. Whisk to a firm meringue.
4. Add the potato flour while whipping.
5. Dissolve the almond mass batter with a bit of meringue, a little at a time, and fold it into the dissolved almond paste in the meringue using a spatula.
6. Spread the meringue on the baking sheets lined with a silicone mat or parchment paper and sprinkle with sliced almonds.
7. Bake until golden brown for about 60 minutes. Ensure that they're thoroughly baked and brittle by trying to loosen the paper. If the paper will not loosen, continue to bake until brittle.

8. Cut the bottoms in the middle after removing from oven.
9. Immediately turn them onto two pieces of parchment paper and remove the silicone mat or paper.

Nougat
10. Melt the sugar until it's a yellow golden caramel and add the toasted almonds. Stir until the almonds are covered with caramel. Pour it on a tea towel and let cool.
11. Smash the nougat in a mortar, but not too finely.

Ice Cream
12. Soak the gelatine in plenty of cold water for at least 10 minutes.
13. Cut the vanilla bean lengthwise and scrape out the seeds with a knife.
14. Bring cream, milk and the vanilla pod with seeds to a boil. Put the pan aside and let stand for 15 minutes in order for the milk and cream to absorb the vanilla flavor.
15. Beat the egg yolks with the sugar and add the vanilla milk. Heat it all to 185° F (85° C).
16. Pass the cream through a fine sieve and stir in the drained gelatine leaves until melted.
17. Whip the cream cold using an electric mixer. Add the butter and stir at low speed until it's a light and fluffy cream. Stir in the crushed nougat.

Assemblage
18. Place one of the bottoms on a tray and cover it with a fourth of the cream using a palette knife. Add on the next layer and repeat the process two more times.
19. Apply the fourth layer and press it flat using a baking tray.
20. Chill the cake for one hour in the freezer or refrigerator.
21. Spread the remaining cream on the cake and sprinkle it with two thirds of a cup (90 g) of sliced and toasted almonds.
22. Roll out the green marzipan until it's one eighth of an inch (3 mm) thick using the confectioners' sugar. Cut out one and one fifth of an inch (3 cm) wide lengths and place them as shown in the picture. Make four bows.

Casablanca Cake

This traditional Swedish cake was one of the first cakes that I made myself. We baked lengths and square cakes in three different sizes each week. The cake was made for the first time in 1945, when the war was over and we were able to import bananas again, and it became very popular.

When it's properly made it's delicious with a crispy meringue and tasty vanilla-flavored ice cream, surrounded by toasted and sliced almonds. With the whipped cream and the bananas as decoration, it's a delicacy that shouldn't be forgotten.

There is a battle about who created the recipe – was it OGO Konditori in Stockholm, Oskar Berg's Hovkonditori or Filip's Hovkonditori on Government Street? I remember that there was a pastry shop in Malmö called Casablanca, which had this cake as their specialty.

10–12 PIECES

One recipe of French meringue made with 4/5 cup egg whites, see page 32
3.5 oz dark chocolate (100 g), preferably Valrhona Grand Cru Guanaja 70%
One Ice Cream recipe, see page 93
1/2 cup toasted and sliced almonds (80 g)

Whipped Cream
10 fl oz whipping cream (300 g)
1 tsp pure vanilla extract (5 g)
3 tsp sugar (15 g)

2 bananas
3 1/2 oz neutral gelatine glaze (100 g), see recipe on page 43

1. Preheat the oven to 210° F (100° C).
2. Draw three squares, 9x9 inch (20x20 cm), on three pieces of parchment paper.
3. Make the meringue and distribute it in the squares as evenly as possible using a palette knife and sprinkle the bottoms with a tiny bit of sugar to make them more brittle.
4. Bake the meringue for about 90 minutes, until they feel light and dry.
5. Melt and temper the chocolate, see page 52.
6. Spread a thin layer of chocolate on the bottoms.
7. Make the ice cream.

Assemblage
8. Spread nearly half of the cream on one of the layers evenly using a palette knife.
9. Add on the next layer and push down with a baking tray to make it flat.
10. Add the remaining cream, saving two thirds of a cup (150 g) to spread on the edges of the cake.
11. Spread the cream and add the last layer. Press until flat using a baking sheet. Place the cake in the refrigerator to set for one hour.
12. Spread evenly on the edges using a palette knife and sprinkle with the toasted almonds. Carefully move the cake to a cake plate.
13. In a chilled bowl, whip the cream, sugar and vanilla extract into a foam.
14. Add the foam to a plastic pastry bag with a fluted nozzle no. 12. Cut the banana into 1/5 inch thick slices. Decorate as shown.
15. Add a thin layer of fruit jelly on top.

Swedish Meringue Cake

This tasty cake was made differently at each place I worked when I was young. This is the way we made it at Blekingsborg pastry shop in Malmö, and we had a lot of meringue cake orders on Saturdays and Sundays. When I was an apprentice I worked every Saturday and every other Sunday as well. On Sundays we always baked wheat cakes, Danish pastry, traditional mayor wreath buns and tasty Karlsbad buns with almond filling. All the orders of cakes were garnished and packed, and we often put to them together on a Saturday to make them succulent and tasty.

APPROX. 10–12 PIECES

One recipe French meringue, see page 32
5 2/3 oz dark chocolate (160 g), preferably Valrhona
    Grand Cru Guanaja 70%, for brushing of the bottoms

Cream / Chocolate Cream
27 fl oz whipping cream (800 g)
2 tbsp sugar (20 g)
2 tsp pure vanilla extract (10 g)
2 tbsp milk, 3% (30 g)
5 oz dark chocolate (140 g), preferably Valrhona Grand
    Cru Guanaja 70%

chocolate spiral for decoration, see page 56
striped chocolate rolls, see chocolate decorations on
    page 59
1 1/2 oz white chocolate (40 g), preferably Valrhona Ivoire
3 oz dark chocolate (80 g), Valrhona Grand Cru
    Guanaja 70%

1. Draw three rings, 7 inches (18 cm) in diameter, with a pencil on parchment paper.
2. Preheat the oven to 210° F (100° C).
3. Make the meringue.
4. Move the meringue to a plastic bag with a large flat nozzle or cut a hole in the front.
5. Pipe three thick circles in the marked sections and pipe a thick cross in the middle of the circles.
6. Put the meringues in the oven and bake until they dry, about 90 minutes.
7. Store the meringues in a dry place until they're ready to use. They can be baked one week in advance.
8. Finely chop and then melt the chocolate in the microwave or in a water bath with a temperature of 130° F (55° C) for brushing.
9. Brush the layers on both sides with chocolate until completely covered. Set in fridge to solidify.
10. In a chilled bowl, whip the cream with sugar and vanilla extract into a foam.
11. Melt the finely chopped chocolate and milk in the microwave oven or in a water bath until it's at a temperature of 140° F (60° C).
12. Weigh one and three quarter cups (400 g) of whipped cream and mix with chocolate milk until it's a smooth paste.
13. Put the two types of cream in two plastic pastry bags with a fluted nozzle, preferably no. 12.

Assemblage
14. Place a layer with a cross on a doily paper, pipe chocolate cream about a twelfth of an inch (2 cm) thick diagonally on two fourths of the pieces and regular cream on the other two.
15. Add one more layer, but pipe the cream conversely this time. Add the third layer.
16. Spread whipped cream evenly on the top and pipe chocolate cream and regular whipped cream as shown in the image.
17. Finish with cream bows around edge of the top and decorate with a chocolate spiral and striped chocolate rolls. (Back in the day the cake was always finished with a marzipan rose and leaves made out of green pickled pears.)

Passion Fruit Cake

I ate this tasty cake as a New Year's Eve dessert at the renowned restaurant Le Gavroche in London, where Albert and Michel Roux reigned in the kitchen - two fantastic professionals. They also run the restaurant Waterside Inn, which is beautifully located beside the Thames. If you visit, you have to try their raspberry soufflé.

Making the mousse with a pâté à bombe instead of Italian meringue makes the cake richer and creamier in its consistency – I hope that you as the reader of this book feel the same way.

Enjoy it with a bowl of fresh raspberries and a chilled glass of Beaumes-de-Venise wine.

12 PIECES

One cake ring, 2x9-inch (5x22 cm)

1/2 recipe Bisquit Joconde, see page 27
3 oz white chocolate (80 g), to cover the lowermost
   bottom

Passion Fruit Mousse with Pâté à bombe
1/3 oz gelatine leaves (10 g/about 5)
4 cups whipped cream (250 g) 40%
2/3 cup sugar (125 g)
1/4 cup water (60 g)
4 oz, or about 6, egg yolks (125 g)
10 1/2 oz passion fruit puree (250 g/about 30 fruits)
   with 10% sugar

Passion Fruit Syrup
2 passion fruits
1/4 cup confectioners' sugar (25 g)

5 1/3 oz neutral gelatine glaze for decoration (150 g), see
   page 43
2 passion fruits for decoration
physalis for decoration

Passion Fruit Mousse
1. Soak the gelatine in plenty of cold water for at least
   10 minutes.
2. In a chilled bowl, whip the cream until firm and
   place in the fridge.

3. Whisk the egg yolks into a foam and bring sugar and water to a boil in a small saucepan, while constantly washing the inside of the saucepan with a brush dipped in water. Boil until the syrup is 250° F (122° C), use the thermometer or do a cold water test, see page 35.

4. Pour the boiling sugar syrup in a steady stream into the whipped yolks while constantly whisking. Continue to whisk on low speed until the egg mixture turns cold.

5. Remove the gelatine from the water and drain the water that's left on the leaves. Melt them to a temperature of 110–120° F (45–50° C).

6. Mix whipped cream, the egg mixture and fruit puree into a light and fluffy mousse using a spatula. Mix two scoops of mousse with the hot gelatin mixture. Finally turn the gelatine into the mousse.

Passion Fruit Syrup

7. Cut the fruits in half and scrape out the fruit content using a teaspoon. Mix with the sugar until melted.

Assembling the cake

8. Place the Bisquit Joconde bottom in the freezer for 1 hour after baking.

9. Turn the bottom on parchment paper and remove the silicone mat or baking mat. Use a ruler to cut out two lengths, 2 inches (5 cm) wide.

10. Line the cake ring with plastic cake wrap and with the bisquit Joconde with the baked part facing the ring. Cut with a knife so that it fits precisely. Place on a baking tray lined with parchment paper.

11. Add a bottom, 8 inches (20 cm) in diameter, to a cake ring.

12. Finely chop and melt the chocolate in a microwave or in a water bath at a 110° F (45° C) temperature. Brush the bottom with chocolate and place it in the fridge to solidify.

13. Place cake base with the chocolate facing down in the ring and half fill it with the mousse.

14. Add the rest of the Bisquit Joconde bottoms in the middle and spread them evenly inside of the cake. Cover them with passion fruit syrup using a brush, so that the bottoms absorb the syrup.

15. Fill the ring with the mousse and even it out with a palette knife. Freeze cake for at least 6 hours.

Completing the cake

16. Take the cake out of the freezer.

17. Mix the jelly with the meat from a passion fruit and apply it on top of the cake resembling a mirror. Let stand for 5 minutes until the jelly hardens.

18. Loosen cake from the ring and remove the plastic cake wrap. Place the cake on a doily paper and decorate with a split passion fruit as shown in the image, as well as a few physalis. Defrost the cake for one hour at room temperature or about three hours in the refrigerator, before serving.

Käse Sahnetorte - Cream Cheese Cake with Strawberries

We always baked this tasty cake for passengers on the Cunard Line. The recipe has been with me ever since, and the cake always tastes crisp and delicious. Remember to use a cottage cheese that is high in fat content, preferably 10%. It's important to add the berries that are going to be on the inside of the cake in syrup before all else, or they will freeze and turn into ice cubes and it turns into a jumble rather than a pleasure.

10–12 PIECES

One cake ring, 2x9-inch (5x22 cm)

One traditional Viennese bottom, see page 20
One recipe of shortcrust pastry, see page 40

Preserved Strawberries
9 oz strawberries (250 g)
2/3 cup sugar (135 g)
2/5 cup water (100 g)

3 1/2 oz quality strawberry jam (100 g)

Quark Creme
1/5 oz gelatine leaves (6 g/about 3)
1 lemon
1 vanilla bean, preferably Tahiti
1 cup cream cheese (250 g) 10%

3/4 cup confectioners' sugar (85 g)
3 tbsp egg yolks (40 g/about 2)
5 fl oz whipping cream (150 g) 40%
2/3 cups milk, 3% (150 g)

Whipped Cream for Decoration
4 cups whipped cream (250 g)
2 tsp sugar (10 g)
1 tsp pure vanilla extract (5 grams)

1/3 cup toasted and sliced almonds (60 g)
17 1/2 oz fresh strawberries for decoration (500 g)
2 tbsp whole pistachios (25 g)
5 1/2 oz neutral gelatine glaze (150 g),
    see recipe page 43

3 oz white chocolate (80 g), preferably Valrhona Ivoire
    for white chocolate feathers, see chocolate decoration on page 61

DAY 1
1. Bake a Viennese cake bottom.

Shortcrust Pastry Bottom
2. Preheat the oven to 375° F (190° C).
3. Roll out the pastry until it's about one eighth of an inch (2.5 mm) thick. Make indentions in the dough with a fork.
4. Place a bottom, 9 inches (22 cm) in diameter, in a cake ring and place it on the sheet with parchment paper.
5. Bake bottom until golden brown for about 10–12 minutes (watch the oven, it will burn easily). Let cool on sheet.

Preserved Strawberries
6. Bring water and sugar to a boil and pour the syrup over the strawberries while still boiling. Allow to cool. Save the mixture for brushing the cake bottom.

DAY 2
Quark Creme
7. Soak the gelatine in plenty of cold water for at least 10 minutes.
8. Wash the lemon and grate the peel with the fine side of the grater.
9. Cut the vanilla bean lengthwise and scrape out the seeds.
10. Beat cream cheese, egg yolk, confectioners' sugar and lemon zest with the vanilla seeds for 5 minutes.
11. Whip the cream to a solid foam in a chilled metal bowl.
12. Remove the gelatine from the water and let the remaining water stay on the leaves.
13. Melt the gelatine leaves to 110–120° F (45–50° C) and stir in milk.
14. Stir the gelatine into the quark mixture and then fold into the whipped cream to form a light cream.

Assembling the cake

15. Place plastic cake wrap in a nine inch (22 cm) by two inch (5 cm) cake ring, or use a springform pan with the same measurements.
16. Cut the cake base into three equally thick bottoms using a serrated knife. Freeze a layer for another day.
17. Spread a layer of strawberry jam on the shortcrust pastry bottom and add a cake bottom. Place it in the cake ring.
18. Brush the cake bottom with half of the strawberry preserve, until absorbed.
19. Spread the drained syrup-soaked strawberries on the bottom.
20. Distribute the quark creme on top and use a palette knife to smoothen.
21. Add another layer and cover it with the remaining syrup. Freeze the cake on a tray lined with baking paper for about 6 hours.

Decoration

22 Remove the cake from the ring and the plastic cake wrap.
23. Spread whipped cream on the edges of the cake using a palette knife.
24. Place the cake in your hand and sprinkle the edges with sliced and toasted almonds.
25. Place strawberries in the middle of the cake, leaving space at the edges.
26. Brush strawberries with jelly and place the cake in the refrigerator for 15 minutes to solidify.
27. In a chilled bowl, whip cream, sugar and vanilla extract into a solid foam.
28. Take the cake out again and add whipped cream to a plastic pastry bag with a fluted nozzle no. 12. Pipe bows around the cake as shown in image.
29. Decorate with white chocolate feathers and pistachios around the entire cake.
30. Thaw cake for one hour at room temperature or in refrigerator for about three hours.

Elderflower and Strawberry Mousse Cake

This summery cake is perfect for summer weddings. The combination of elderflowers, strawberries and almond bottoms is bound to taste good. It's best if you make your own elderflower squash. Please refer to my book, *Jam and Marmalade,* for recipes.

10–12 PIECES

One cake ring, 2x9-inch (5x22 cm) or a springform pan with the same diameter measurement

Dough for decoration - Pate à cigarette
1 3/4 tbsp egg whites (25 g/about 1)
2 tbsp soft unsalted butter (25 g)
1/4 cup confectioners' sugar (25 g)
1/4 cup all-purpose flour (25 g)
One drop of food color, preferably green natural vegetable color

1/2 recipe Bisquit Joconde, see page 27

3 oz white chocolate (80 g), preferably Valrhona Ivoire, for brushing of the cake ring bottom

1/2 recipe of strawberry syrup, see Strawberry and Rhubarb Charlotte on page 73

Elderflower bavaroise
1/5 oz gelatine leaves (6 g /about 3)
4 cups whipped cream (250 g)
1 cup elderflower squash (200 g)
3 1/2 tbsp lemon juice (50 g)
2 oz, or about 3, egg yolks (60 g)

One recipe of strawberry mousse, see Strawberry and Rhubarb Charlotte on page 73

Decoration
3 1/2 oz neutral gelatine glaze (100 g), see page 43
17 1/2 oz strawberries for decoration (500 g)
3 oz white chocolate chips (80 g), preferably Valrhona Ivoire, see chocolate decorations on page 56

Decoration Dough - Pate à cigarette
1. Take out the egg white and butter to make them room temperature.
2. Sift confectioners' sugar and wheat flour.
3. Use a spatula and stir butter, confectioners' sugar and flour, until barely mixed. Add egg whites one at a time until smooth and pass it through a sieve.
4. Add a drop of food coloring.
5. Spread the dough out as evenly as possible on a silicone mat or a kitchen towel using a palette knife.
6. Create a pattern using a paint scraper (can be purchased in paint stores) and freeze the mat or cloth for 10 minutes. Next, spread the Bisquit Joconde mixture.
7. Quickly peel off the paper after baking, to prevent the decoration dough from sticking to the paper, or freeze the bottom for one hour before you remove the paper.
8. Make one baking sheet of Bisquit Joconde, see page 27, patterned with pâté à cigarette.

Assemblage
9. Cut out two lengths of Bisquit Joconde using a ruler, making them two inches (5 cm) wide.
10. Attach plastic cake wrap inside the ring and place it on parchment paper. Line it with the bottom and cut with a knife to ensure that the seam isn't visible.
11. Melt the finely chopped chocolate in a microwave or a water bath with a temperature of 110° F (45° C). Brush the chocolate on the paper inside the ring to form a protective layer for the first bottom.
12. Cut a layer from the remaining bottoms, 9 inches in diameter. Place it in the bottom of the cake ring. You might have to cut the edges a little bit for it to fit. Place on a tray lined with parchment paper.
13. Brush the lowermost bottom lightly with strawberry preserve.

Elderflower Bavaroise

14. Soak the gelatine in plenty of cold water for at least 10 minutes.
15. In a chilled bowl, whip the cream until firm and place it in the fridge.
16. Mix elderflower squash, lemon juice and egg yolks in a saucepan and heat to 185° F (85° C), while constantly stirring. Pass through a fine sieve, a so-called chinoise.
17. Add the drained gelatine leaves and leave the remaining water on the leaves. Stir until the gelatine has melted. Make sure that the temperature does not exceed 122° F (50° C).
18. Cool the mixture in a cold water bath under continuous whipping until the temperature is 70° F (20° C).
19. Add half of the bavaroise mixture with the whipped cream using a spatula until it is a smooth paste and then add the remaining mixture.
20. Move the mixture into the ring and place on the remains of the Joconde bottom. Brush the bottom with the remaining strawberry preserve and set everything in the freezer for 30 minutes.
21. Add the strawberry mousse and freeze the cake for at least 6 hours. Smooth out the top using a palette knife.

Decoration

22. Remove the cake from the freezer. Glaze the surface with jelly using a palette knife. Remove the ring and plastic cake wrap from the cake.
23. Decorate with halved strawberries and cover with neutral gelatine glaze. Add white chocolate shavings in the middle and move the cake onto a doily paper.
24. Thaw cake, about one hour at room temperature or three hours in refrigerator.

If the cake is well packaged it will keep in the freezer for several weeks without the decor.

Malakoff Cake

This tasty cake originates from the Mecca of pastry bakers, that is, Vienna. Nobody does it better than Kurcafe Oberla. If you are in Vienna, make sure to visit it, because they are great at making pastries. They have a store at St. Stephen's Square in downtown Vienna, where all the pastries are delicious. They are also famous for their panettone. It is indeed an Italian specialty, but they make them just as well as they do in Motta in Milan.

10–12 PIECES

One cake ring, 2x9-inch (5x22 cm) or a springform pan with the same diameter measurement

Lady Finger Mixture
4 oz, or about 6, egg yolks (120 g)
8 tsp sugar (38 g)
2 tsp pure vanilla extract (8 g)
6 1/2 oz, or about 6, egg whites (180 g)
1 tsp lemon juice (5 g)
1/2 cup sugar (105 g)
1 1/3 cup all-purpose flour (165 g)

Cointreau Fromage
1/3 oz gelatine leaves (8 g/about 4)
1 vanilla pod, preferably Tahiti
3 tbsp egg yolks (40 g/about 2)
8 1/2 tsp sugar (40 g)
1 2/5 tbsp Cointreau (20 g)
6 cups whipped cream (350 g) 40%

Whipped Cream
8 1/3 fl oz whipping cream (250 g) 40%
2 tsp sugar (10 g)
1 tsp of pure vanilla extract (5 grams)

3 1/2 tbsp Cointreau (50 g)
1/3 cup toasted and sliced almonds (60 g) for decoration

Bottom and Lady Fingers
1. Preheat oven to 390° F (200° C). Draw a circle that's nine inches (22 cm) in diameter on parchment paper with the help of a cake ring.
2. Beat the egg yolks with two tablespoons of sugar and vanilla extract into a solid foam for four minutes.
3. Sift the flour on a parchment paper.
4. In a very clean bowl, beat the egg whites and lemon juice until fluffy and gradually add half cups (105 g) of sugar until it's a solid meringue.
5. Add the egg yolk mixture to the meringue using a spatula and finally add the flour gently and make it into a light and fluffy mixture (don't overdo the mixture, or it will become watery).
6. Add the mixture to a plastic pastry bag with a flat nozzle no. 12 and pipe a cake layer in a spiral from the inside and out, within the marked ring.
7. Place the bottom in the oven and bake it golden brown for about 8–10 minutes.
8. Immediately transfer the bottom to cool on a baking rack.
9. Pipe biscuits as thick as a finger, two and a half inches (7 cm) long, on parchment paper.
10. Sprinkle a little sugar and let it melt for 5 minutes.
11. Bake the biscuits until golden brown for 8–10 minutes. Let cool on baking rack.

Cointreau Fromage

12 Soak the gelatine in plenty of cold water for 10 minutes.

13. Cut the vanilla bean lengthwise and scrape out the seeds with a knife. Add the vanilla seeds to a clean bowl together with the egg yolks and sugar and whisk into a foam for 5 minutes.

14. Remove the gelatine from the water and drain the remaining water on the leaves.

15. Melt the gelatine leaves to 110–120° F (45–50° C).

16. Stir the alcohol into the gelatine mixture and add it into the egg yolk foam, while whisking. Fold the mixture into the whipped cream until it's a light and fluffy fromage.

Assembling the cake

17. Place the cake ring on a tray lined with parchment paper. Line ring with plastic cake wrap.

18. Remove the round cake base from the paper and place it in the ring.

19. Brush the bottom with the liqueur.

20. Save six biscuits for garnishing of the cake and drench the remaining biscuits in liquor. Place them in the ring and alternate with the cream two to three times until the ring is full.

21. Smooth the top evenly using a palette knife and set the cake in the freezer for six hours.

22. Remove the cake from the ring and remove the plastic cake wrap.

23. In a chilled bowl, whip the cream, sugar and vanilla extract into a solid foam. Spread whipped cream as evenly as possible using a palette knife.

24. Place the cake in your hand and sprinkle it with sliced almonds around the edges.

25. Mark the cake in twelve pieces using a sharp knife dipped in hot water. Decorate each piece with a pipe of cream, using a plastic pastry bag with a fluted nozzle no. 12.

26. Add half a biscuit on each cream peak and add sliced almonds in the middle of the cake.

27. Let the cake thaw for one hour at room temperature or three hours in the refrigerator.

Mango Mousse Cake with Raspberries

This delicious combination of tasty mango mousse, raspberries and succulent almond biscuit is perfect as a dessert after a tasty dinner and it isn't too difficult to make. Try to get a hold of a perfectly ripe mango, that's the most important part. I personally prefer the Thai version.

Use a cake ring to make the shape of a drop, as it appears in the picture. It's quite easy to do, as cake rings are easy to bend. You can make the cake round, but it's fun to bake a cake in a different shape every now and then.

10–12 PIECES

One cake ring, 2x9-inch (5x22 cm)

Lightly Preserved Raspberries
9 oz fresh raspberries (250 g)
2/3 cup sugar (135 g)
2/5 cup water (100 g)
1 3/4 tbsp glucose (25 g)

Italian Meringue
2 oz, or about 2, egg whites (60 g)
1 tsp lemon juice (5 g)
2 tbsp sugar (20 g)
1/2 cup sugar (100 g)
1/6 cup water (40 g)

Mango Mousse
1/3 oz gelatine leaves (10 g/about 5)
2 1/2 cup mango puree (500 g) with 10% sugar
1 tbsp lemon juice (15 g)
1 3/4 tbsp white rum (25 g)
5 cups whipped cream (300 g) 40%

1/2 recipe of Bisquit Joconde, see page 27
One recipe of dough decoration, a so-called pate a
    cigarette see page 104, but with yellow color instead
    of green

3 1/2 oz dark chocolate (100 g), preferably Valrhona
    Manjari, for chocolate feathers and for brushing of
    the bottom
1/2 oz white chocolate (15 g) to marble the chocolate
    feathers
5 1/3 oz neutral gelatine glaze, (150 g) see page 43
3 1/2 oz raspberries (100 g) for decoration

Lightly Preserved Raspberries
1. Bring sugar, water and glucose to a boil and add
   the boiling syrup over the berries. Let the berries
   stand to absorb the sugar, while cooling down.

Mango Mousse
2. Start off by making an Italian meringue,
   see page 34.
3. Soak the gelatine in plenty of cold water for at least
   10 minutes.
4. Mix the room temperature mango puree with
   lemon juice and white rum.

5. Beat the Italian meringue into the mixture using a
   whip and then fold in the whipped cream using a
   spatula until it's a light and fluffy mousse.
6. Remove the gelatine from the water and leave the
   remaining water on the leaves when melting the
   gelatine to 110–120° F (45–50° C).
7. Whisk about half a cup of the mousse into the
   gelatine mixture and fold the gelatin mixture into
   the mousse.

Assemblage
8. Make a Bisquit Joconde with decoration dough,
   see preparation on page 104, Elderflower bavaroise
   and strawberry mousse cake.
9. Remove the paper from the patterned Bisquit Joconde. Line the cake ring with plastic cake wrap.
10. Cut two lengths with a ruler, 2 inches (5 cm) wide.
    Line the cake ring with the lengths and make sure
    that the seams fit by cutting them with a knife.
    Place on a tray lined with parchment paper.
11. Cut a bottom the same shape as the inside of the
    ring.
12. Melt the finely chopped chocolate to 130° F (55° C)
    in the microwave or in a water bath. Spread choco-
    late over the bottom using a brush and put the rest
    of the chocolate aside for the feathers. Place the
    bottom in the fridge to solidify.
13. Place the bottom in the lined ring with the choco-
    late side facing down.
14. Add mango mousse and fill half full. Add the drai-
    ned preserved raspberries.
15. Add the Bisquit Joconde wastage in the middle
    and brush the bottom with a little raspberry syrup
    from the berries, until the biscuit has absorbed the
    syrup.
16. Add the rest of the mousse to the cake ring and
    smooth it out using a palette knife. Freeze cake for
    at least six hours.

Decoration
17. Take out the cake and cover it with the jelly.
    Spread it evenly using a palette knife.
18. Remove the ring and the plastic cake wrap.
19. Melt the chocolate one more time and shape marb-
    led feathers, see chocolate techniques on page 61.
20. Decorate with the feathers and fresh raspberries.
    Move the cake to a tray and let it sit and thaw at
    room temperature for about 60 minutes or three
    hours in the refrigerator.

Sicilian Chocolate Mousse Cake

This is a chocolate mousse cake with orange, which I ate in Palermo when I worked on cruise ships and had Armando as my Sicilian sous chef. Armando's father owned a small Pasticceria in Palermo, where they served the world's tastiest lemon juice and lemon sorbet, not to mention the strawberry ice cream... But this is a cake book, so I will have to control myself!

Orange Bottoms
One cake ring, 9 inches (22 cm) in diameter
5 oz, or about 3, eggs (150 g)
1 orange
1 oz preserved orange zest (30 g) (recipe can be found in *Jams and Marmalades* or *Desserts*)
1/5 cup almond meal (45 g), see page 37
1 tsp lemon juice (5 g)
1/3 cup sugar (60 g)
1/2 cup corn starch (50 g)

Truffle Cream
14 oz dark chocolate (400 g), Valrhona Grand Cru Pur Caribe 66%
6 2/3 cups whipped cream (400 g)

Chocolate Feathers
3 oz white chocolate (80 g), preferably Valrhona Ivoire
Marbled chocolate for decorating the edges
3 oz dark chocolate (80 g), preferably Valrhona Grand Cru Guanaja 70%

1/4 recipe chocolate jelly, see page 159
1/3 cup cocoa (25 g), preferably Valrhona 20/22

1. Preheat oven to 390° F (200° C).
2. Separate the egg yolks and whites.
3. Beat the egg yolks with the orange zest, preserved orange peel, almond meal and one and a half tablespoons of sugar.
4. In a very clean bowl, beat the egg whites with lemon juice into foam and add three tablespoons of sugar in batches. Whisk until the meringue is firm.
5. Mix meringue with the egg yolk mixture, sift the flour and create a fine mixture using a spatula.
6. Add the mixture to the ring and bake until golden brown for about 25 minutes. Use a stick to ensure that it's baked through.
7. Sprinkle sugar on top of the layer and place it on a baking grid lined with baking paper.

Truffle Cream
8. Heat the chocolate to 130° F (55° C).
9. Whip the cream into light foam in a chilled bowl.
10. Mix half of the whipped cream with the melted chocolate into a smooth cream and fold in the remainder of the mousse.
11. Make chocolate feathers out of the white chocolate, see picture on page 61.

Decoration of edges
12. Temper the dark chocolate, see page 52.
13. Spread chocolate thinly on an acetate sheet using a palette knife and create waves in it using a paint scraper, see image on page 58.
14. Mix the remaining chocolate with the leftover white chocolate and temper it again. Apply it over the marked parts of the acetate sheet using a palette knife.
15. Let it solidify at room temperature, apply an acetate sheet and place a heavy item on top of it, to prevent the chocolate from warping.

Assemblage
16. Remove the bottom from the cake ring using a knife. Line the cake ring with plastic cake wrap. Put down the baked orange bottom and place the cake on a tray lined with parchment paper.
17. Fill the ring with the mousse and bang it on the table to prevent holes on the sides. Smooth it using a palette knife and let it sit for at least three hours in the fridge.
18. Loosen the cake from the plastic cake wrap and pour a little of the chocolate jelly, at about 95° F (35° C), over the cake in a creative manner. Dust with cocoa using a sieve.
19. Decorate with the white feathers and dust a tiny bit of cocoa on top of them.
20. Remove the chocolate from the acetate sheet and break off pieces of it. Nudge them around the edges of the cake.
21. Carefully move the cake to a doily paper.

Praline Cake from Piemonte

This explosion that consists of luscious roasted hazelnuts is among the most delicious things one can eat, together with a strong espresso. The nuts should ideally be from Piedmont in Italy or from Spain, the Turkish ones aren't the same. In Turin there are a lot of good pastry shops that have amazing pastries filled with nuts, chestnuts, apricots and cherries.

10–12 PIECES

Hazelnut Meringue Bottoms
1 2/3 cups ground hazelnuts (200 g)
1 cup sugar (200 g)
9 oz, egg whites (250 g)
1 tsp lemon juice (5 g)
1/2 cup sugar (100 g)

Praline Buttercream
2 cups vanilla cream (500 g), see page 46
5 2/3 oz hazelnut praline paste (160 g), see page 39
1 1/3 cups unsalted butter (320 g)

confectioners' sugar to dust with

Hazelnut Meringue Bottoms
1. Preheat the oven to 340° F (170° C). Trace three circles on parchment paper, 9 inches (22 cm) in diameter.
2. Make a tpt by running hazelnuts and sugar in a food processor.
3. Whisk the egg white and lemon juice with two tablespoons of sugar into a foam, increase the speed and add the remaining sugar, while constantly whisking into a firm meringue.
4. Fold in the nut mixture using a spatula, into a light and porous mass.
5. Add the mixture to a plastic pastry bag with a flat nozzle No. 10, or cut a suitable hole in the tip of the cone.
6. Pipe three bottoms of the meringue, from the inside out. Use the remaining meringue to pipe small balls of meringue for decoration, making them about the size of a thumb. Bake until golden brown for 35–40 minutes.
7. Remove the bottoms from the oven and immediately turn them around and remove the paper. The bottoms should be brittle; if they aren't, bake them a little longer until they are dry.

Praline Butter Cream
8. Mix all the ingredients into a light and porous cream, similar to whipped cream.

Assemblage
9. Apply one third of the cream to one of the bottoms. Repeat with the next base. Add the third bottom and press cake flat using a plate.
10. Add the remaining cream and cover the sides.
11. Smooth out the top and decorate with the small meringues.
12. Place on a cake plate and let stand in the fridge for 60 minutes.
13. Dust with confectioners' sugar.

Blueberry and Yogurt Cake

We used to bake this cake in Switzerland, as the blueberries would arrive, and it was very popular among the ladies in the cafeteria on the second floor. I think they assumed that it contained fewer calories than the other cakes. The cake is just as easy to bake year-round, just add frozen blueberries, lingonberries or strawberries instead.

10—12 PIECES

One cake ring, 2x9-inch (5x22 cm) or a springform pan with the same diameter measurement

One Viennese bottom, see page 20
One recipe of shortcrust pastry, see page 40

Preserved Blueberries
2/3 cup sugar (135 g)
1/2 cup water (100 g)
1 3/4 tbsp glucose (25 g)

Yogurt Bavaroise
1/3 oz gelatine leaves (8 g/about 4)
1 lemon
1/4 cup sugar (45 g)
1 3/4 oz, or about 4, egg yolks (50 g)
1/5 cup milk, 3% (50 g)
a dash of salt (1 g), preferably fleur de sel
8 fl oz plain Turkish yogurt (200 g)
3 1/2 cups whipped cream (225 g)

3 1/2 oz apricot jam (100 g), see page 44

Whipped Cream for decoration
8 1/3 fl oz whipping cream (250 g) 40%
1 tbsp sugar (10 g)
1 tsp pure vanilla extract (5 g)

Marbled Chocolate pieces for decoration of edges
1 1/2 oz dark chocolate (40 g), Valrhona Grand Cru
    Guanaja 70%
1 1/2 oz white chocolate (40 g), preferably Valrhona Ivoire
2 acetate sheets
See preparation on page 60

17 1/2 oz blueberries (500 g)
5 1/3 oz neutral gelatine glaze (150 g), see page 43

DAY 1
1. Bake the Viennese bottom.

Shortcrust Pastry Bottom
2. Preheat the oven to 375° F (190° C).
3. Roll out the pastry until it's about one eighth of an inch (2.5 mm) thick. Make indentions in the dough by using a fork.
4. Make a bottom by using a 9-inch (22 cm) ring. Place on a baking sheet lined with parchment paper.
5. Bake bottom until golden brown for 10–12

minutes, and keep a close eye on the oven, as the thin dough easily burns.

Preserved Blueberries
6. Bring sugar, water and glucose to a boil and pour it over the berries. Let stand and cool, in order for the berries to absorb the syrup.

DAY 2
Yogurt Bavaroise
7. Drain the preserved blueberries in a sieve. Soak the gelatine in plenty of cold water for at least 10 minutes.
8. Wash the lemon and grate the outer rind from half of the lemon. Rub the zest with the sugar on a cutting board, until the etheric oil has dissolved the sugar.
9. Mix the egg yolk with the sugar for 5 minutes.
10. Mix the egg yolk with milk and heat to 185° F (85° C), while constantly stirring.
11. Remove the gelatine from the water and let the remaining water on the leaves follow. Add the milk mixture and stir until the gelatine has melted.
12. Add the yogurt and whisk until smooth.
13. In a chilled bowl, whip the cream into foam and add it together with the drained blueberries using a spatula into a light and porous mousse.

Assembling the cake
14. Place a cake ring on a tray lined with parchment paper. Line the inside with plastic cake wrap.
15. Spread a layer of apricot jam on the shortcrust pastry bottom using a palette knife.
16. Divide the cake base into three equally thick bottoms, using a serrated knife. Freeze a bottom for another occasion.
17. Add the mousse and spread it evenly. Apply a second bottom and press it flat, using a baking sheet. Place in freezer for about 6 hours.
18. Loosen the cake from the ring and the plastic and cover the edges with whipped cream.
19. Remove the chocolate from the acetate sheet and attach the chocolate pieces around the cake.
20. In a chilled bowl, whip the cream, vanilla and sugar into a firm foam.
21. Pipe little balls of whipped cream around the cake with a fluted nozzle no. 12.
22. Fill the hole with blueberries and spread the neutral gelatine glaze over it.
23. Allow the cake to thaw for one hour at room temperature or three hours in the refrigerator.

Cake of a Thousand Sheets · Gâteau mille feuille

This tasty, crispy and crunchy cake that was most likely created by the great chef Marie Antoine Câreme (1784–1834), is always delicious when it is freshly baked and brittle. The French version consists of a crispy pastry, fine vanilla cream as the filling and a thin layer of raspberry jam on the bottom. The legendary restaurateur Tore Wretman also loved this cake, so much that Dag Öster, the head pastry chef at Operakällaren, had to bake it every day.

In this case it isn't necessary to make a classic shortcrust pastry, the so-called Quick Puff Pastry works just as well.

Gâteau Glacé is a version of the Cake of a Thousand Sheets. It is baked in circles, and it has vanilla ice cream with cotton candy in the middle. It is served with hot chocolate sauce.

The recipe can be found in my book *Desserts*.

I have chosen to decorate with fresh rose petals, which suits this beautiful cake.

12 PIECES

One 9 inch cake ring (22 cm)

One Quick Puff Pastry recipe, see page 39
confectioners' sugar (50 g)

Cream
1/6 oz gelatine leaves (4 g/about 2)
2 tbsp water (25 g)
One recipe vanilla cream, see page 46
5 fl oz whipping cream (150 g)
One recipe apricot preserve, see page 45
3 1/2 oz raspberry jam (100 g), see recipe page 44
5 1/2 oz fondant (150 g), see page 43
2 tsp dark rum (10 g)
One red rose, pesticide-free

Shortcrust Pastry
1. Divide dough in half and roll out each part onto a baking sheet, about one eighth of an inch (3 mm) thin, using all-purpose flour and a roller.
2. Roll out the pieces of dough onto two baking sheets lined with parchment paper. Make indentions using a fork, to prevent the dough from bubbles. Leave in the refrigerator for one hour.
3. Preheat oven to 390° F (200° C). Bake bottoms until golden brown for about 20–25 minutes, until they are thoroughly baked, yet not too brown.
4. Sprinkle confectioners' sugar over the bottoms and increase the oven temperature to 480° F (250° C).

5. Bake bottoms until the sugar is caramelized and is developing a brown color.
6. Make four bottoms using a cake ring, as soon as they are out of the oven. Let the bottoms cool on a baking rack.
7. Cut the pastry residues with a knife and save the crumbles for decoration of the edges of the cake.

Cream
8. Soak the gelatine in plenty of cold water for at least 10 minutes.
9. Pass the cold vanilla cream through a fine sieve.
10. Whip the cream into foam in a chilled metal bowl.
11. Remove the gelatine from the water and melt it in two tablespoons (25 g) of water at 110–120° F (45–50° C).
12. Rapidly whisk the warm gelatine mixture and add it to the vanilla cream. Carefully add the whipped cream using a spatula.

Assemblage
13. Spread a thin layer of raspberry jam on the first bottom and add bottom number two. Spread nearly half of the cream on top. Add one more bottom and repeat the procedure.
14. Apply the last bottom with the flat side facing upwards. Press down on the cake using a baking sheet to ensure that it's even. Use the remaining cream to cover the edges.

15. Cover the top of the cake with apricot preserve.
16. Heat the fondant and liquor to 95–105° F (35–40° C) and pour glaze in the middle of the cake. Quickly glaze it using a palette knife.
17. Sprinkle the edges of the cake with pastry crumbs and place it on a cake plate. Decorate with fresh rose petals, as shown. I felt so exclusive when we took the picture, that I added a gold leaf.

Let cake stand in the refrigerator until ready to serve, the sooner the better.

Another classic puff pastry cake is the **Zola Cake**, which is named after the author Émile Zola. It consists of two thin pastry bottoms; the bottom one is covered with a layer of tasty apple jam and next, a nine inch (22 cm) cake ring is placed around it, which is filled with Zola fromage, see page 49.

When the cake has settled in the fridge, you remove it from the ring and top it off with a shortcrust pastry base that has been glazed with pink rum fondant, just like the cake of a thousand sheets.

Another very tasty traditional Swedish cake is the **Napoleon Cake**, similar to the pastry, but in the shape of a cake. It consists of a shortcrust pastry base covered with apple jam, a shortcrust pastry bottom, vanilla cream and whipped cream. It is topped off with a shortcrust pastry base that is covered in raspberry jam and thinly glazed with white fondant.

Flocken Sahnetorte – snöflingetårta med lingon

We often served this cake during afternoon tea, when I worked on the cruise ship Vista/Fjord. The passengers would eat enormous amounts of cakes and pastries, and our American passengers particularly loved this beautiful cake. Chief Steward Per Sjöström would sometimes also have a piece of Flocken Sahnetorte, although Black Forest Cake was his favorite.

The Petits-choux and lingonberry cream gives this cake a delicious texture. When the Chaine de Rotisseurs used to come on board in Hamburg, we served an orgy of cakes, and we always placed a dome of caramel on top. Enjoy it with a cup of strong coffee or a freshly brewed tea.

10–12 PIECES

One cake ring, 2x9-inch (5x22 cm) or a springform pan with the same diameter measurement

If you want to make a sugar dome on top of the cake, the way I did it:

Use a round glass jar or a metal bowl, with a diameter of 10 inches (24–26 cm).

Lubricate it lightly on the inside using regular cooking oil.

Cook the caramel, see page 123, see image on how to make a sugar dome.

Butter Sprinkles
1/3 cup butter (80 g)
1/2 cup sugar (90 g)
2 tsp pure vanilla extract (10 g)
3/4 cup all-purpose flour (100 g)

One recipe of shortcrust pastry, see page 40
One recipe of petits-choux, see page 40

Vanilla and Kirsch Fromage
1/3 oz gelatine leaves (8 g/about 4)
1 vanilla pod, Tahiti
1/2 cup confectioners' sugar (50 g)
1 1/2 oz, or about 2, egg yolks (40 g)
16 4/5 fl oz whipped cream (500 g) 40%
Kirsch Wasser (60 g), or dark rum

10 1/2 oz fine lingonberry jam (300 g)
1/2 cup toasted and sliced almonds for decoration (80 g)
confectioners' sugar

Butter Sprinkles
1. Mix all the ingredients in a food processor into a dough.
2. Squeeze the dough through a potato ricer and let it solidify in the refrigerator for about one hour.

Shortcrust Pastry Bottom
3. Preheat the oven to 375° F (190° C).
4. Mix the shortcrust pastry and leave it standing in a cold place.
5. Roll out the dough until it's about one eighth of an inch (2.5 mm) thick. Make indentions using a fork and cut out a bottom using a cake ring, nine inches (22 cm) in diameter. Place it on parchment paper.
6. Bake the bottom until golden brown for 10–12 minutes (keep a close eye on it, as pastry bottoms burn easily).

Petit-choux bottoms
7. Preheat the oven to 430° F (220° C).
8. Make the petits-choux according to recipe.
9. Draw three circles on parchment paper using a pencil and a cake ring, nine inches (22 cm) in diameter.
10. Add the mixture to a plastic pastry bag, cut a hole in the tip and pipe within the marked lines, from the inside and out. Sprinkle with the butter sprinkles.
11. Bake the bottoms until golden brown for 8–12 minutes and place on a grid.

Vanilla and Kirsch Fromage

12. Soak the gelatine leaves in cold water for at least 10 minutes.
13. Cut the vanilla bean lengthwise and scrape out the seeds using a knife.
14. Rub the seeds on the cutting board with one quarter of a cup (50 g) of sugar using a palette knife to distribute the vanilla evenly.
15. Whisk the vanilla sugar with egg yolks in a 104°F (40–45° C) simmering water bath. Whisk the egg mixture to a solid and cool foam.
16. In a chilled bowl, whip the cream to solid foam.
17. Remove the gelatine from the water and drain the remaining water. Melt it to a temperature of about 115–125° F (45–50° C).
18. Stir the liquor into the gelatin solution and turn it into the cream. Quickly add it to the egg yolk foam, to make a smooth fromage.

1 Drizzle caramel in the greased mold, see page 46.
2 Gently loosen as the candy begins to harden.
3 The finished caramel dome.

Assembling the cake

19. Spread a thin layer of cranberry jam on the short-crust pastry bottom and place it into a cake ring or a springform pan.

20. Add a baked petit-choux bottom on top of the shortcrust pastry bottom and push down. Cover the bottom with half of the remaining lingonberry jam using a palette knife.

21. Spread half of the fromage on top. Add another petit-choux bottom and cover with the remain-ing lingonberry jam. Spread out the rest of the fromage on top and add another petit-choux bot-tom with the sprinkles facing upwards.

22. Use a baking sheet to push down on the cake. Set the cake in the refrigerator for 60 minutes to solidify.

23. Loosen the cake from the ring. Dust with confec-tioners' sugar.

24. If it's a special occasion, add a dome of caramel on top of the cake, or serve this tasty cake the way it is.

Tricolor Cake

My good friend Erik Rotcliff invented this tasty chocolate cake when he and his future wife visited me. Erik was in reality working on the recipe for his own wedding cake, an elderflower mousse cake with strawberry jelly, coated with white chocolate and decorated with two swans made out of white caramel. Erik has a PhD in microbiology, but his passion is gastronomy, so whenever we meet, we always talk about desserts, food and wine.

Almost everyone loves chocolate cake, even Maria Escalante who is sometimes difficult to humor. Bertil Forsberg, the property manager of the The Crown Prince of Malmo, also agreed that it was very tasty.

The gold leaf isn't necessary as it doesn't taste of anything, but it makes the cake very special.

GOOD TO KNOW

It is possible to make flour-free chocolate bottoms, thanks to the chocolate that binds the water in the eggs and makes the cake set.
The fat in the chocolate crystallizes, and in combination with the proteins in the eggs, the cake will set.

12 PIECES

One springform pan, 2x9-inch (5x22 cm)

Chocolate Bottom without Flour
5 ⅓ oz dark chocolate (150 g), preferably Valrhona Grand Cru Guanaja 70%
3 tbsp unsalted butter (40 g)
3 tbsp egg yolks (40 g/about 2)
5 oz, or about 5, egg whites (150 g)
1 tsp lemon juice (5 g)
¼ cup sugar (55 g)

Crème Anglaise
½ cup milk, 3% (120 g)
4 fl oz 40% whipping cream (120 g)
¼ cup egg yolks (60 g/about 3)
2 tsp sugar (10 g)

For the Milk Chocolate Mousse
½ gelatine leaf (1 g)
6 oz chocolate (175 g), preferably Valrhona Jivara Lactée 40%
2 ½ cups whipped cream (150 g)
For the White Chocolate Mousse
½ gelatine leaf (1 g)

6 oz white chocolate (175 g), preferably Valrhona Ivoire
2 ½ cups whipped cream (150 g)

For the Dark Chocolate Mousse
4 oz dark chocolate (110 g), preferably Valrhona Grand Cru Guanaja 70%
2 ½ cups whipped cream (150 g)

One recipe of Opéra Frosting, see page 48

Chocolate Rolls, see Chocolate Decorations on page 59
3 oz dark chocolate (80 g), preferably Valrhona Grand Cru Guanaja 70%
1 sheet of gold leaf

Chocolate Bottom without Flour
1. Preheat oven to 350° F (175° C). Draw a circle, nine inches (22 cm) in diameter, on a pastry cloth or a silicone mat. This type of bottom would stick to parchment paper.
2. Chop the chocolate finely. Gently melt it in the microwave oven or in a water bath until the chocolate has a temperature of 113° F (45° C), using a thermometer to measure.
3. Beat the butter into the chocolate. When it's melted, add and whisk the egg yolks into a smooth paste.
4. Whisk the cold egg whites with lemon juice and a third of the sugar into foam on medium speed. Increase the speed and add the remaining sugar while constantly whisking the batter into a firm meringue.
5. Fold the chocolate cream into the meringue using a spatula and make a light and airy batter.

6. Add the mixture to a plastic pastry bag and cut a hole in the tip, or use a flat nozzle no. 10.
7. Use the mixture to pipe a round bottom within the marked field.
8. Bake for about 12 minutes until the mixture feels firm, but a little soft. Freeze the bottom as soon as it has cooled down. (This base can be stored in the freezer for several weeks when it's wrapped in plastic film.)

Creme Anglaise
9. Bring the milk and whipped cream to a boil.
10. Lightly whisk the yolks with the sugar. Turn the hot mixture over the egg yolks and mix well.
11. Pour it back into the saucepan. Stir constantly while heating to 185°F (85°C), using a thermometer or performing a spoon test.
12. Pass through a fine sieve, a chinoise, and use the cream immediately.

Chocolate Mousse
13. Divide the crème anglaise into three bowls, about a half of a cup in each bowl.
14. Chop the different chocolate varieties finely.
15. Start making the milk chocolate mousse. Soak half of the gelatine leaf in plenty of cold water for at least 10 minutes.
16. Pour the hot crème anglaise over the finely chopped milk chocolate and stir until melted. Use a thermometer to ensure that the temperature is 95°F (35°C). If it's not hot enough, heat it up to the correct temperature in a water bath or in a microwave oven.
17. Remove the gelatine leaf from the water and leave the remaining water on the leaves when melting the gelatine to a temperature of 105–120°F (40–50°C).
18. Pour the gelatin into the cream and mix well.
19. In a chilled bowl, whip two cups (450 g) of whipping cream into a fluffy, not too firm foam. Use two thirds of a cup (150 g) and gently turn it into the cream using a spatula. Put the remaining cream in the fridge.

20. Place a circular piece of parchment paper in the bottom of a springform pan. Line it with plastic cake wrap.
21. Divide the mousse into the ring and spread it as evenly as possible using a palette knife. Tap the pan on the table to make the mousse spread out evenly. Place it back in the freezer.
22. Make the white chocolate mousse in the same manner as the milk chocolate mousse (heat the crème anglaise before you add it to the chocolate, or it won't melt).
23. Move the mousse into a plastic pastry bag and cut a hole in the tip. Remove the ring from the freezer and pipe white chocolate mousse around the edges. Spread the rest of the mousse in the middle.
24. Spread the mousse as evenly as possible using a palette knife and tap the pan on the table to ensure that the mousse is spread evenly. Set it back in the freezer.

Dark Chocolate Mousse
25. Chop the chocolate finely and heat to 120–130°F (50–55°C), add the crème anglaise, stir and make sure that the temperature is 104°F (40°C). If it isn't, heat it in a water bath or in the microwave.
26. Fold the whipped cream using a spatula into a light and airy mousse.
27. Add the mousse on top of the white chocolate mousse and smooth it evenly using a palette knife. Tap the pan on the table to even out the mousse.
28. Add the frozen chocolate bottom and press evenly on top of the mousse.
29. Wrap the pan in plastic film and freeze the cake.
30. Glaze the cake with Opéra glaze, leaving the ring on and the bottom facing down.
31. Carefully loosen the ring and remove the plastic cake wrap, set the cake on a cake plate and decorate with a chocolate roll. Feel free to decorate with a few gold leaves for that extra touch.

Rhubarb Käsekuchen – Cheesecake with Rhubarb

This tasty cake is a classic in the German pastry shops and when it's freshly baked and warm it's a real delicacy. Serve it with strawberry ice cream or preserved strawberries and it will taste even better. I personally love rhubarb in tarts and pastries. Brigitte was one of my German pastry chefs on Vista/Fjord, and her father owned a large bakery in Hanover. Brigitte was in charge of the cakes on board, and all her Käsekuchen were perfectly made.

10–12 PIECES

One cake ring, 2x9-inch (5x22 cm)

Marinated rhubarb
⅔ pound diluted pink rhubarb (300 g)
⅓ cup sugar (60 g)

Quark Cream Filling
1 cup 10% cream cheese (250 g)
¼ cup corn starch (30 g)
1 tbsp pure vanilla extract (15 g)
2 oz, or about 3, egg yolks (60 g)
1 small lemon, grated rind
3 tbsp dark rum (40 g)
3 oz, or about 3, egg whites (90 g)
1 tsp lemon juice (5 g)
¼ cup sugar (45 g)

Almond sprinkles
⅓ cup almond meal (50 g)
¼ cup sugar (50 g)
3 ½ tbsp butter (50 g)
½ cup all-purpose flour (50 g)

One recipe of traditional shortcrust pastry, see page 40

DAY 1
Marinated Rhubarb
1. Cut the rhubarb into one twelfth of an inch (2 cm) pieces and mix thoroughly with the sugar. Place them in a plastic bag and let stand in refrigerator overnight.

DAY 2
Quark Cream Filling
2. Assure that the quark is room temperature and sift corn starch and vanilla extract. Mix it with egg yolk, lemon zest and rum until fluffy.
3. In a very clean metal bowl, whisk egg whites and lemon juice into foam and add the sugar. Whisk to a firm meringue, start at medium speed and then increase the speed.
4. Fold meringue into the quark cream.

Almond Sprinkles
5. Mix all the ingredients into a dough and press it through a potato ricer.

Shortcrust Pastry
6. Roll out the pastry until it's about one eight of an inch thick and shape a 9-inch (22 cm) bottom. Make indentions in the dough using a fork.
7. Place dough in a springform pan. Roll out one third of a pound of the remaining dough and shape it into a string and place it around the edges of the ring. Dip your thumb in a little flour and press one edge a little higher than the edge of the ring. Cut away excess dough using a knife.
8. Place the ring in the freezer for 30 minutes. Preheat the oven to 340° F (170° C).
9. Add the quark cream mixture and spread the drained rhubarb on top. Scatter the sprinkle.
10. Bake cake for 60 minutes, ensure that it's baked using the tip of a knife.
11. Remove cake from the oven and let stand for 10 minutes.
12. Dust with a little confectioners' sugar. Serve with a little lightly whipped cream on the side.

Almond Cake L'Alcazar

You can find this tasty traditional French almond cake at Pâtisserie Millet in Paris on Rue de Saint Dominique. Jean Millet worked as an international Pastry Chairman for many years and he was also a juror in Malmo when I took my exam. The censors and pastry chef masters Hans Eichmüller and Calle Widell were obviously there as well.

The name of the cake originates from a mosque called Alcazar, in the beautiful Spanish city of almonds, Cordoba. It is simple, tasty, long lasting and the perfect cake to bring to picnics.

10–12 PIECES

One springform pan, 2x9-inch (5x22 cm)

Almond Filling
1 ⅔ cups almond meal (375 g)
3 ⅔ cups confectioners' sugar (365 g)
2 ⅓ tsp pure vanilla extract (10 g)
¾ cup unsalted butter (190 g)
⅕ cup dark rum (50 g)
5 oz, or about 3, eggs (150 g)
4 oz, or about 6, egg yolks (120 g)

One recipe of traditional shortcrust pastry, see page 40

3 ½ oz apricot jam (100 g), see recipe on page 44
3 tbsp sliced almonds (30 g)
confectioners' sugar for decoration

Almond Filling
1. Make a tpt of almond meal, confectioners' sugar and vanilla extract in a food processor or a blender.
2. Add the room temperature butter and mix the tpt until it's slightly creamy. Add the rum and the room temperature eggs and egg yolks one by one into a smooth filling.

Assemblage
3. Work the pastry with your hands and roll out until it's about one eighth of an inch (2.5 mm) thick. Shape a bottom using the springform pan and add it to the pan. Make indentions in the dough using a fork.
4. Roll out one third of a pound of the remaining pastry and place it inside the pan. Nudge the dough around the edges making them slightly higher than the pan, and cut away the excess dough.
5. Place the ring in the freezer for 30 minutes. Preheat the oven to 340° F (170° C). Spread a thin layer of apricot jam on the bottom of the ring.
6. Fill the shortcrust pastry pan with the almond filling and spread it on the sides using a palette knife.
7. Sprinkle on the chopped almonds.
8. Bake the cake until golden brown for about 50 minutes, checking with a stick that it's thoroughly baked.
9. Let cool for 10 minutes and sprinkle with a little sugar. Place on a rack and turn the cake upside down. Let it cool completely.
10. Loosen cake from the ring and turn it with the baked side facing up. Dust with confectioners' sugar.

Serve cake at room temperature with a bowl of fresh berries.

Traditional American Cheesecake

There are hundreds of recipes on how to make this cake. This is the way we baked it at Cunard Line on Vista/Fjord and Saga/Fjord and we always served it with preserved raw strawberries, which our passengers loved. It should be snow white inside and tall and creamy - everyone's American dream.

It's important to use real Philadelphia cream cheese and nothing else. Remember that the cheese should be at room temperature before you bake it, to make it extra creamy inside.

Always bake it the day before, to let it mature.

At Olof Viktor bakery in Glemminge we vary our cheesecakes with strawberries, apples, rhubarb and mango, depending on the season.

10–12 PIECES

One springform pan, 2x9-inch (5x22 cm)

Bottom
2 tbsp butter for the pan (25 g)
⅓ cup butter (75 g)
7 oz digestive biscuits (200 g)
¼ cup sugar (45 g)

Filling
4 ⅓ cup Philadelphia cream cheese (1 kg), not light!
1 ¾ cups confectioners' sugar (175 g)
2 tbsp pure vanilla extract (25 g)
1 lemon, grated rind
1 tsp salt (5 g), preferably fleur de sel
7 oz, or about 4, eggs (200 g)

17 ½ oz strawberries (500 g) for decoration
confectioners' sugar

Raw Preserved Strawberries
17 ½ oz strawberries (500 g)
⅓ cup sugar (75 g)

Bottom
1. Preheat the oven to 300°F (150°C). Spread the pan with plenty of soft butter.
2. Grind the biscuits into crumbs in a food processor.
3. Melt the butter in a saucepan and stir in crumbs and sugar.
4. Pour the mixture into the pan and press it down using the back of a spoon, until the bottom is covered.
5. Bake the bottom until golden brown for about 13–15 minutes, take it out of the oven and let cool on a rack.

Filling
6. Mix cream cheese with the sugar, lemon zest, and salt in a food processor. Mix well with an S-shaped blade, to prevent too much air getting into the mixture.
7. Add the eggs one by one to form a creamy paste.
8. Add the mixture to the bottom in the pan and smoothen it out on top. Bake it for about 90 minutes.
9. Turn the oven off, open the oven door and let the cake cool for 1 hour. Place it in the fridge and leave for at least 12 hours.

Raw Preserved Strawberries
10. Rinse and hull strawberries and slice them. Mix them with the sugar until melted. Pour in a bowl.

Serving
11. Remove the ring by heating the sides of the pan with your hands until the butter causes it to detach from the sides. Carefully remove it.
12. Place the cheesecake on a cake plate and decorate with whole small strawberries. Dust with a little confectioners' sugar and serve with raw preserved strawberries.

TIP:
Dip the knife in hot water between cutting each piece, for beautiful slices of cake.

Margaretha Cake

This is a typical cake for Midsummer's Eve and for Mother's Day – it's tasty and long-lasting.

The cake was presumably named after Princess Margaretha, but I remember the recipe also existing in Switzerland, Germany, Italy and Spain, where they used apricot jam instead of raspberry jam and an almond bottom with a little lemon zest in the batter, rather than the traditional cake bottom that we use.

Some pastry shops don't use a shortcut pastry bottom in the bottom of the cake, which causes the heavy cake to stick to the cake doily. I bake my almond paste lattice separately, as opposed to baking it on top of the cake as most others do, for the reason that the cream will flow out a little on the sides.

The cake looks better this way, the way my master confectioner Kurt Lundgren always made it at Blekingborgs Konditori in Malmö.

One recipe of Swedish classic Viennese bottom, see page 20
One recipe of shortcrust pastry, see page 40
9 oz almond paste 50/50 (250 g)
half a recipe of vanilla cream, see page 46
3 ½ oz raspberry jam (100 g), see page 44

⅓ cup toasted and sliced almonds (60 g)
17 ½ oz fresh berries and fruit (500 g) for decoration
5 ⅓ oz neutral gelatine glaze (150 g), see page 43
2 tbsp pistachio (25 g)

1. Bake a Viennesse bottom, preferably the day before the cake is made, in order for it to solidify and to make it easier to slice.

Shortcrust Pastry
2. Preheat the oven to 375° F (190° C).
3. Work the cold pastry until it's smooth using your hands and roll out until it's about one eighth of an inch thick. Make indentions in the dough using a fork. Shape a bottom using a nine inch cake ring.
4. Bake it until golden brown for about 10–12 minutes. Keep an eye on it, as it burns easily. Let cool on sheet.

Almond Paste Lattice
5. Sketch a nine-inch (22 cm) circle on a piece of parchment paper.
6. Little by little, dissolve the almond paste with the vanilla cream, until it's a lump-free, pipeable batter. It shouldn't be too loose.
7. Pipe a lattice on the paper with a fluted nozzle no. 12 and decorate with bows around it, as shown in the image. Let stand for one hour to dry.

8. Preheat the oven to 445° F (230° C).
9. Bake the lattice until golden brown for about 5 minutes, keep a close eye on it as it easily burns. Let cool and place in freezer to solidify.

Assemblage
10. Apply a layer of raspberry jam on the shortcrust pastry bottom.
11. Divide the cake base into three equally thick bottoms using a serrated knife.
12. Add a layer on top of the raspberry jam.
13. Spread four inches of vanilla cream using a palette knife.
14. Add another bottom and press down the cake using a sheet, to make it flat and even.
15. Apply another layer of vanilla cream and add the third layer. Put pressure on this layer too, using a sheet.
16. Spread a thin layer of vanilla cream on top and around the cake using a palette knife. Sprinkle the cake around the sides with sliced almonds and nudge it with a palette knife.
17. Carefully remove the almond lattice gently from the parchment paper. Brush a little water on the back of the paper to make it easier to remove. Place the lattice on the cake and fill the squares with fruit and berries. Brush them with neutral gelatine glaze and sprinkle a few chopped pistachio nuts.

Optionally decorate the cake in an old fashioned way, with a marzipan rose and green leaves.

Paris–Brest

This tasty petits-choux wreath was created in 1891. It's named after a famous bike race and is a classic pastry at every pâtissérie around the country. We only baked wreaths that were 8 inches in diameter at Pâtisserie Dupont in Paris, just about enough for 8 people. When I looked in my recipe book, I noticed that we were producing nine of them on weekdays and 27 on Saturdays and Sundays. Sunday is cake day in France.

In Swedish pastry shops, the petits-choux wreaths were filled with vanilla cream, raspberry jam and whipped cream and they had a lid that was dusted with confectioners' sugar.

Petits-choux pastries are a real delight to eat when they're freshly baked.

12 PIECES

Crème Praliné
1 ⅓ cups unsalted butter (320g)
5 ⅔ oz almond praline paste (160 g), see page 39
2 cups vanilla cream (500 g), see page 46

One recipe of petits-choux, see page 40
1 egg
a dash of salt (1 g)
⅓ cup sliced almonds (60 g)

confectioners' sugar for decoration

Petits-choux
1. Preheat the oven to 355°F (180°C). Sketch a circle, twelve inches (30 cm) in diameter, on parchment paper.
2. Cut a hole, four inches (1 cm) in diameter, in the tip of a disposable pastry bag. Add the petits-choux batter to the pastry bag and start off by piping a circle around the lines. Pipe an identical circle next to it and finally another one on top.
3. Whip egg and salt and cover the entire wreath using a soft brush. Sprinkle with sliced almonds.
4. Place the wreath in the oven and bake until golden brown for about 30–35 minutes, but don't let it get too brown.
5. Allow the wreath to cool on a baking rack.

Crème Praliné
6. Mix room temperature butter with the praline paste until it becomes light and fluffy, preferably with an S-shaped blade in a food processor. The cream should be as light as whipped cream.
7. Add the cold vanilla cream and mix until it's light and fluffy.

(The ideal temperature is 72°F (22°C), use a thermometer to check.)

Assemblage
8. Cut the wreath in half using a serrated knife.
9. Add the cream to a plastic pastry bag with a fluted nozzle no. 12 and spread the cream over the bottom as shown in image.
10. Put the lid on and set it in the fridge to solidify.
11. Dust cake with confectioners' sugar before serving.

Othello Cake

This tasty classic cake isn't as tragic as the play Shakespeare wrote in 1603. It was most likely invented in Milan in 1887 when the opera based on the play was performed at the famous La Scala opera stage. I've never seen an Othello cake in Italy, but it's common in Sweden and Denmark, and also in Norway as I recall.

12 PIECES

One cake ring, 2x9-inch (5x22 cm) or a springform pan with the same diameter measurement

Sarah Bernhardt Cream
½ gelatine leaf (1 g)
8 ⅓ fl oz 40% whipping cream (250 g)
1 ¾ oz dark chocolate (50 g), preferably Valrhona Grand Cru Pur Caribe

Cream
⅛ oz gelatine leaves (3 g/about 1 ½)
1 cup vanilla cream (250 g), see page 46
4 cups whipped cream (250 g)

Chocolate Glaze
3 ⅔ fl oz whipping cream (110 g)
1 tbsp glucose (15 g)
3 oz dark chocolate (90 g), preferably Valrhona Grand Cru Pur Caribe

One classic Viennese bottom, see recipe page 20
12 ⅓ oz almond paste 50/50 (350 g) for decoration

Whipped Cream
8 ⅓ fl oz 40% whipping cream (250 g)
2 tsp sugar (10 g)
1 tsp pure vanilla extract (5 g)

Sarah Bernhardt Cream
1. Soak the gelatine leaf in plenty of cold water for at least 10 minutes.
2. Bring half of the cream to a boil, add it to the gelatin and stir until melted.
3. Add the chopped chocolate and stir until melted.
4. Add the cold cream and mix the cream with a hand blender to an emulsion. Put the cream in the fridge.

Cream
5. Soak the gelatine in plenty of cold water for at least 10 minutes.
6. Whip the cream into solid foam in a cool bowl.
7. Pass the custard through a fine sieve.

8. Gently mix the vanilla cream into the whipped cream until it's a fluffy cream.
9. Remove the gelatine from the water and leave the remaining water on the leaf.
10. Melt the gelatine to a temperature of 110–120° F (45–50° C).
11. Whisk about one fifth of the cream into the gelatine mixture until melted and turn the gelatine mixture into the cream.

Chocolate Glaze
12. Bring cream and glucose to a boil, pour it over the chopped chocolate and stir until it melts.

Assembling the cake
13. Divide the Viennese bottom into three bottoms using a serrated knife.
14. Whip the Sarah Bernhardt cream into solid foam; the same way you would make whipped cream. It's important that it's very chilled.
15. Spread the cream on the first bottom using a palette knife.
16. Add another layer. Add 90 percent of the cream and spread it evenly with a palette knife.
17. Add one more bottom and spread a thin layer of cream on top. Set the cake in the freezer. Roll out the marzipan until it's about one eighth of an inch thick and shape a bottom, 9 inches in diameter, with a cake ring.
18. Add the almond paste base to the cake and press it flat using a baking sheet. Glaze it with the chocolate glaze, about 110–120° F (45–50° C), using a palette knife.
19. Roll out the remaining almond paste into a nine inch (22 cm) long and two and a half inch (6 cm) wide ribbon.
20. Place the ribbon around the cake and put it together using a drop of water at the joint.
21. Whip the cream, vanilla extract and sugar into foam in a chilled bowl.
22. Add the cream to a plastic cone with a fluted nozzle no. 12.
23. Decorate with bows of whipped cream.

Dobos Cake

József Dobos in 1884, a famous pastry chef in Budapest, created this cake. The first time it was introduced was in 1885 at the National General Exhibition of Budapest, and Franz Josef I and his Empress Elisabeth were among the first to taste the cake, which quickly became popular throughout Europe. It's a five layer cake with thin bottoms covered in chocolate butter cream and a thin caramel.

The recipe was secret until 1906, when József Dobos retired and other pastry chefs in Hungary were able to bake it. At Gerbaud's pastry shop in Budapest the Dobos cake is always available and also at the famous Café New York, New York. When Gerbaud's pastry shop guested the NK bakery in Stockholm we baked lots of this tasty classic cake.

12 PIECES

1 recipe of Dobos bottoms, see page 20

Chocolate Buttercream (follow the method for Crème Anglaise)
⅓ cup milk, 3% (75 g)
2 oz, or about 3, egg yolks (60 g)
2 tbsp sugar (30 g)
1 tsp pure vanilla extract (5 g)
⅛ tsp salt (2 g), preferably fleur de sel
4 ¼ oz dark chocolate (120 g), preferably Valrhona Grand Cru Guanaja 70%
5 ⅓ oz nut paste (50 g), see page 39
1 ¼ cups unsalted butter (300g)
3 oz, or about 3, egg whites (90 g)
½ cup sugar (90 g)
1 tsp lemon juice (5 g)

Dobos Glaze
3 tbsp glucose (40 g)
½ cup sugar (100 g)

Chocolate Buttercream
1. Bring the milk to a boil.
2. Beat the egg yolks with the sugars and salt and mix with milk. Heat the mixture while constantly stirring to 185° F (85° C), or perform a spoon test.
3. Pass the cream through a fine sieve (chinoise) and stir in the chopped chocolate and hazelnut paste until melted.
4. Whip the cream until cold 70° F (20° C), add the room temperature butter and slowly mix on low speed until it becomes a light and fluffy cream.

5. Place a water bath with boiling water on the stove. In a metal bowl, whisk egg whites, sugar and lemon juice and stir constantly while heating in a water bath to (55–60° C).
6. Beat the meringue until cool and add it to the butter cream.

Assemblage
7. Set aside the best looking bottom for the glazing.
8. Place a bottom on the table, add one fifth of the cream and spread it as evenly as possible with a palette knife. Add another layer and repeat procedure until the five layers are filled.
9. Smoothen the cake on the top and sides, and carefully transfer the cake to a doily paper. Chill cake for about one hour.

Dobos Glaze
10. Bring the glucose to a boil until it becomes yellow. Add a little sugar bit by bit, stirring constantly until it's a golden caramel.
11. Quickly spread the caramel on the sixth bottom using a palette knife and immediately mark twelve pieces using the back of a knife. Cut in pieces according to the markings, before the caramel is completely solidified.
12. Take the cake out of the refrigerator and place the caramelized pieces on top as shown in the image.

A dobos cake keeps in the fridge for at least three days.

Apple Meringue Cake

This tasty autumn cake with apple compote probably has its origins in the pastry shop Fahlmans in Helsingborg. Pierre and Mikael cherish their nearly 100-year-old family business with founder George Fahlman and then Lasse Fahlman, the brother's father. I remember that this cake paired with vanilla sauce was a bestseller in the fall, at Conditori Lundagård in Lund. Confectioner Master Thure Collbring learned much about the pastry chef profession at Fahlmans in Helsingborg, and he brought some specialties back to Lund.

12 PIECES

One recipe shortcrust pastry, see page 40

Apple Compote

⅓ oz gelatine leaves (8 g/about 4)
10 ½ oz green tart apples (300 g) (35 oz/1 kg peeled weight)
1 lemon, juice
¾ cup sugar (150 g)

One classic Swedish cake base, see page 16
One recipe of hot whipped meringue, see page 34
¼ cups confectioners' sugar (25 g)

Crème Anglaise with Whipped Cream (real vanilla custard)

2 vanilla beans, preferably Tahiti
3 cups milk, 3% (700 g)
5 oz, or about 7, egg yolks (140 g)
1 cup sugar (200 g)
10 fl oz 40% whipping cream (300 g)

1. Preheat the oven to 375° F (190° C).
2. Roll out the pastry about one eighth of an inch thick. Shape a bottom with a cake ring, 9 inches in diameter, and make indentions in the dough with a fork.
3. Place the shortcut pastry ring on a baking sheet lined with parchment paper.
4. Roll out one third of a pound of the remaining pastry into a dough strand and wrap it around the edge on the inside of the ring. Use your thumb to push the dough to half of the height of the ring. Set in freezer for 30 minutes.
5. Bake pastry until golden brown for about 15–17 minutes and let cool on the sheet

Apple Compote

6. Soak the gelatine in plenty of cold water for at least 10 minutes.
7. Peel and core the apples, cut them into wedges and place in a roomy saucepan. Squeeze the juice from the lemon over it.
8. Add the sugar and cook on high heat until the apples begin to fall apart and you are easily able to smash them with a spoon. Constantly stir, as they burn easily.
9. Remove the gelatine from the water and drain the water. Mix them into the compote and stir until melted.
10. Pour the compote in a container and cover with plastic film to cool. Keep it in the fridge.

Assembling the cake

11. Preheat the oven to 445° F (230° C).
12. Remove the ring from the shortcrust pastry bottom and apply half of the cold apple compote on the pastry bottom.
13. Divide the classic cake base into two parts using a serrated knife, and freeze the other half for another occasion.
14. Place the bottom on the compote and apply the remaining compote on top of the cake base.
15. Apply a layer of warm whipped meringue and mark twelve bits on top using a knife.
16. Move the remaining meringue into a disposable plastic pastry bag with a flat nozzle no. 12.
17. Pipe a border around the cake and pipe a pattern with the meringue in each marking on top of the cake, as shown in the image.
18. Dust with confectioners' sugar, place the cake in the oven and bake it beautifully golden brown for about 5 minutes.
19. Let cake cool before it's cut into pieces, using a knife that's been dipped in hot water. Serve at room temperature with delicious vanilla custard.

Crème Anglaise wtih Whipped Cream

20. Cut the vanilla beans lengthwise. Scrape the seeds out and add to a saucepan as well as the rod. Add the milk and bring to a boil. Set aside and allow it to absorb the vanilla.
21. Remove the rod.
22. Whisk yolks and sugar until fluffy. Pour the hot milk over top and stir well.
23. Pour the mixture into a saucepan. Gently heat while constantly stirring with a wooden spoon.
24. Stir until sauce begins to thicken, to 185° F (50° C). If you don't have a thermometer, you can perform a spoon test.
25. Strain the sauce through a fine sieve into a bowl. Refrigerate as quickly as possible in a cold water bath. The consistency of the sauce is at it's peak after twelve hours when the proteins of the yolk swell and the butter fat is crystallized; so try cooking it the day before you are going to use it.
26. When serving, whip the cream into solid foam in a chilled bowl and fold the cold sauce into the cream using a spatula, until it becomes a light and fluffy vanilla custard.

Apple and Chiboust Cake

Vary the apple pie on St. Martin's Day with this delicious light version, with a lid made out of caramelized sugar. The chiboust cream was invented in the 1840s by a skilled Parisian pastry chef named Chiboust. His pastry shop was located on the fashionable Rue Saint Honoré in the middle of the Paris fashion district. He also invented the world famous cake Gateau Saint Honoré (the recipe can be found in my book *Passion for desserts*). The cream is also referred to as a light vanilla cream, because the meringue is mixed until it's light and fluffy.

The combination of apple, caramel and Calvados makes this a fantastic cake.

Macaron Bottom
5 ⅓ oz almond paste 50/50 (150 g)
2 tbsp egg whites (30 g/about 1)
⅓ cup sugar (75 g)

Chiboust Cream with Vanilla and Calvados
⅓ oz gelatine leaves (8 g/about 4)
⅔ cup sugar (120 g)
⅖ cup water (100 g)
4 ½ oz, or about 4–5, egg whites (125 g)
1 tsp lemon juice (5 g)
2 tbsp sugar (20 g)
1 cup milk, 3% (200 g)
1 vanilla bean, preferably Tahiti
4 oz, or about 6, egg yolks (120 g)
2 tbsp sugar (25 g)
3 tbsp corn starch (25 g)
⅕ cup Calvados (50 g)

One recipe of shortcrust pastry, see page 40
One recipe of apple compote, see apple meringue cake
　on page 142

⅕ cup Calvados (50 g) for brushing the biscuit bottom
¼ cups confectioners' sugar (25 g)

Macaron Bottom
1. Preheat the oven to 350° F (180° C).
2. Dissolve the room temperature almond paste with half of the egg whites and sugar into a smooth paste, add the remaining egg whites and work it into a smooth substance.
3. Sketch an 8 inch ring on a parchment paper.
4. Add the mixture to a plastic pastry bag and cut a hole in the top. Pipe the batter in the ring from the inside out.
5. Bake bottom until golden brown for about 20–25 minutes.
6. Leave the bottom to cool and place it in the freezer to solidify.

Chiboust Cream with Vanilla and Calvados
7. Soak the gelatine in plenty of cold water for at least 10 minutes.
8. Bring sugar and water to a boil in a small saucepan. Brush the inside of the pan using a brush drenched in water. Boil to 252° F (122° C).

9. Whisk the egg white, lemon juice and one and a half tablespoons of sugar into a meringue.
10. Pour the boiling syrup into the meringue in a steady stream while constantly stirring. Slowly whisk into a firm meringue.
11. Pour the milk into a small heavy saucepan. Cut the vanilla bean lengthwise and scrape out the seeds with a knife into the milk.
12. Bring the milk to a boil, adding the seeds and pod. Put pot aside and let it sit to absorb the vanilla flavor. Remove the vanilla pod.
13. Whisk egg yolk, sugar and corn starch until fluffy. Pour the vanilla milk into the egg mixture while whisking. Stir until you have a smooth mixture.
14. Pour the mixture into a saucepan. Heat while carefully stirring with a whisk until the cream has been brought to a boil.
15. Remove cream from heat and add the drained gelatine leaves. Stir until completely melted. Add liquor and stir.
16. Immediately turn the cream into the meringue using a spatula and stir until it's a light and fluffy cream.

Assemblage
17. Roll out and make a shortcrust pastry bottom the same way you would for an apple meringue cake on page 142.
18. Place the pastry bottom on a tray lined with parchment paper and add the cold apple compote. Add the macaron bottom and brush it with the liquor.
19. Place a nine inch cake ring around it and line it with plastic cake wrap.
20. Add the chiboust cream to the ring and smoothen out with a palette knife. Set in the freezer for 30 minutes to solidify.
21. Gently remove the cream from the plastic cake wrap by using a knife and remove the cake ring.
22. Dust confectioners' sugar evenly over the cake. Caramelize it with a gas flame until it's a beautiful golden brown color.
23. Cut a pretty little apple in half and dust with plenty of powdered sugar. Use a gas flame to caramelize it beautifully and place it on the cake as decoration. Place the cake on a doily paper and serve refrigerated.

Hazelnut Toffee Cake

Ulla Rosander is a dietician and a good friend of mine, and this tasty succulent cake is her favorite. Maria Escalante and I both love nuts from Piedmont in Italy, just like Ulla.

Mary and I ate stunningly tasty hazelnut pastries in a pastry shop in the city, during the Slow Food festival in Turin. We must have tried about 30 different petit fours and pastries, and everything tasted fantastic. It was a dietitian's nightmare.

12 PIECES

One springform pan, 9 inches in diameter

Hazelnut Mazarin Paste
1 ⅔ cups roasted and peeled hazelnuts (250 g)
2 ½ cups confectioners' sugar (250 g)
3 tbsp corn starch (25 g)
1 tbsp dark rum (15 g)
1 cup unsalted butter (250g)
9 oz, or about 5, eggs (250 g)

One classic shortcrust pastry recipe, see page 40

Hazelnut Toffee
2 ½ fl oz 40 whipping cream (75 g)
⅓ cup butter (75 g)
⅓ cup sugar (75 g)
⅓ cup glucose (75 g)
200 roasted and peeled hazelnuts

Hazelnut Mazarin Paste
1. Make a tpt by mixing hazelnuts, confectioners' sugar and cornstarch in a blender or a food processor. Add the liquor and the soft butter and mix it into a smooth paste.
2. Stir in the eggs one by one.
3. Roll out the pastry dough until it's about one eighth of an inch thick and shape a bottom, 9 inches in diameter, with a cake ring and place it in a springform pan.
4. Measure one third of a pound of the remaining pastry and roll it into the shape of a roll and place it inside the pan. Use your thumb to shape an edge that's a little higher than the pan. Cut away excess dough.

5. Place the pan in the freezer for about 30 minutes.
6. Fill the pan with the mixture and smoothen it out around the edges.
7. Preheat the oven to 340° F (170° C).
8. Bake cake until golden brown for about 60 minutes, testing with a knife to ensure that it's thoroughly baked.
9. Sprinkle a little sugar on top, place on a baking sheet lined with parchment paper and turn the cake upside down to cool down and flatten out.

Hazelnut Toffee
10. Bring cream and butter to a boil and set aside.
11. Bring glucose and sugar to a boil in a saucepan until it turns into a golden brown caramel. Stir the cream and butter and boil to 240° F (115° C), while constantly stirring, using a thermometer or performing the cold-water candy test, see page 35. Add the toasted nuts until they are completely covered with caramel.

Finishing up the cake
12. Carefully turn cake, add the nut caramel to the pan and spread it evenly using a palette knife. Let cool and put it in the fridge to cool for 1 hour.
13. Cut the candy out of the ring, remove the pan from the cake and move to a cake plate.

Eat immediately and enjoy with an espresso or a strong coffee, and maybe a grappa on the side, and you are in Piedmont.

Mazarin Cake with Fresh Fruits and Berries

Östen Brolin always bakes this tasty cake. His pastry shop Vetekatten in Stockholm is famous for its pastries throughout the city. His wife Agneta helps him to manage the lovely bakery shop. The mazarin is important to Östen and me. Make sure that all ingredients are at room temperature so that the mazarin substance doesn't clash. If the butter and eggs are cold, the water will be squeezed out of the butter and the substance will clash. It's not a disaster however; just let the mixture stand until it's at room temperature, mix again and the problem is solved. It does take a bit of time though, so it is better to temper the ingredients first.

One recipe of classic shortcrust, see page 40
One recipe of almond paste, see page 45
fresh fruits and berries
One recipe of apricot preserve, see page 45

1. Line the mazarin cake in the same manner as the hazelnut toffee cake, see page 146. Fill it with almond paste in the same manner and bake for about 60 minutes at 340°F (170°C). Use a knife point to check that it's thoroughly baked.
2. Sprinkle sugar on the cake and place on a parchment paper with a baking sheet on top. Turn the cake upside down. Let cool.
3. Turn the cake the right way and move it to a cake dish. Brush the top with apricot preserve. Decorate with fresh fruits and berries, as shown in the image. Dust with confectioners' sugar.

This tasty cake should be enjoyed at room temperature.

Fraisier

This beautiful traditional French cake isn't only beautiful to behold, it's also tasty. The creamy mousseline cream and the juicy pistachio bottom go very well together. One of the best I've tried was at the Ritz Hotel in Paris, at Place De Vendome, during their afternoon tea with harp music playing in the background. Visit The Hemingway bar on the bottom floor if you're in the Ritz or treat your loved one to a Karen Blixen in the bar, served with an orchid on the rim. Then walk to the Paul Hèvin chocolatier that's only a stone's throw away and taste some of Paris's best pralines.

Naturally this amazing cake is as good without the sugar dome, but it certainly is beautiful, isn't it?

One springform pan and one cake ring, 2x9-inch (5x22 cm)

Pistachio Bottom
⅔ cup pistachio meal (105 g)
1 cup confectioners' sugar (105 g)
2 tbsp unsalted butter (35 g)
⅔ cup all-purpose flour (80 g)
5 oz, or about 3, eggs (150 g)
7 oz, or about 7, egg whites (195 g)
1 tsp lemon juice (5 g)
¼ cup sugar (50 g)
1 drop of orange blossom water

Orange Mousseline Cream
⅕ oz gelatine leaves (6 g/about 3)
1 vanilla pod, preferably Tahitian
1 large ripe orange
1 cup sugar (200 g)
1 ⅔ cups milk, 3% (375 g)
⅓ cup corn starch (35 g)
3 ½ oz, or about 5, egg yolks (100 g)
¾ cup unsalted butter (185 g)
⅛ cup Cointreau (25 g)

Strawberry Syrup
3 ½ oz strawberry puree (100 g) with 10 % sugar
2 tbsp confectioners' sugar (15 g)
1 tsp lemon juice (5 g)
⅛ cup Cointreau (25 g)

⅓ cup white chocolate (80 g), preferably Valrhona Ivoire
26 oz large beautiful strawberries (750 g)

9 oz green marzipan (250 g)
confectioners' sugar for rolling

Caramelized Strawberries
12 large beautiful strawberries
One recipe of caramel, see page 46

green food coloring, preferably natural vegetable color

Pistachio Bottom
1. Preheat oven to 375° F (190° C). Place a cake ring, nine inches in diameter, on a baking sheet lined with parchment paper.
2. Make a tpt by mixing confectioners' sugar and pistachio meal into powder.
3. Melt butter and set aside, sift flour on paper.
4. Whisk the eggs with the tpt and orange blossom water for 10 minutes until firm.
5. Whisk the egg whites with the lemon juice on average speed in a clean metal bowl. Add sugar and whisk on high speed until meringue is firm.
6. Fold the egg substance into the meringue with a spatula and then add the sieved flour.
7. Add a scoop of the substance and stir it into the butter and fold it too.
8. Fill the cake ring with the substance and spread on sides to ensure that it will be evenly baked.
9. Bake for 25–30 minutes until golden brown, using a knife to ensure that it is thoroughly baked.
10. Sprinkle sugar on top, place on parchment paper laid out on a baking tray on top. Turn upside down. Add another plate to prevent the bottom from drying out.

Orange Mousseline Cream

11. Soak the gelatine leaves in plenty of cold water for at least 10 minutes.
12. Cut the vanilla bean lengthwise and scrape out the seeds with a knife.
13. Rinse and dry the orange and strip away the outermost skin with a grater.
14. Add a quarter of a cup of the sugar and knead it with the help of a palette knife until the essential oil has dissolved the sugar.
15. Bring milk to a boil with the orange skin, vanilla bean and marrow. Set the pot aside and let stand for 10 minutes.
16. Beat the egg yolk, sugar and corn starch until it thickens.
17. Pour the milk over the roux and mix well with a whisk.
18. Transfer it all back into the pot and bring to boil while constantly stirring.
19. Remove the gelatine leaves from the water and place in pot. Also add the spare water from the leaves to the mixture. Stir until the gelatine is completely dissolved.
20. Strain the cream through a fine sieve.
21. Add the refrigerated butter and whisk at the lowest speed until it becomes a light and fluffy cream. Add the liquor (if the cream is too loose, refrigerate for 30 minutes and lightly mix after it has been cooled).

Strawberry Syrup

22. With a hand blender, mix puree, lemon juice and liqueur into a puree.

Assemblage

23. Place a circular parchment paper on the bottom of a springform pan. Line it with plastic cake wrap.
24. Divide the tier into three bottoms with a serrated knife, place one in the freezer for another occasion.
25. Finely chop and melt the chocolate to 110° F (45° C) in a microwave oven or in a water bath.
26. Brush the cake bottom with chocolate and place it in the fridge to solidify.
27. Place the chocolate covered pistachio bottom with the chocolate facing the cake mold.
28. Rinse and clean the strawberries dry on a towel.
29. Cut the largest and best looking strawberries and place them around the cake with the cut surface facing outwards as shown in the picture.
30. Brush the lowermost bottom with half of the strawberry syrup.
31. Spread a layer of strawberries on the bottom.
32. Add mousseline cream, fill the pan with the cream and spread it evenly with a palette knife. Save some cream for later.
33. Add the second pistachio tier and brush it with the remaining syrup. Set in fridge to solidify for an hour.
34. Roll out the marzipan about one eighth of an inch thick with a rolling pin and confectioners' sugar. Use a plate, nine inches in diameter, with a cake ring.

Completing the cake

35. Loosen the cake from the ring and make sure to stick the plastic cake wrap with a piece of adhesive tape. It must stay on until the cake is served to ensure that the cut surface of the strawberries don't dry up.
36. Spread a thin layer of cream on top of the cake and add the marzipan plate. Press it with a baking tray.

Caramelized Strawberries

37. Dip the strawberries in the caramel while holding the green part so that you don't burn yourself. Shape a horn on the front of the caramel and place on parchment paper to solidify.

Sugar Dome

38. Rub a one quart round pan, a so-called fluted dome mold, on the inside with cooking oil and color the rest of the caramel from the strawberries with a drop of dye.
39. Make a sugar dome, see page 123.
40. Dust the cake with confectioners' sugar and decorate with caramelized strawberries as shown in the picture.
41. Place the dome in the center of the cake and carefully decorate it with a strawberry on the top.

The cake tastes best if kept cool in the refrigerator until just before serving.

Almond Praline Cake with Raspberry Puree

This is the perfect dessert cake after an autumn dinner consisting of fried hare with fried chanterelles, glazed chestnuts and a nice glass of red wine - hare is one of my favorites.

The cake is decorated with a petit-choux on top.

I ate a similar cake the last time I visited Konditorei Heinemann in Dusseldorf.

Make sure not to miss it, one of the shops is located on the famous Konig's Avenue. Dusseldorf is a town of bakeries, with the famous Konditorei Otto Bittner and Georg Maushagen, among others.

12 PIECES

One cake ring, 2x9-inch (5x22 cm)

One classic génoise cake, see page 16

Petit-choux
½ cup all-purpose flour (60 g)
¼ cup water (50 g)
¼ cup 3% milk (50 g)
⅛ tbsp sugar (2 g)
⅛ tbsp salt (2 g)
2 tbsp butter (30 g)
3 ½ oz, or about 2, egg (100 g)

Raspberry Syrup
3 ½ oz raspberry puree (100 g), with 10% sugar
⅓ cup confectioners' sugar (35 g)
⅛ cup water (25 g)

Bavaroise Praline
⅕ oz gelatine leaves (6 g/about 3)
8 ⅓ fl oz whipping cream (250 g)
¾ cup milk, 3% (175 g)
2 oz, or about 3, egg yolks (60 g)
4 ⅖ oz hazelnut praline paste (125 g), see recipe page 39

Raspberry Jelly
17 ½ oz raspberries (500 g)
⅓ cup sugar (80 g)
⅙ oz gelatine leaves (4 g/about 2)

8 ⅓ fl oz whipping cream (250 g)
1 tbsp sugar (10 g)
1 tsp pure vanilla extract (5 g)

⅓ cup sliced and toasted almonds
confectioners' sugar to dust with

Petit-choux
1. Preheat oven to 390° F (200° C). Draw a circle, nine inches in diameter, on a baking sheet with parchment paper.
2. Sift the flour on a parchment paper.
3. Bring water, milk, sugar, salt and butter to a boil in a small saucepan.
4. Toast the batter, stirring until it starts to separate from the edges of the pan and shapes into the form of a ball.
5. Pour the mixture into a bowl and let cool for two minutes. Add eggs, one at a time, until the batter is smooth and resilient.
6. Transfer the batter to a plastic pastry bag and cut a small hole in the front. Pipe a baking grid from two directions.
7. Bake the petit-choux until golden brown, about 12–15 minutes. Let cool on a rack.

Bavaroise Praline
8. Soak the gelatine in plenty of cold water for at least 10 minutes.
9. In a cold bowl, whip the cream into foam and put in the fridge.
10. Mix milk and egg yolks and heat in a saucepan while constantly stirring to 185° F (85° C). Put the mix through a chinoise strainer and add the drained gelatine. Stir until it melts.
11. Mix in the hazelnut praline paste with a hand blender.
12. Cool the custard in a water bath at 70° F (20° C), while constantly stirring. Fold the cream into the whipped cream in two rounds and mix until it becomes a light and airy cream.

Raspberry Jelly

13. Combine raspberries and sugar in a glass bowl and cover with plastic film.
14. Place the bowl in a simmering water bath for 60 minutes.
15. Strain through a fine sieve and drain the gel until all the liquid has passed through the strainer. There should be about one cup of juice.
16. Soak the gelatine in plenty of cold water for at least 10 minutes.
17. Heat the juice to 120° F (45–50° C). Remove the gelatine from the water and let the water run off. Melt the gelatine in the juice and pour it into a round-sheet form, nine inches in diameter, and let cool. Cover with plastic film and freeze.

Assemblage

18. Remove the base of the cake from the ring and divide it into three equally thick bottoms with a serrated knife. Wrap one of the pieces in plastic wrap and freeze for another day.
19. Place a cake ring, nine inches in diameter, on a tray with parchment paper. Line the ring with plastic cake wrap and place the bottom in the ring.
20. Mix raspberry jelly, confectioners' sugar and water with a whisk, until sugar dissolves. Use half of the raspberry syrup to brush on the cake base.
21. Fill with half of the bavaroise.

22. Remove the gel from the mold by flushing a little warm water on the outside of the pan so it falls out. Place it on top of bavaroise.
23. Fill with remaining bavaroise and smoothe with a palette knife.
24. Add one more cake and brush with remaining raspberry syrup. Freeze cake for at least 6 hours.

Completing the cake

25. Loosen the cake from the ring and plastic cake wrap.
26. In a chilled bowl, whip the cream with the sugar and vanilla extract into solid foam.
27. Spread cream on the cake as evenly as possible, with the help of a palette knife. Lift it up and sprinkle the edges with sliced almonds.
28. Pipe a couple of cream peaks on top of cake, using a plastic pastry bag. Cut a hole in the tip of it, so that the baking grid floats a little.
29. Remove the baking grid from the baking paper. Place it on top of the cream peaks and dust with confectioners' sugar.
30. Place cake on a cake doily. Let it thaw for one hour at room temperature or three hours in the refrigerator.

Irish Coffee Cake

According to stories, this drink was born at an airport in Ireland. Most people agree that it's a nice drink. I made this cake for an Arla Foods food course in Stockholm.

I came to think of the tasty cooked chocolate mousses that we made at Montana School in Lucerne. François Gatti was the pastry chef and professor, a dessert master who is the author of our textbook, *Entremets for Working Hotels and Restaurants*. Every class was an adventure, and chocolate mousse was one of his passions.

12 PIECES

1 cake ring, 9 inches in diameter and 2 inches tall

Cocoa Biscuit
5 oz, or about 7, egg yolks (145 g)
½ cup sugar (100 g)
¾ cup all-purpose flour (100 g)
½ cup cocoa powder (50 g), preferably maroon Valrhona
½ cup finely ground and roasted hazelnuts (60 g)
5 oz, or about 5, egg whites (145 g)
1 tsp lemon juice (5 g)
½ cup sugar (100 g)

One recipe of traditional shortcrust pastry, see page 40

Coffee and Chocolate Mousse
1/12 oz gelatine leaves (2 g/about 1 leaf)
16 ⅘ fl oz 40% whipping cream (500 g)
6 oz of chocolate (175 g), preferably Valrhona Jivara Lactée 40%
½ oz dark roasted Nescafé (15 g)
¼ cup Irish whiskey (50 g), preferably Jameson

White Chocolate Mousse
½ gelatine leaf (1 g)
8 ⅓ fl oz 40% whipping cream (250 g)
3 oz of white chocolate (85 g), preferably Valrhona Ivoire

3 ½ oz apricot jam (100 g), see page 44

Whiskey Syrup
½ cup Irish whiskey (100 g)
¾ cup confectioners' sugar (75 g)
2 ½ fl oz strong coffee (75 g)

12 Marzipan Coffee Beans
1 ¾ oz marzipan (50 g)
3 tsp cocoa (5 g), preferably Valrhona 20/22
3 tsp Nescafé (5 g)

8 ⅓ fl oz 40% whipping cream (250 g)
1 tbsp sugar (10 g)
1 tbsp pure vanilla extract (5 g)

Chocolate Chip, see page 56
3 oz Valrhona Grand Cru dark chocolate, (80 g) Guanaja 70%

5 ⅓ oz white marzipan (150 g), see page 38
confectioners' sugar
cocoa for decoration, Valrhona 20/22
5 crushed walnuts

Cocoa Biscuit
1. Preheat oven to 375° F (190° C).
2. Whisk egg yolks and sugar on medium speed until light and fluffy.
3. Sift flour and cocoa powder on a paper and add the nuts.
4. Whisk the egg whites, lemon juice and sugar until it becomes a meringue. Begin whisking on medium speed and then increase the speed until the meringue is firm.
5. Fold the egg yolk foam into the meringue with a spatula. Add cocoa, flour and nuts and mix to a light and porous batter.
6. Add the mixture to a cake ring placed on a baking sheet lined with parchment paper. Spread on the edges of the ring, to make sure that the bottom becomes flat when baked.
7. Bake the bottom for about 25 minutes, until golden brown. Test with a knifepoint to make sure that it's baked.
8. Sprinkle some sugar on top, place on parchment paper and a baking sheet and turn the bottom upside down. Place on a baking tray so that it doesn't dry out.

Shortcrust Pastry

9. Preheat oven to 375° F (200° C).
10. Roll out the shortcut pastry until it's one twelfth of an inch thick and make indentions with a fork. Add a cake ring to the 9-inch bottom.
11. Place the bottom on a baking sheet and bake it until golden brown, about 10–12 minutes. Watch it carefully, as it's easy to burn shortcrust pastry bottoms.

Coffee and Chocolate Mousse

12. Soak the gelatine in plenty of cold water for at least 10 minutes.
13. Bring half of the whipped cream and Nescafe to a boil and put aside. Remove the gelatine from the water and leave any remaining water on the leaf. Mix the gelatin with the cream and stir until it's melted.
14. Add the finely grated chocolate and stir until it's melted.
15. Add the remaining cream and whiskey and mix with a hand blender until an emulsion is formed. Cover with plastic film and place in the fridge.

White Chocolate Mousse

16. Soak the gelatine in plenty of cold water for at least 10 minutes.
17. Bring half of the cream to a boil and put aside. Remove the gelatine from the water, add the cream and the remaining water from the leaf. Stir until melted.
18. Add the hot cream to the finely chopped chocolate and stir until completely melted.
19. Smoothly mix with a hand blender and add remaining cream. Mix until it forms an emulsion, cover with plastic film and store in the fridge until the next day.

Marzipan Coffee Beans

20. Knead the marzipan, cocoa and coffee and shape twelve small balls. Press lightly with a knife to make them resemble coffee beans.
21. Mix whiskey, sugar, and coffee until it becomes a whiskey syrup.

Assemblage

22. Use a cake ring or a springform pan, nine inches in diameter and two inches tall, and place on a tray lined with parchment paper.
23. Spread the preserve on the shortcrust pastry.
24. Cut the cake base out of the ring and divide it into three equal pieces with the help of a serrated knife. Wrap one of the cake bottoms with plastic film and save for another occasion.
25. Add a cake bottom to the jam-covered shortcrust pastry and spread half of the whiskey syrup on the bottom.
26. Whisk the coffee mousse in the same manner as the whipped cream. Spread the mousse on the cake using a palette knife.
27. Attach the cake ring with plastic cake wrap inside. Add another bottom and spread out the remaining whiskey syrup.
28. Whip the white chocolate mousse in the same manner as the whipped cream. Spread out evenly using a pallet knife. Freeze cake for at least six hours.
29. In a cool bowl, whip the cream, sugar and vanilla extract to solid foam.

Completing the cake

30. Loosen cake from the ring and plastic cake wrap and fill the entire cake with whipped cream using a palette knife.
31. Place the cake in your hand and sprinkle it with dark, slightly crushed chocolate shavings around the edges. Place on a cake plate.
32. Roll out the marzipan with the help of confectioners' sugar, about one twelfth of an inch thick. Form a circle by using a nine-inch cake ring.
33. Add the circle on top of the cake. Place a saucer in the middle and dust with cocoa. Remove the saucer.
34. Add the remaining cream to a plastic pastry bag with a fluted nozzle, no. 12. Decorate with whipped cream and coffee beans.
35. Sprinkle on some crushed walnuts in the middle.

Let thaw for one hour at room temperature or three hours in a refrigerator.

Marbled Chocolate Mousse Cake

I can't imagine anything better tasting than this cake. Creamy crème brûlée and a smooth aromatic dark chocolate mousse, glazed with two kinds of cocoa jelly – doesn't it sound amazing?

It doesn't get any prettier or tastier than this.

12 PIECES

One cake ring, 2x9-inch (5x22 cm)

Chocolate Bottom
2 tbsp all-purpose flour (18 g)
3 ½ oz dark chocolate (105 g), preferably Valrhona Grand Cru Guanaja 70%
¼ cup unsalted butter (60 g)
3 ½ oz, or about 3, egg whites (100 g)
1 tsp lemon juice (5 g)
¼ cup sugar (55 g)
2 oz, or about 3, egg yolks (60 g)

Chocolate Shavings
Try to get hold of plastic transfer sheets with printed cocoa butter (available for purchase online).

3 oz dark chocolate (80 g), preferably Valrhona Grand Cru Guanaja 70%
2 plastic transfer sheets

Crème Brûlée filling for Chocolate Cake
⅙ oz gelatine leaves (4 g/about 2)
4 oz, or about 6, egg yolks (120 g)
⅔ cup sugar (125 g)
1 vanilla bean, preferably Tahiti
16 ⅘ oz 40% whipping cream (500 g)

Chocolate Mousse
⅓ cup sugar (70 g)
⅛ cup water (35 g)
8 ⅓ fl oz 40% whipping cream (250 g)
7 oz dark chocolate (225 g), preferably Valrhona Grand Cru Guanaja
2 oz, or about 3, egg yolks (60 g)
1 ¾ oz, or about 1, egg (50 g)

Chocolate Jelly
¼ oz gelatine leaves (8 g/about 4)
1 cup water (225 g)
⅘ cup sugar (185 g)
3 tbsp liquid glucose (40 g)
1 cup cocoa powder (75 g), preferably Valrhona 20/22
¾ oz dark chocolate (20 g), preferably Valrhona Grand Cru Guanaja 70%
5 fl oz 40% whipping cream (150 g)

White Chocolate Jelly
1 gelatine leaf (2 g/about 1)
2 ½ oz white chocolate (75 g), preferably Valrhona Ivoire
¼ cup milk, 3% (50 g)
1 ¾ tbsp glucose (25 g)
2 tsp unsalted butter (10 g)
Approx. 1 tsp titanium dioxide (5 g) (white food coloring that can be purchased in craft stores)

Chocolate Bottom
1. Preheat oven to 350° F (180° C). Place a cake ring on a parchment paper.
2. Sift the flour on a baking paper.
3. Melt the chopped up chocolate and butter to a temperature of 120° F (50–55° C).
4. Whisk egg whites, lemon juice and sugar on medium speed to a stiff meringue. It should be whipped for a lengthy time.
5. Whisk the egg yolks into the chocolate butter until smooth. Fold it into the meringue with a spatula and fold in the flour. Spread the batter in the ring and bake for about 18–20 minutes. Don't leave it in too long because it becomes dry. Test it using a stick.
6. Place the ring on a rack to cool down and remove the bottom. Put it in the freezer to make it easier to handle.

Chocolate Shavings

7. Temper the chocolate, see page 52, and roll it out thin on the two sheets using a palette knife.

8. Let set compressed in the refrigerator, to prevent the chocolate from warping.

Crème Brûlée filling for Chocolate Cake

9. Soak the gelatine in plenty of cold water for at least 10 minutes.

10. Whisk yolks and sugar until light and fluffy.

11. Cut the vanilla bean lengthwise and scrape out the seeds with a knife.

12. Bring the whipping cream, vanilla bean and seeds to a boil. Set the pan aside and let the cream sit for about 15 minutes, for it to absorb the vanilla flavor.

13. Add the egg yolk foam and mix well. Heat to 185° F (85°C), while constantly stirring.

14. Add the drained gelatine leaves and stir until melted. Pass through a fine sieve, a chinoise, into an eight inch tin foil pan.

15. Let the brûlée sit in the freezer for about two hours.

Chocolate Mousse

16. Whip the cream in a cold bowl to a loose foam and set in the fridge.

17. Beat the egg yolks and the egg into foam.

18. Boil sugar and water to 250°F (123°C), or perform the cold-water candy test, see page 35. Add the syrup to the egg foam while constantly whipping, whisk until it's cold.

19. Chop the chocolate finely and melt it to 130°F (55° C) in microwave.

20. Fold half of the cream into the chocolate and mix until smooth. Fold it into the cream with a spatula until it becomes a smooth mousse and finally fold in the egg foam.

Assemblage

21. Line the ring with plastic cake wrap and place on parchment paper. Add half of the mousse to the ring and spread it evenly.

22. Remove the tin foil pan from the brûlée, add the brûlée to the mousse and press it down so that the chocolate mousse is pushed aside around the outside.

23. Add the remaining mousse and spread it evenly using a palette knife. Add the frozen chocolate bottom and press it on using a baking sheet.

24. Freeze cake for at least six hours before glazing.

Chocolate Jelly

25. Soak the gelatine in plenty of cold water for at least 10 minutes.

26. Bring water, sugar and glucose to a boil. Sift the cocoa and chop the chocolate. Add the chocolate mixture and the cream.

27. Bring to a boil and reduce heat until the mixture just about simmers. Whisk or stir occasionally to prevent the bottom from burning.

28. Carefully simmer at 225° F (107° C) for about one hour. Use a sugar thermometer or test it by lifting the whisk to see if a drop remains. If it's the case, you know that the glaze can cover an area.

29. Remove the gelatine from the water and drain. Add the sheets to the mixture and stir until melted.

30. Pour through a sieve. Quickly cover the surface with plastic film to avoid a white sheen on the surface. Cool to 95°F (35°C), which is the right temperature for glaze. (Cover the jelly with plastic film and it will keep for two weeks in the fridge. You can also freeze it.)

White Chocolate Jelly

31. Soak the gelatine leaves in plenty of cold water for a minimum of 10 minutes.

32. Chop the chocolate finely and melt it in microwave or a 120° F (50° C) water bath.

33. Bring the milk and glucose to a boil and pour the boiling mixture over the chocolate. Stir with a ladle or hand blender until it becomes a chewy ganache.

34. Mix in the butter.

35. Remove the gelatine leaf from the water and melt on the stove or in the microwave oven to 110–120° F (45–50° C). Use a thermometer.

36. Pour the gelatine and titanium oxide into the ganache and mix well.

Glazing the cake

37. Loosen the cake from the ring, remove the plastic cake wrap and place the cake with the baked bottom facing down.

38. Pour the brown jelly around the cake and the white chocolate jelly in the middle. Glaze the cake, creating a marble pattern on top.

39. Allow the cake to settle and gently place it on a cake doily.

40. Loosen the chocolate shavings from the transfer sheets and garnish the cake with them.

Let it thaw for one hour at room temperature or about three hours in the fridge until it's ready to serve.

Gâteau roulé au Kirsch – Cherry Charlotte Cake

My old friend René Qurin always used to bake this tasty cake when we worked together at the Savoy Hotel in Malmö when we were young. Rene comes from Sellestadt in Alsace in France and is an accomplished pastry chef. We served the cake as a Sunday dessert at Falsterbohus and Skanörs Gästgifvaregård simultaneously, and it was finished off every Sunday. If you don't have Kirschwasser you can use rum instead, it won't be the same but good nonetheless. Kirschwasser suits all baked goods, chocolates and ice cream – make sure to stock up when you're abroad.

One cake ring, 2x9-inch (5x22 cm)

One jelly roll cake base, see page 24
One traditional Swedish cake bottom, see page 16
5 ⅓ oz apricot jam (150 g), see page 44
Two recipes of apricot preserve see page 45

Diplomat Cream with Kirschwasser
⅕ oz gelatine leaves (6 g/about 3)
10 fl oz whipping cream (300 g)
1 ¼ cup vanilla cream (300 g), see page 46
3 ½ tbsp Kirschwasser (50 g), or dark rum
⅔ cup candied red cherries (100 g)

Diplomat Cream with Kirschwasser
1. Soak the gelatine in plenty of cold water for at least 10 minutes.
2. Whip the cream to solid foam in a chilled bowl.
3. Pass the vanilla cream through a sieve.
4. Remove the gelatine from the water and let the remaining water stay on the leaves. Melt the gelatine to a temperature of 110–120° F (45–50° C).
5. Stir in the liquor in the gelatine and whisk the mixture into the vanilla cream. Beat until it's smooth.
6. Fold in the whipped cream and candied cherries to a light and fluffy mousse.

Assemblage
7. Loosen the paper from the jelly roll cake base and cut in half using a sharp knife.
8. Place the halves on two parchment papers and spread jam on both bottoms. Divide the apricot jam evenly, roll them into jelly rolls and tighten them using a ruler. Place in freezer for 60 minutes.
9. Cut the frozen jelly rolls with a serrated knife into half-inch-thick slices.
10. Place a cake ring on a tray lined with parchment paper.
11. Line the ring with plastic cake wrap and then cover the bottom of the ring with a layer of swiss roll slices.
12. Line the jelly roll slices along the inside of the ring.
13. Fill the cake ring with cream and spread it evenly with a pallet knife.
14. Divide the traditional cake into three equally thick bottoms using a serrated knife.
15. Place one cake base on top of the cream, place on a parchment paper and press it smooth with a baking sheet (save the remaining wrapped up cake bottoms in the freezer for another time). Freeze cake for at least six hours.

Completing the cake
16. Loosen the cake from the ring and plastic band and place it face-down on a rack.
17. Bring the apricot preserve to a boil and spread it on the entire cake. Place the cake on a cake doily.

Let cake thaw for about one hour at room temperature or in the fridge for about three hours.

I've decorated with some beautiful cherries dipped in caramel and then sprinkled on some pistachios. The cake however is beautiful as is and doesn't need to be decorated.

Charlotte Forestier cake

This beautiful silky mousse cake has delicious flavors of raspberries and blueberries and is a treat for the mouth as well as they eye. It's important that the berries have been soaked in syrup, or they will freeze to ice in the cake. This results in a runny and bad-looking cake when cutting it.

12 PIECES

One cake ring, 2x9-inch (5x22 cm)

Almond Dacquoise Bottom
¾ cup confectioners' sugar (75 g)
⅔ cup almond flour (75 g)
3 oz, or about 3, egg whites (90 g)
1 tsp of lemon juice (5 g)
2 tbsp sugar (30 g)

3 oz dark chocolate (80 g), preferably Valrhona Grand Cru Manjari for brushing
One roll cake base, see page 24
5 ⅓ oz cup raspberry jam (150 g), see page 44, to fill the roll cake

Preserved Raspberries and Blueberries
⅔ cup sugar (135 g)
⅖ cup water (100 g)
4 oz blueberries (100 g)
4 oz raspberries (100 g)

Diplomat Cream
⅕ oz gelatine leaves (6 g/about 3)
1 ¼ cup vanilla cream (300 g), see page 46
5 cups whipped cream (300 g)
1 ¼ tbsp Kirschwasser (25 g), or Eau de Framboise

1 ¾ oz raspberry jam (50 g), see page 44
 (150 g) see page 43
17 ½ oz fresh raspberries (500 g)
1 ½ oz white chocolate (40 g) for feathers, see page 113
confectioners' sugar

Almond Dacquoise Bottom
1. Preheat oven to 350°F (175°C). With a pencil, draw a circle nine inches in diameter on a sheet of parchment paper.
2. Mix confectioners' sugar and almond flour into a tpt.
3. Whisk egg white and lemon juice on medium speed into foam, increase speed and add sugar. Beat to a solid meringue.
4. Fold in the tpt with a spatula until smooth.
5. Fill a plastic pastry bag with the mixture. Use a flat nozzle, no. 12 or cut a hole in the front.
6. Pipe a bottom that's nine inches in diameter inside of the marking. If there is leftover meringue, use it to pipe a few meringues.
7. Bake for about 20 minutes, or until the bottom is baked, without it being completely baked in the middle. Allow to cool and then place it in the freezer, to make it easier to detach from the parchment paper.

8. Finely chop the chocolate and melt in microwave or in a water bath to a temperature of 130°F (55°C).
9. Spread chocolate on the bottom and let it sit in the fridge.
10. Bake the roll cake base. Sprinkle some sugar on top, place on parchment paper, turn it upside down and put in a cold place to settle.
11. Stir and spread the raspberry jam on top of roll cake and divide it into eight equal squares using a sharp knife. Place the squares on top of each other and press with a baking sheet, so that they stick together. Set the squares in the freezer for one hour.

Preseved Raspberries and Blueberries
12. Bring sugar and water to a boil and pour the boiling mixture over the berries. Leave to cool for the berries to soak up the syrup.

Diplomat Cream
13. Soak the gelatine in plenty of cold water for at least 10 minutes.
14. Whip the cream to solid foam in a cold bowl.
15. Pass the vanilla cream through a sieve.
16. Remove the gelatine from the water and let the remaining water stay on the leaves. Melt the gelatine to a temperature of 110–120°F (45–50°C).
17. Stir in the liquor in the gelatine and whisk the mixture into the vanilla cream. Beat until it's smooth.
18. Fold in the whipped cream to a light and fluffy mousse.

Assemblage
19. Line the cake ring with plastic cake wrap. Place the dacquoise bottom in the ring with the chocolate covered side facing down.
20. Cut half an inch wide slices of the square and cut them into two-inch-wide pieces. Place them inside the ring side by side, with the jam creating vertical stripes as shown in the picture.
21. Fill the cake with half of the diplomat cream and add the drained blueberries and raspberries.
22. Add the remaining cream and create a smooth surface using a palette knife. Set the cake in the freezer for at least 60 minutes.
23. Spread a little raspberry jam on the cake spread the jelly on top of the cake. Remove the ring and plastic cake wrap.
24. Decorate the top with fresh raspberries and white chocolate feathers. Dust with a little confectioners' sugar.

Place the cake on a cake doily.

Honold Hasselnuss Rahmtorte – Hazelnut Cream Cake

When I was working at the crèmerie at Confiseries Honold in Zurich I often baked this tasty hazelnut cake. It was almost as popular as their famous Schwarzwälder Torte that we made hundreds of every week. We baked some amazing cakes there! Genueser Torte was the hardest one to make, with a shortcrust pastry bottom covered with cherry and caramelized vanilla chiboust cream. Everyone was there to learn Swiss pâtisserie from the best.

On the second floor was the confiserie with the praline department. Mr. Fey was the master there, as he was the candy chef and in charge of all the pralines. On average, we made nearly nine thousand pounds of pralines each month.

In November and December we made about 26 500 pounds of pralines, which meant that we had to work sixteen hours every day for two months.

Be sure to visit Honold Confiserie in Zurich on Rennweg, which is a side street of Banhofstrasse.

12 PIECES

One cake ring, 2x9-inch (5x22 cm) or a springform pan with the same diameter measurement

One recipe of shortcut pastry, see page 40

Hazelnut Mousse
⅕ oz gelatine leaves (6 g/about 3)
7 ½ cups whipped cream (450 g)
⅔ cup vanilla cream (100 g), see recipe page 46
3 ½ oz hazelnut praline paste (100 g), see page 39
⅓ cup of crushed roasted hazelnuts (50 g)

3 ½ oz apricot jam (100 g), see page 44
One hazelnut cake bottom, see page 23

4 oz green marzipan (100 g), see page 38, or purchase one of good quality
confectioners' sugar for rolling
2 tbsp egg white (30 g)
12 roasted hazelnuts

Whipped Cream for decoration
8 ⅓ fl oz whipping cream (250 g)
2 tsp sugar (10 g)
1 tsp g pure vanilla extract (5 g)

1 ⅓ cup roasted, crushed hazelnuts (200 g) for decoration of the edges and to sprinkle on top

whole roasted hazelnuts for decoration
chocolate shavings from 3 oz of dark chocolate (80 g), Valrhona Grand Cru Guanaja 70%, see chocolate decoration on page 56

Shortcrust Pastry Bottom
1. Preheat oven to 375° F (190° C).
2. Roll out pastry until it's about a twelfth of an inch thick, and make indentions with a fork.
3. Shape a circle with a nine-inch cake ring and place it on a baking sheet lined with parchment paper.
4. Bake bottom until golden brown for about 8–10 minutes. Watch it carefully, as it's easy to burn shortcut pastry bottoms.

Hazelnut Mousse
5. Soak the gelatine in plenty of cold water for at least 10 minutes.
6. Whip the cream to solid foam in a chilled bowl.
7. Pass the vanilla cream through a sieve and mix it with the praline paste until it's a smooth cream.
8. Remove the gelatine from the water and keep the remaining water on the leaves. Melt it to a temperature of 110–120° F (45–50° C).
9. Whisk the gelatine into the vanilla cream and praline paste and mix until smooth.
10. Fold in the whipped cream and crushed hazelnuts until it's a light and fluffy mousse.

Assemblage

11. Line a cake ring with plastic cake wrap.
12. Spread the apricot jam on the shortcut pastry bottom using a palette knife and place it in the ring.
13. Divide the bottom into three equally thick bottoms using a serrated knife. (Freeze one of them for another occasion).
14. Add a bottom on top of the shortcut pastry bottom and fill the ring with the hazelnut mousse, use a palette knife to smooth it out and add another bottom. Place cake in the freezer.
15. Roll out the green marzipan until it's an eighth of an inch thick and use a fluted cookie cutter to form bottoms about the size of a quarter.
16. Spread a little egg white over the marzipan. Place a hazelnut with the tip facing up and press the marzipan around it.

Completing the cake

17. In a chilled bowl, whip the cream, sugar and vanilla extract to solid foam.
18. Loosen cake from the ring and plastic cake wrap and spread whipped cream over the edges and on top. Lift it up and sprinkle with crushed hazelnuts around the edges.
19. Pipe balls of whipped cream. Use a flat nozzle no. 12 or cut a hole in the front of the cone. Decorate each ball with a roasted shelled hazelnut.
20. Garnish with chocolate shavings in the middle, chopped toasted hazelnuts and the marzipan-wrapped hazelnuts.
21. Place the cake on a cake doily. Let it thaw for about 1 hour at room temperature or about 3 hours in the refrigerator.

Walnut Cake from Grenoble

This tasty walnut cake really tastes of walnuts. Try to get hold of the French ones, as they are the best tasting. In the city of Grenoble there are walnut trees everywhere. Confectioner Master Calle Widell and I once visited Grenoble to study the walnut pastry in the city, and when we conveyed out impressions to our colleagues they almost passed out from excitement.

You can drink coffee with this cake and it will taste amazing.

12 PIECES

One cake ring, 2x9-inch (5x22 cm) or a springform pan with the same diameter measurement

Walnut Bottoms

½ cup walnuts (65 g)
½ cup unpeeled almonds (65 g)
⅓ cup sugar (65 g)
5 oz, or about 8, egg yolks (150 g)
4 ½ oz, or about 4–5, egg whites (125 g)
1 tsp. lemon juice (5 g)
⅓ cup sugar (60 g)
⅔ cup all-purpose flour (75 g)

Butter Ganache

⅓ cup unsalted butter (75 g)
3 oz dark chocolate, preferably Valrhona Grand Cru Pur Caribe (75 g)

Rum Syrup

⅕ cup dark rum (50 g)
⅓ cup confectioners' sugar (40 g)
1 tbsp water (15 g)

Walnut Cream

½ recipe of French buttercream, see page 46
½ cup crushed walnuts (50 g)
2 ⅔ tbsp dark rum or Kirschwasser (40 g)

9 oz marzipan (250 g)
confectioners' sugar for tucking
9 oz fondant (250 g), see recipe page 43
2 ⅔ tbsp of dark rum (40 g)
whole walnuts for decoration
confectioners' sugar

Walnut Bottoms

1. Preheat the oven to 375°
2. Make a tpt by mixing walnuts, almonds and one third of a cup (65 g) of sugar in a food processor or a blender.
3. Use an electric mixer for about 10 minutes to whisk the egg yolk with the tpt into solid foam.
4. On medium speed, whisk the egg white and lemon juice into foam. Add the sugar, increase the speed and whip into a firm meringue.
5. Fold the egg yolk mixture into the meringue using a spatula and sift in the flour. Fold it into a smooth mixture.
6. Add the mixture to a cake ring or a springform pan. Spread the mixture to the edges.
7. Bake the bottom until golden brown for about 25 minutes, check with a stick that it's thoroughly baked.
8. Sprinkle a little sugar on top and place on a baking sheet lined with parchment paper. Turn the bottom upside down and cover with a sheet so that it doesn't dry out. As soon as it has cooled down, place it in the freezer for one hour. This will make it easier to cut up.

Butter Ganache

9. Chop the chocolate finely, cook the butter and pour it over the chocolate while still boiling. Stir until melted.
10. Mix with a hand blender to an emulsion, cover with plastic film and let stand at room temperature to solidify.

Assemblage

11. Cut the cake base out of the ring. Place on a tray lined with parchment paper. Divide the cake base into three pieces using a serrated knife.
12. Whisk rum, confectioners' sugar and water to make the rum syrup until the sugar is dissolved.
13. Mix the butter cream with the liquor to make the walnut cream and add the crushed walnuts to half of the cream.

14. Apply half of the walnut buttercream on the first bottom and add the next bottom. Brush it with a little rum syrup.

15. Repeat with the next base and apply rum syrup to the top one.

16. Spread butter cream on top of the cake as evenly as possible. Set the cake in the refrigerator for one hour.

17. Roll out the marzipan until it's about one eighth of an inch thick, roll it up on the rolling pin and unroll it over the cake. Make sure that there are no folds on the sides and remove excess marzipan using dough cutter or a knife.

18. Heat the fondant with the liquor to approximately 95° F (35° C). Place the cake on a rack with parchment paper underneath.

19. Pour the fondant over the cake in one go and remove excess fondant with a palette knife. Move over to a doily paper.

20. Spread the ganache all around the cake using a spoon and create a beautiful marbled pattern. Garnish with a few walnut halves and dust a little confectioners' sugar on top.

A **traditional Swedish walnut cake** is much easier to make, and it was very popular when I started working in the profession. One classic Swedish cake base was divided into three parts. On the bottom layer you would spread a layer of apple jam or walnut paste and then you applied the following bottom. The second layer was covered in whipped cream containing walnuts. It was decorated with whipped cream, just like a cream cake, and with whole walnuts.

Diplomat Cake

This exclusive cake that forms a beautiful checkerboard pattern when you cut it into pieces isn't that common these days. It was a specialty at Confiserie Brändli in Basil and it is safe to say that it still is. Head Confiseur Béni Schmid audited each cake before we were allowed to bring it into the store. If you're travelling to Basel, try their truffles au framboise and marrons glacés marinated in whiskey, and get a Swiss crumpet to go – you won't find any better than at Brändli.

You'll have to bake at least two cakes, since you need one chocolate génoise bottom and one light génoise bottom, but it's well worth it. You can freeze the leftover bottoms and use at another time.

2 CAKES, 24 PIECES

Two cake rings, 2x9-inch (5x22 cm) or two springform pans with the same diameter measurement

Chocolate Decoration
2 acetate sheets
3 oz dark chocolate (80 g), Valrhona Grand Cru Guanaja 70%
3 oz white chocolate (80 g), preferably Valrhona Ivoire

One recipe of chocolate génoise, see page 16
One recipe of plain genoise, see page 16
One recipe of shortcrust pastry, see page 40

Diplomat Cream
⅓ oz gelatine leaves (8 g/about 4)
2 ⅔ cups vanilla cream (600 g), see recipe page 46
20 fl oz whipping cream (600 g)
⅓ cup brandy (75 g)

Brandy Syrup
½ cup brandy (100 g)
¾ cup confetioner's sugar (75 g)
⅛ cup water (25 g)

7 oz apricot jam (200 g), see page 44
One recipe opéra glaze, see page 48

One gold leaf sheet for decoration

Chocolate Decoration
1. Temper the chocolate, see tempering on page 52.
2. Spread the chocolate on two acetate sheets using a palette knife.
3. Shape round bottoms using a round cookie cutter, just as the chocolate has hardened. Press firmly.
4. Place the sheets on top of each other in the fridge and put something heavy on top so that the chocolate doesn't warp.

Génoise Bottoms
5. Divide the bottoms into three pieces and freeze one chocolate bottom and one light bottom for another occasion. Place the four bottoms on the pastry board.
6. Using round cookie cutters or cake rings, shape one six-inch, one five-inch, one three-inch and a one and a half-inch bottom using the chocolate bottoms, and repeat with the white bottoms. Change the rings and alternate with the light and dark bottoms to form a checkerboard pattern.

Shortcrust Pastry Bottoms
7. Preheat the oven to 375° F (190° C).
8. Roll out pastry until it's about one eighth of an inch thick, make indentations in the dough with a fork.
9. Shape two bottoms with a cake ring, nine inches in diameter, place them on a baking sheet and bake until golden brown for about 8–10 minutes. Keep a close eye on them, as shortcrust pastry bottoms burn easily.

Diplomat Cream

10. Soak the gelatine in plenty of cold water for at least 10 minutes.
11. Pass the vanilla cream through a fine sieve.
12. Whip the cream until firm in a chilled bowl.
13. Remove the gelatine from the water and let the remaining water on the leaves follow.
14. Melt the gelatine to a temperature of 110–120° F (45–50° C). Add the brandy and stir.
15. Gently mix the vanilla cream with the whipped cream using a spatula until it's a light and fluffy cream. Add the melted gelatine and carefully mix.

Mounting the cakes

16. Spread apricot jam on the shortcrust pastry bottoms and add one third of the cream. Spread it evenly using a palette knife.
17. Whisk brandy and confectioners' sugar until the sugar has dissolved for the brandy syrup.
18. Carefully move two of the layers on to two shortcrust pastry bottoms and drench them in brandy syrup using a brush.
19. Place two cake rings around the bottoms and line them with plastic cake wrap.
20. Distribute another third of the diplomatic cream on the génoise bottom using a palette knife and add the last bottoms. Press them flat using a tray.
21. Drench these bottoms with brandy syrup as well and spread the rest of the cream on top. Freeze the cakes.

Completing the cakes

22. Remove the cakes from the rings and the plastic cake wrap. Place them on a container of some sort so they are at a high level, and on a foundation of parchment paper.
23. Make sure that the temperature of the opéra glaze is around 100° F (38° C) and pour half the glaze over one of the cakes and smoothen it out. Repeat the procedure with the next one. Transfer the cakes to doily paper.
24. Remove the chocolate from the plastic sheets and lay the pieces around the cakes as shown in the picture.
25. Decorate with a gold leaf.

Thaw the cakes for approximately 1 hour at room temperature or 3 hours in the fridge.

Messina Cake

When I was a young boy, Yngve Malmqvist was the Pâtissière Chef at the Savoy in Malmö. He was a skilled craftsman who taught me a lot. He had learnt this recipe at Pâtisserie Arnold Zurcher in Montreux, Switzerland, where he studied for a while.

The slightly chewy pistachio dacquoise bottom, the tart orange cream and the luscious chocolate bottom is the perfect combination. The fact that it's beautiful doesn't hurt either. Whenever you cut the cake, the filling stands out.

You need to make two cakes for this recipe, but you can freeze one of them for another day. When you decide to take it out, I can promise you that it won't last for long. That's how delicious the cake is.

TWO CAKES, 24 PIECES

Pistachio Dacquoise

1 ½ cup confectioners' sugar (150 g)
⅓ cup almond meal (75 g)
½ cup pistachio (75 g)
6 ½ oz, or about 6, egg whites (180 g)
1 tsp lemon juice (5 g)
⅓ cup sugar (60 g)
3 oz dark chocolate (80 g), preferably Valrhona Grand
    Cru Guanaja 70%, for brushing

Orange Diplomat Cream

⅓ oz gelatine leaves (10 g/about 5)
3 oranges
¼ cup sugar (50 g)
2 cups vanilla cream (500 g), see page 46
1 ¾ tbsp lemon juice (25 g)
2 cups whipped cream (500 g)

1 almond chocolate bottom, see page 31
½ cup Cointreau (100 g)

16 ⅘ fl oz whipping cream (500 g)
2 tbsp sugar (20 g)
2 tsp pure vanilla extract (10 g)

1 cup roasted and sliced almonds (150 g)
9 oz almond paste 50/50 (250 g), see page 37
⅓ cup cocoa powder for garnishing (25 g), preferably
    Valrhona 20/22

For Delicate Chocolate Rolls

5 ⅓ oz dark chocolate (150 g), Valrhona Grand Cru
    Guanaja 70%, see chocolate decoration on page 62

Pistaschio Dacquoise

1. Preheat oven to 350° F (175° C). Sketch two circles,
   9 inches in diameter, on parchment paper.
2. Mix confectioners' sugar, almond meal and
   pistachios into a tpt in a food processor or a
   blender.
3. In a very clean bowl, whisk the egg white and lemon juice on medium speed until it turns into a
   foam. Add sugar and increase the speed. Whip into
   a solid meringue and fold the tpt into the meringue using a spatula.
4. Pipe the meringue inside of the rings using a
   plastic pastry bag. Use a flat nozzle no. 12, or cut a
   hole in the tip. (If there is leftover meringue mixture, pipe some meringues and bake for coffee.)
5. Bake the bottoms for about 20 minutes and make
   sure that they aren't too baked in the center. Let
   the bottoms cool completely.

6. Melt chocolate in the microwave or in a water bath
   with a temperature of 130° F (55° C).
7. Cover both sides of the bottoms with chocolate
   and place in the fridge.

Orange Diplomat Cream

8. Soak the gelatine in plenty of cold water for at least
   10 minutes.
9. Rinse and dry the oranges. Tear off the skin using a
   grater and rub the zest with one fourth of a cup of
   sugar using a palette knife until the sugar starts to
   flow.
10. Pass the vanilla cream custard through a sieve and
    mix with orange sugar and lemon juice into a
    smooth paste.
11. Remove the gelatine from the water and leave the
    remaining water on the leaves. Melt the gelatine to
    a temperature of 110–120° F (45–50° C).
12. Whisk about half a cup of vanilla cream into the
    gelatine and mix until smooth. Add it to the paste
    and fold in the cream using a spatula.

Assemblage

13. Remove the almond chocolate bottom from the
    paper and cover it with Cointreau. Spread the
    orange cream on top using a pallet. Set in fridge to
    set for 1 hour.
14. Carve one-inch wide strips out of the chocolate
    bottom using the orange cream, a ruler and a knife
    that has been dipped in hot water.
15. Roll the strip like a cake roll and place a roll in the
    middle of each pistachio dacquoise bottom. Conti-
    nue to roll the lengths around the roll on the cake
    until the bottoms are filled to the edge. Form them
    into beautiful round shapes and set in the freezer
    for 1 hour to stiffen.

Completing the cakes

16. In a chilled bowl, whip the cream, sugar and
    vanilla extract into solid foam.
17. Spread the whipped cream over the cakes and
    smoothen out evenly around the sides and on top.
18. Sprinkle the side of the cakes with sliced and
    toasted almonds.
19. Roll out the marzipan with the confectioners' su-
    gar, one twelfth of an inch tick, and shape to fit the
    bottoms using a nine-inch cake ring.
20. Add the almond paste bottoms on top of the cakes
    and the even them out using a baking sheet.
21. Sift the cocoa and decorate with two chocolate
    rolls on each cake.
22. Move over to doily paper and allow the cakes to
    thaw for about 1 hour at room temperature or for
    about 3 hours in refrigerator.

Rubinstein Cake

We often baked this classic Danish cake at the Savoy in Malmö, since several of the confectioners there had worked at the Hotel d'Angleterre in Copenhagen. Gösta Wennberg was the Chef Pâtissière, and he was known all over Scandinavia for his baking skills. The cake was named after the composer and pianist Anton Rubinstein (1829–1894), not to be confused with his Polish namesake, Artur Rubinstein. Rubinstein often visited Copenhagen, where he became acquainted with Hans Christian Andersen.

The chewy almond bottom, raspberry jam, rum fromage and the small glazed petits-choux make this cake a delicacy, and it's also beautiful to behold. You can try it at the fine pastry shop La Glacé in Copenhagen, although they are best known for their sportskage. Don't forget to try one if you are in the city of the Queen. When I was young I tried all of them, and they are all delicious.

12 PIECES

One cake ring, 2x9-inch (5x22 cm) or a springform pan with the same diameter measurement

half a recipe of petits-choux, see page 40

Egg Wash
1 egg
a dash of salt (1 g)

⅔ cup vanilla cream for petits-choux filling (150 g),
    see page 46

Chocolate Glaze for the Petits-choux
3 ⅔ fl oz whipping cream (110 g)
3 oz dark chocolate (90 g), preferably Valrhona Grand
    Cru Pur Caribe
1 ¾ tbsp glucose (25 g)

3 oz dark chocolate (80 g), Valrhona Grand Cru
    Guanaja 70% for chocolate decoration

Macaron Bottom
9 oz almond paste 50/50 (250 g)
⅔ cup sugar (125 g)
2 oz, or about 2, egg whites (60 g)

3 ½ oz raspberry jam (100 g), see recipe page 44

Rum Fromage
⅕ oz gelatine leaves (6 g/about 3)
3 tbsp egg yolks (40 g/about 2)
⅓ cup confectioners' sugar (40 g)
16 ⅘ fl oz whipping cream (500 g)
¼ cup dark rum (60 g)
2 oz crushed nougat (50 g), see page 93

Whipped Cream for Decoration
8 ⅓ fl oz 40% whipping cream (250 g)
2 tsp sugar (10 g)
1 tsp pure vanilla extract (5 g)

Petits-choux
1. Preheat the oven to 430°F (220°C).
2. Use the mixture to pipe balls the size of a walnut on parchment paper using a plastic pastry bag. Cut a hole in the tip, or use a flat nozzle no. 12.
3. Lightly beat the eggs and salt for the egg wash.
4. Brush the balls with the egg wash and nudge them with a fork.
5. Bake the balls until golden brown for about 15–20 minutes and allow to cool on a rack.
6. Fill the balls with the vanilla cream using a paper cone.
7. Bring cream and glucose to a boil for the chocolate glaze and pour the boiling glaze over the chopped chocolate. Stir until melted.
8. Mix the glaze into an emulsion using a hand blender.
9. Dip the top of the petits-choux in the chocolate glaze and let them solidify on parchment paper.

Chocolate Decoration

10. Temper the chocolate, see tempering on page 52.
11. Add an acetate sheet on top of the pattern, transfer the chocolate into a small plastic pastry bag and cut a hole in the tip. Pipe the arches according to the drawings and leave to harden at room temperature.

Pipe chocolate after the monster (see page 235).

Macaron Bottom

12. Preheat the oven to 355°F (180°C).
13. Mix the room temperature almond paste with sugar and half of the egg white into a smooth paste. Add the remaining egg whites and mix it into a lump-free batter.
14. Move the batter into a plastic pastry bag and cut a hole in the tip.
15. Wrap the cake ring in a sheet of parchment paper to prevent the batter from flowing out.
16. Pipe the mixture and bake it until golden brown for about 25 minutes. Take it out of the oven and immediately brush the bottom with nearly one fluid ounce of dark rum and let cool.

Rum Fromage

17. Soak the gelatine in plenty of cold water for at least 10 minutes.
18. Heat the egg yolks and sugar in a water bath while constantly whisking to 105–120°F (45–50°C). Remove from the water bath and whisk the egg mixture to a cold foam.
19. In a chilled bowl, whip the cream into foam and fold in the egg foam using a spatula.
20. Remove the gelatine from the water and keep the remaining water on the leaves. Melt the gelatine to a temperature of 110–120°F (45–50°C). Stir the liquor into the gelatine, add the gelatine mixture and the nougat into the fromage and stir.
21. Pour the fromage into a two-quarter round pan, similar to an ice cream bombe mold. Set it in the freezer for about one hour.

Assembling the cake

22. Place the macaron bottom on a cake doily and apply raspberry jam using a palette knife.
23. Release the fromage by pouring lukewarm water over the mold and place it in the middle of the almond bottom.
24. Whisk the cream, sugar and vanilla extract into foam in a chilled bowl.
25. Pipe cream daubs around the dome using a plastic pastry bag and a fluted nozzle no. 12.
26. Place the glazed petits-choux around the cake and pipe cream daubs between them.
27. Garnish the cake with chocolate scrolls as shown in the image. Gently remove them from the plastic film.
28. Optionally decorate with candied violets and candied rose petals.

Charlotte Russe

This was one of the finest desserts on the menu at restaurants and pastry shops when I was working as a young pastry chef. It's a beautiful and tasty dessert that was invented by the king of chefs, Marie Antoine Câreme, for a dinner when he was working as the head chef for the Tsar of Russia.

All desserts or cakes that are called Charlotte are always lined with some sort of cake base. Back in the old days you would always wrap a fabric ribbon around it, which makes it a little extra festive if you ask me.

8 PIECES

One cake mold, 4x7 inches (10x18 cm) (you can get a mold that's specifically made for Charlotte cake, but it also works well with any mold that's high enough)

1 ¾ oz dark chocolate (50 g), preferably Valrhona Grand Pur Cru Caribe 66%, for decor

One recipe of bisquits cuillère, see page 23
One recipe of apricot preserve, see page 45

One recipe of fondant, see page 43
One drop of red food color, preferably natural vegetable color
⅕ cup rum (50 g)
3 ½ tbsp lemon juice (50 g)
One drop of yellow food color, preferably natural vegetable color

Preserved Raspberries
9 oz raspberries (250 g)
⅔ cup sugar (135 g)
⅖ cup water (100 g)

⅕ cup rum for soaking the biscuits (50 g)

Rum Fromage
11 ½ fl oz 40% whipping cream (335 g)
⅕ oz gelatine leaves (6 g/about 3)
⅓ cup egg yolks (80 g/about 4)
⅓ cup sugar (65 g)
1 tbsp water (20 g)
⅓ cup dark rum (85 g)

Whipped Cream for Garnishing
8 ⅓ fl oz 40% whipping cream (250 g)
2 tsp sugar (10 g)
1 tsp pure vanilla extract (5)

candied rose petals

Chocolate Decoration
1. Temper the chocolate, see page 52, and spread it on a strip of acetate paper, two and a half inches wide and two and a half inches long. Sweep a glue scraper over the strip and roll it together. Set it down in a glass and let it harden in the fridge for 30 minutes. Carefully remove the plastic from the chocolate.

Preserved Raspberries
2. Bring sugar and water to a boil and pour the boiling syrup over the berries. Allow to cool completely. Drain the raspberries in a sieve.

Glazing the Biscuits
3. Line the mold with an acetate sheet and cut into a circle that fits in the bottom of the mold, to prevent the biscuits from sticking to the pan.
4. Cut the biscuits in the middle and carve them into triangles, so that they create a pattern of a star in the bottom of the mold.
5. Line the mold with the biscuits to see how many you need, you usually need 12 pieces.
6. Remove the biscuits from the mold and cover them with boiling apricot jam using a brush, before glazing them.
7. Heat five ounces of fondant to 95–100° F (35–38° C) and season with rum and a drop of red color.
8. Dip half of the biscuits in the glaze with the sugar coated part facing down and place them on parchment paper to solidify. Repeat with half of the tips.
9. Repeat with the remaining biscuits, but instead, add lemon juice and a little yellow food coloring, preferably natural vegetable color. Let the glaze harden for 30 minutes.

Rum Fromage

10. Whip the cream to solid foam in a chilled bowl. Place in the fridge.
11. Soak the gelatine in plenty of cold water for at least 10 minutes.
12. Beat the egg yolks into foam.
13. Bring sugar and water to a boil and pour it in a stream into the egg yolks while constantly stirring. Beat until egg mixture is light and fluffy.
14. Remove the gelatine from the water and keep the water on the leaves. Melt the gelatine at 110–120° F (45–50° C).
15. Add the rum to the gelatine and whisk it into the egg foam.
16. Fold the whipped cream to a light fromage.

Assembling the cake

17. Add the stars to the bottom of the mold, alternating red and yellow, and nudge it with the glazed side facing down.
18. Trim the glazed biscuits with a knife and place them inside the mold, alternating between yellow and red. Remember that the glazed surface should face the plastic. Trim them until they fit. Cut the biscuits along the edge of the mold using scissors.
19. Moisten four biscuits with 3 tablespoons of rum and cut them into pieces the size of a sugar cube.
20. Fill one third of the mold with fromage and add drained preserved raspberries and a few pieces of soaked biscuits. Add more fromage, raspberries and soaked biscuits.
21. Fill the mold with fromage and add the last raspberries and pieces of biscuits, cover the mold with biscuits and wrap plastic film over it.
22. Set the mold in the refrigerator for about six hours.
23. When serving, place the cake on a beautiful silver plate and remove the plastic.
24. In a chilled bowl, whip the cream, sugar and vanilla extract into foam.
25. Add a little cream to a small paper cone and cut a small hole in the end.
26. Pipe the cream in between the biscuits. Decorate with chocolate rings and candied rose petals.
27. Wrap a white silk ribbon neatly around the cake.

You can serve a raspberry coulis with the cake, see page 75, but make sure to replace the strawberries with raspberries.

Lemon Fromage Cake with a Tosca Cover

This is the perfect summer cake with its fresh lemon flavor, tasty lemon curd and crispy tosca lid. You will have leftover lemon curd when you make the cake, but you can enjoy it on toast, it's quite tasty.

Sven Malmborg was a talented pastry chef at Conditori Lundagård. He worked at the cake station for several decades and I remember that lemon fromage was one of his favorites, in spite of the fact that it annoyed him having to grate so many lemons every day. But it is divine.

12 PIECES

One cake ring, 2x9-inch (5x22 cm) or a springform pan with the same diameter measurement

Tosca
¼ cup sugar (50 g)
2 ⅓ tbsp honey (50 g)
3 ½ tbsp unsalted butter (50 g)
4 tsp all-purpose flour (10 g)
¼ cup sliced almonds (35 g)

One recipe of shortcrust pastry, see page 40
One traditional Swedish cake base, see page 16
One recipe of lemon curd, see page 46

Lemon Syrup for soaking the cake base
3 ½ tbsp lemon juice (50 g), ¼ cup confectioners' sugar (25 g)

½ recipe of lemon fromage, see page 185

For decoration
one lemon
granulated sugar

Tosca
1. Preheat the oven to 355° F (180° C).
2. Bring sugar, honey and butter to a boil at a temperature of 240° F (115° C).
3. Stir in the sliced almonds and flour.
4. Spread out the batter on a tea towel or a silicone mat in the shape of a ring, about one twelfth of an inch thick and nine inches in diameter.
5. Bake the mixture until golden brown for about 12–13 minutes, let cool a little and shape a bottom using a cake ring.
6. Spread the remaining tosca mixture on a tea towel or a silicone mat. Bake until golden brown in the same manner and let stand for 5 minutes. Use a knife or a dough cutter to cut lengths that are two inches long and divide them into two-inch-wide squares.

Shortcrust Pastry Bottom
7. Preheat the oven to 375° F (190° C).
8. Roll out the pastry until it's about one eighth of an inch thick and shape a bottom using a 9 inch cake ring.
9. Bake bottom until golden brown for about 8–10 minutes.

Assembling the cake
10. Apply one quarter of an inch thick layer of lemon curd on the shortcrust pastry bottom using a palette knife.
11. Divide the cake base into three pieces using a serrated knife (freeze the remaining bottoms for another occasion).
12. Whisk the lemon juice and confectioners' sugar for the lemon syrup until the sugar has melted.
13. Add a cake bottom, drench it in lemon syrup and let it absorb the juice.
14. Fill the cake bottom with another quarter inch layer of lemon curd and place a ring lined with plastic cake wrap around it.
15. Fill the ring with lemon fromage and smoothen it using a palette knife.
16. Freeze the cake.

Serving the cake
17. Remove the ring and the plastic around the cake.
18. Gently place the tosca cover on top of the cake. Move it to a cake plate and decorate around it with the pieces of tosca.
19. Cut the lemon in half and sprinkle with plenty of sugar. Caramelize the surface with a gas flame, the same one that is used for crème brûlée. Decorate with the lemon as shown in the image, and add a few mint leaves.

Lemon Fromage

P eople used to order this light crisp dessert ordered from the confectioner. It was molded in a cake ring and served with a cream garnish. You could also put a couple of biscuits inside the fromage.

My mother often made fromage as a Sunday dessert when I was a child. Later in life I made it for my mom. This is the way we made it at the Savoy Hotel in Malmö, and I've never tried a better lemon fromage than this one.

Grating the lemons on sugar cubes instead of grating them on a grater makes all the difference; the flavor is more intense and the fromage tastes much better, even if it does involve a little more work.

8–10 PIECES

One ring mold cake pan, a so-called bundt pan,
2 quarters
confectioners' sugar for the mold

Lemon Fromage Wreath
⅓ oz gelatine leaves (8 g/about 4)
2 yellow ripe lemons
1 ¾ oz sugar cubes (50 g)
3 oz, or about 4, egg yolks (80 g)
½ cup sugar (100 g)
⅕ cup dry white wine (50 g)
8 ⅓ cup whipped cream (500 g)

Whipped Cream for Garnishing
8 ⅓ fl oz 40% whipping cream (250 g)
3 tsp sugar (15 g)

17 ½ oz fresh raspberries (500 g)

Lemon Fromage Wreath
1. Soak the gelatine leaves in cold water for at least 10 minutes.
2. Rinse the lemons in lukewarm water and dry them. Grate the lemon peel with one and three quarter ounces of lump sugar until it's absorbed by the sugar cubes and has a yellow color and starts to crumble. Squeeze the juice from the lemons.
3. Beat the egg yolks into foam.
4. In a saucepan, bring the lemon sugar cubes, sugar and the white wine to a boil. Turn the boiling mixture over the egg yolks and whisk until the foam is cold.
5. Fold the whipped cream into the egg foam using a spatula.

6. Remove the gelatine from the water and leave the water that's left on the leaves. Melt the gelatine to 110–120° F (45–50° C).
7. Add the lemon juice to the gelatine and mix well. Fold the gelatine mixture into the egg and cream mixture until it's a light and porous fromage.
8. Rinse the pan in cold water and dust it with some confectioners' sugar, to simplify the process of removing the fromage from the pan later. Add the fromage to the pan and smoothen it out using a palette knife.
9. Set the fromage in the freezer for at least 1 hour.

Serving
10. In a chilled bowl, whip the cream and sugar into solid foam.
11. Dip the pan in cold water, dry it off and carefully remove the fromage to a beautiful plate. (You may under no circumstances use warm water when removing the fromage from the pan. The frozen dessert has a temperature of −18° F (−8° C) and water from the tap has a temperature of about 43–50° F (6–10° C), which is enough for the fromage to loosen from the pan.)
12. Decorate with whipped cream and raspberries as shown in the image. If you want to, you can fill the hole in the middle of the ring with fresh raspberries.
13. If you want to decorate with a couple of striped chocolate rolls, see page 59, chocolate decoration.

Enjoy it with a cold glass of Sauternes. I can guarantee you that it doesn't get any better than this.

Chocolate Charlotte Grand Cru Valrhona

This beautiful and tasty chocolate charlotte was very popular among our passengers on the Cunard Line, and most people took two pieces, even though we had at least 20 different types of cakes at our afternoon tea. The smooth milk chocolate bavaroise and the light and fluffy dark chocolate mousse is the perfect combination, in my opinion. You can pair it with fresh raspberries if you want to serve the cake as a dessert. This recipe requires you to make two cakes, as it isn't possible to make fewer cake bottoms.

TWO CAKES, 24 PIECES

Two cake rings, 2x9-inch (5x22 cm) or two springform pans with the same diameter measurement

Long Chocolate Rolls for Decoration
14 oz dark chocolate (400 g), preferably Valrhona Grand Cru Manjari 64%

Half a recipe two-colored charlotte bisquit, see page 28
One chocolate génoise bottom, see page 16

Milk Chocolate Bavaroise
8 ⅓ fl oz whipping cream (250 g)
⅕ oz gelatine leaves (6 g/about 3)
1 cup milk, 3% (250 g)
⅓ cup sugar (70 g)
2 oz, or about 3, egg yolks (60 g)
5 ⅓ oz milk chocolate (150 g), preferably Valrhona Jivara Lactée 40%

Raspberry Syrup
5 ⅓ oz raspberries (150 g)
½ cup confectioners' sugar (50 g)

Dark Chocolate Mousse with a Pâte à bombe
11 ¾ fl oz whipping cream (350 g)
1 ¾ oz, or about 1, egg (50 g)
3 oz, or about 4, egg yolks (80 g)
½ cup sugar (95 g)
⅕ cup water (45 g)
8 ¼ oz dark chocolate (235 g), preferably Valrhona Grand Cru Guanaja 70%

⅓ cup cocoa (25 g), preferably Valrhona 20/22

1. Start by making the chocolate rolls that will be used as decoration for the cake, see striped chocolate cigarettes on page 59, but use only dark chocolate.

Milk Chocolate Bavaroise
2. Whip the cream into solid foam in a chilled bowl and set it in the fridge.
3. Soak the gelatine leaves in cold water for at least 10 minutes.
4. Mix milk, sugar and egg yolks in a saucepan and heat to 185° F (85° C), while constantly stirring. Pass it through a fine sieve, a so-called chinoise.
5. Add the drained gelatine leaves and stir until melted. Add the chopped chocolate and stir until it melts.

6. Cool in a water bath to 77° F (25° C), turning down the whipped cream and stirring well until it's a smooth bavaroise.

Dark Chocolate Mousse
7. Whip the cream into loose foam in a chilled bowl.
8. Beat eggs and egg yolks into a foam.
9. Bring sugar and water to a boil until the temperature is 252° F (122° C), or perform the cold-water candy test, see page 35, while constantly brushing the inside of a pan with a brush dipped in water.
10. Add the boiling sugar syrup in a stream into the egg foam and whisk it on low speed until cold.
11. Chop and melt the chocolate in the microwave or in a water bath at a temperature of 130° F (55° C) (use a thermometer).
12. Mix the chocolate with half a cup of whipped cream into a ganache, pour the ganache into the remaining cream and mix well.
13. Fold the egg foam into a light and porous mousse.

Assemblage
14. Place two cake rings on a baking sheet lined with parchment paper. Turn the two-colored bisquit upside down and cut out four two-inch wide lengths.
15. Line the rings with plastic cake wrap and line them inside with the top side facing the inside of ring.
16. Cut the half-thawed chocolate genoise into four equally thick bottoms using a serrated knife.
17. Place a génoise bottom in each ring.
18. Add milk chocolate bavaroise and place in the refrigerator to solidify for 30 minutes.
19. Mix the raspberries and confectioners' sugar for the raspberry syrup into a purée.
20. Add an additional cake bottom and spread raspberry syrup over it.
21. Add the dark chocolate mousse and put the cakes in the freezer.
22. Take out the cakes 1 hour before serving. Loosen them from the rings and remove the plastic cake wrap.
23. Place the cakes on a cake dish and decorate with chocolate shavings as shown in the image. Dust with cocoa and place on a doily paper.

You can save one of the cakes for another occasion; it keeps in the freezer for at least one month if it's well wrapped.

Piña Colada Cake

This tasty cake reminds me of happy days in the Caribbean on the Cunard Line, when we cruised around all of the islands and treated the cold buffet managers to Piña Coladas served in hollowed-out pineapples. I tried the most delicious Piña Colada during a cocoa trip in Mexico.

Everyone fell in love with their Piña Colada and Mathias Dahlgren, a world champion in cooking, called it fantastic. Maria Escalante and I could only agree.

12 PIECES

One cake ring, 2x9-inch (5x22 cm)

3 oz toasted and shredded coconut (80 g)

Coconut Dacquoise Bottoms
4 ¼ oz grated coconut (120 g)
⅓ cup almond meal (50 g)
⅘ cup sugar (170 g)
4 oz, or about 6, egg whites (120 g)
½ cup sugar (80 g)
1 tsp lemon juice (5 g)

Bavaroise
1 ½ cups pineapple flesh (315 g)
3 tbsp sugar (35 g)
⅓ oz gelatine leaves (10 g/about 5)
7 fl oz coconut milk (200 g), not light!
4 oz, or about 6, egg yolks (120 g)
½ cup sugar (100 g)
½ cup white rum (100 g)
15 fl oz whipping cream (450 g)

3 ½ oz dark chocolate (100 g), preferably Valrhona Grand Cru Pur Caribé, for brushing the cake bottom and palm trees
3 ½ oz, neutral gelatine glaze (100 g), see recipe on page 43

Whipped Cream
8 ⅓ fl oz 40% whipping cream (250 g)
2 tsp sugar (10 g)
1 tsp pure vanilla extract (5 g)

1 ½ oz white chocolate (40 g), preferably Valrhona Ivoire, for chocolate shavings, see page 56

fresh pineapple slices

1. Pour the coconut onto a baking sheet and roast until golden brown at 390° F (200° C). Stir occasionally so that it doesn't burn.

Coconut Dacquoise Bottoms

2. Preheat the oven to 340° F (175° C). Draw two circles, nine inches in diameter, on parchment paper.
3. Make a tpt by mixing coconut, almond meal and three quarters of a cup of sugar into a powder in a food processor or blender.
4. Whisk the egg whites, sugar and lemon juice into a solid meringue. Start mixing on medium speed and increase the speed at the end.
5. Using a spatula, fold the tpt into a smooth meringue.
6. Pipe two bottoms using a plastic pastry bag. Use a flat nozzle no. 12 or cut a hole on the tip of the cone. Pipe from the inside out.
7. Bake bottoms for 15–20 minutes. They should be crisp on the surface but also sturdy. Use bottoms immediately to prevent them from becoming dry.

Bavaroise

8. Mix pineapple with two and a half tablespoons of sugar to a purée and pass it through a fine sieve.
9. Soak the gelatine in plenty of cold water for at least 10 minutes.
10. Bring the coconut milk and pineapple purée to a boil and set aside.
11. Whisk egg yolks and sugar light and fluffy and pour it into the fruit purée. Mix well and heat to 185° F (85° C), while stirring. If you don't have a thermometer you can perform a spoon test.
12. Remove the gelatine from the water and let the remaining water on the leaves follow into the bavaroise. Stir until gelatine is melted and add the rum.

13. Cool the cream in a 70° F (20° C) water bath.

14. Whip the cream lightly and fold in the cream in two rounds.

Assemblage

15. Finely chop and melt the chocolate in a microwave or in a water bath. Spread a thick layer of chocolate on one of the sides of the bottom and place in the fridge to solidify.

16. Line a cake ring with plastic cake wrap. Place it on a tray with parchment paper and fill half of the ring with bavaroise.

17. Add a chocolate-free dacquoise bottom and gently press down. Fill the ring with bavaroise.

18. Finally add the chocolate covered dacquoise bottom with the chocolate facing up.

19. Freeze the cake for at least 6 hours.

Completing the cake

20. Turn the cake upside down leaving the ring on and glaze it with neutral gelatine glaze using a palette knife.

21. In a chilled bowl, whip the cream, sugar and vanilla extract into solid foam.

22. Remove the ring and plastic cake wrap. Spread whipped cream around the sides using a palette knife.

23. Place the cake in your hand and sprinkle it with roasted coconut around the edges. Place the cake on a doily paper.

24. Heat the chocolate and temper it, see page 52. Move it to a paper cone and cut a small hole in the top. Pipe palm trees on an acetate sheet and leave to harden.

25. Sprinkle toasted coconut on top of the cake, sprinkle with white chocolate shavings and add pineapple slices like in the image. Arrange the palm trees.

26. Allow cake to thaw for one hour at room temperature or for about three hours in refrigerator.

Pipe tempered chocolate into palm trees on an acetate sheet.

Cherry and Brandy Cake

This tasty moist cake is beautiful when it's cut up, and the succulent cherries and chocolate bottoms go well together. It's an adult cake that is suitable at a nice dinner, maybe with saddle of venison or a tasty duck as the main course.

12 PIECES

1 cake ring, 9 inches in diameter and 2 inches tall or a springform pan with the same diameter measurement

Brandy Mousse with White Chocolate
½ gelatine leaf (1 g)
16 ⅘ fl oz 40% whipping cream (500 g)
6 oz white chocolate (175 g), preferably Valrhona Ivoire
3 ½ tbsp brandy (50 g)

One recipe of shortcrust pastry, see page 40
3 ½ oz raspberry jam (100 g), see page 44
One chocolate génoise bottom, see page 16

Brandy Syrup
½ cup brandy (100 g)
¾ cup confectioners' sugar (75 g)
⅛ cup water (25 g)

8 oz brandied cherries (250 g), so-called griottes, or see my books, *Chocolate Passion* or *Chocolate: more of the delectable*, for recipes.

One recipe of opéra glaze, see page 48
fresh cherries for decoration (optional)
pistachios for decoration
1 oz neutral gelatine glaze (25 g)

Garnish
1 acetate sheet
3 oz milk chocolate (80 g), preferably Valrhona Jivara Lactée 40%
1 ¾ oz white chocolate (50 g), preferably Valrhona Ivoire

1. Start by tempering the milk chocolate. Spread it thinly over the sheet and make a marble using a wooden scraper or a brush, see chocolate decorations on page 60. Spread the tempered white chocolate using a palette knife. Allow to solidify and place in the fridge under pressure to prevent the chocolate from warping.

Chocolate Filigree Disc
1 acetate sheet
3 ½ oz chocolate (100 g), Valrhona Jivara Lactée 40%

2. Temper the chocolate, see chocolate decorations on page 52. Fill a paper cone with the chocolate and cut a small hole in the front. Pipe a zigzag pattern in a seven-inch circle on top of the acetate sheet, as illustrated, and allow to solidify under pressure in the fridge to prevent it from warping.

Brandy Mousse with White Chocolate

3. Soak the gelatine in plenty of cold water for at least 10 minutes.
4. Bring half of the cream to a boil and put aside. Remove the gelatine and add the water that's left on the leaves to the cream. Stir until melted.
5. Pour the cream over the finely chopped white chocolate and stir until completely melted. Add the remaining cream and mix to an emulsion using a hand blender.
6. Mix in the brandy and cover with plastic film. Put it in the fridge, the cream should be very cold.

Shortcrust Pastry Bottom

7. Preheat the oven to 375° F (190° C).
8. Roll out pastry until it's about one eighth of an inch thick and make deep indentations using a fork.
9. Shape a bottom with a nine-inch cake ring and place on a baking sheet lined with parchment paper.
10. Bake the bottom until golden brown for 10–12 minutes, don't lose sight of the oven, as shortcrust pastry bottoms burn easily.

Assemblage

11. Spread a layer of raspberry jam on the shortcrust pastry bottom using a palette knife.
12. Place a nine inch cake ring on a tray lined with baking paper and line the inside of the ring with plastic cake wrap. Place the shortcrust pastry bottom in the ring.
13. Divide the cake base into three equally thick bottoms and freeze one of the bottoms for another occasion.
14. Whisk bandy, confectioners' sugar and water into a brandy syrup until the sugar dissolves.
15. Place one bottom on top of the shortcrust pastry bottom and brush it with half of the brandy syrup.
16. Whip the freezing brandy mousse in the same manner as whipped cream; put it in a plastic pastry bag with a flat nozzle no. 12. Pipe a thick spiral and leave room for the drained brandied cherries in the interstices.
17. Place the cherries in the spiral until the entire ring is full. Pipe a layer of brandy mousse on top.
18. Add another chocolate bottom and brush it with the remaining brandy syrup.
19. Add the remaining mousse and smoothen out using a palette knife. Freeze cake for at least 6 hours.

Completing the cake

20. Loosen the cake from the ring and the plastic cake wrap, and place it on a container covered with parchment paper.
21. Heat the opéra glaze to 95–105° F (35–40° C).
22. Pour glaze over the cake and glaze it in one single stroke using a palette knife. Move the cake onto a cake tray.
23. Release the chocolate shavings from the acetate sheet and nudge them around the edges of the cake. Place the grid on top and decorate with pistachios and possibly some fresh cherries covered in neutral gelatine glaze.
24. Leave cake to thaw for 1 hour at room temperature or for 3 hours in the fridge.

Miroir au Cassis

I would say that this is when French patisserie is at its best. It's the perfect elegant dessert cake after a nice meal. It would go well with Orange Duck as the main course, with its tangy orange sauce. When you make the sauce for the duck, don't forget to caramelize the sugar until it has a very brown color, as it is very important for the taste.

12 PIECES

One cake ring, 2x9-inch (5x22 cm) or a springform pan with the same diameter measurement

Black Currant Jelly
14 oz black currants (400 g)
½ cup (80 g)
⅕ oz gelatine leaves (6 g/about 3)

Chocolate Biscuit without Flour
7 oz dark chocolate (200 g), preferably Valrhona Grand Cru Pur Caribe 66.5%
3 ½ tbsp unsalted butter (50 g)
3 tbsp egg yolks (40 g/about 2)
7 oz, or about 6–7, egg whites (200 g)
1 tsp lemon juice (5 g/about 1 tsp)
⅓ cup sugar (70 g)

Black Currant Mousse
⅕ oz gelatine leaves (6 g/about 3)
⅓ pound Italian meringue (165 g), see recipe page 34
4 oz black currant puree (225 g) with 10% sugar
8 ⅓ cup 40% whipped cream (500 g)

3 oz dark chocolate (80 g), preferably Valrhona Grand Cru Pur Caribe 66.5% for brushing of the cake base and chocolate sheets
One acetate sheet

Temper two ounces of the chocolate, see page 52, and spread it out thinly using a palette knife. Set in fridge under pressure to solidify.

White and Dark Feathers
1 ¾ oz dark chocolate (50 g), Valrhona Grand Cru Pur Caribe 66.5%
1 ¾ oz white chocolate (50 g), preferably Valrhona Ivoire
For instructions, see chocolate decorations on page 61

Black Currant Jelly
1. Soak the gelatine leaves in cold water for at least 10 minutes.

2. Mix the blackcurrants with the sugar in a bowl and place in a simmering water bath for 45 minutes.
3. Strain the juice through a fine sieve (there will be about two and a half cups of juice).
4. Remove the gelatine from of the water and add the juice. The remaining water on the leaves can go into the mixture as well.
5. Stir until gelatine is melted. Pour into a jar and refrigerate.

Chocolate Biscuit without Flour
6. Preheat the oven to 350° F (175° C). Draw two nine-inch circles on parchment paper.
7. Melt the finely chopped chocolate to 120–130° F (50–55° C).
8. Whisk in the butter until melted and add egg yolks.
9. Whisk the egg whites, lemon juice and sugar to a meringue. Start on medium speed and increase the speed until you have a firm meringue.
10. Fold the chocolate mixture into the meringue using a spatula to form a light and fluffy substance.
11. Fill a plastic pastry bag with the mixture. Use a flat nozzle no. 12 or cut a hole in the front. Pipe two bottoms from the inside and out.
12. Bake the bottoms for 12–15 minutes until they feel solid, but not dry. Cool on the sheet and place them in the freezer for at least 1 hour.

Black Currant Mousse
13. Soak the gelatine in plenty of cold water for at least 10 minutes.
14. Make the Italian meringue. Whisk the meringue with the black currant puree.
15. Remove the gelatine from the water and leave the remaining water on the leaves.
16. Heat the gelatine to 110–120° F (45–50° C) and pour it into the meringue mixture while constantly stirring.
17. Fold in the whipped cream using a spatula to form a light and fluffy mousse.

Assembly

18. Remove the chocolate bottoms from the paper and cover one of them with four teaspoons of melted chocolate. Set it in the fridge to solidify.

19. Place a cake ring on a tray lined with parchment paper. Line the ring with plastic cake wrap.

20. Place the chocolate-covered bottom in the ring with the chocolate side facing down.

21. Add the mousse to the ring and smoothen it using a palette knife. Apply the second chocolate bottom and spread a little mousse on it, so that the surface is completely smooth.

22. Freeze for at least 6 hours.

23. Heat the jelly to 86°F (30°C) and cool it in a water bath to about 68°F (20°C). Take the cake out of the freezer and spread jelly on the cake bottom, leaving the ring on.

24. Remove the ring and plastic cake wrap. Place the cake on parchment paper.

25. Remove the chocolate from the acetate sheet and place chocolate sheets around the cake.

26. Decorate with chocolate feathers, as shown in the image.

27. Thaw cake for about one hour at room temperature of for about three hours in refrigerator.

Gianduja Mousse Cake with Caramelized Walnuts and Rum Marinated California Raisins

Ilearned how to make this fabulous cake during a cake course at the legendary school of Lenôtre in Paris. The school's director Gilbert Phone, who I knew from the Coba School in Basel, invented the cake. Master Confectioner Gilbert Phone was from Alsace and every morning he would arrive in Basel by train from Colmar. He was a specialist at working with caramel and it was a great pleasure for us as students, who came from all the corners of the world.

Julius Perlia was from Luxembourg and he was the director of the school and an amazing pastry chef and teacher.

The time I spent at the school of Coba, was the best part of my education in becoming a skilled craftsman.

12 PIECES

One cake ring, 2x9-inch (5x22 cm) or a springform pan with the same diameter measurement

Brownie Base
4 ¼ oz dark chocolate (120 g), preferably Valrhona Grand Cru Guanaja 70%
½ cup unsalted butter (120 g)
1 cup walnuts (150 g)
½ cup cassonade sugar (100 g)
⅛ tsp salt (2 g)
1 cup confectioners' sugar (100 g)
3 ½ oz, or about 2, egg (100 g)
1 cup all-purpose flour (120 g)
1 tsp pure vanilla extract (5 g)

Gianduja
4 ½ oz roasted hazelnuts (125 g), shelled
1 ¼ cups confectioners' sugar (125 g)

Caramelized Walnuts
6 ⅓ oz walnuts (180 g)
¼ cup confectioners' sugar (25 g)
1 tsp lemon juice (5 g)
1 tsp unsalted butter (5 g)

Mousse
2 ⅔ oz california raisins (75 g)
1 ¾ tbsp dark rum (25 g)
7 fl oz 40% whipping cream (415 g)
9 oz gianduja paste (250 g)
7 ½ oz caramelized walnuts (210 g), see above

¼ cup dark rum (60 g) for brushing of the bottom
10 ½ oz dark chocolate (250 g), preferably Valrhona Grand Cru Pur Caribe 66.5%

Brownie Base
1. Preheat the oven to 430° F (220° C).
2. Chop the chocolate finely and melt in the microwave or in a 130° F (55° C) water bath while stirring constantly.
3. Add the room temperature butter and stir until butter is melted.
4. Chop the walnuts coarsely and add them, along with the other ingredients. Mix into a smooth paste.
5. Place a cake ring on a baking sheet lined with parchment paper. Add the mixture to the ring and spread it up along the edges, so that the bottom is flat.
6. Bake the base until golden brown for about 8–10 minutes (it should definitely not be thoroughly baked).
7. Place the bottom on a baking grid to cool, to prevent it from baking on the hot baking sheet and becoming hard.

Gianduja
8. Mix nuts and confectioners' sugar in a blender into a dough-like substance, with a temperature of about 160° F (70–72° C).

Caramelized Walnuts
9. Preheat the oven to 300° F (150° C).
10. Heat the walnuts in the oven.
11. Combine the warm nuts with the confectioners' sugar and lemon juice in a saucepan.

12. Caramelize the walnuts while stirring constantly until they are golden brown. Put aside and stir in the butter to separate the nuts.
13. Place the nuts on a parchment paper and let cool.

Mousse

14. Marinate the raisins in the liquor for one hour.
15. In a chilled bowl, whip the cream to loose foam. Set in the fridge.
16. Crush the walnuts coarsely using a rolling pin wrapped in a towel.
17. Heat the gianduja paste to 95° F (35° C) and dissolve it with one third of the whipped cream.
18. Mix all the ingredients into a mousse.

Assemblage

19. Place a cake ring on a baking sheet lined with parchment paper.
20. Line the ring with plastic cake wrap and add the brownie bottom. Cover it with rum.

21. Add the mousse to the ring and smoothen out using a palette knife.
22. Freeze cake for at least 6 hours.

Completing the cake

23. Loosen the cake from the ring and plastic cake wrap and set it on a cake plate.
24. Heat chocolate in microwave or in a water bath to 130° F (55° C).
25. Spread a thin layer of chocolate on a plastic ribbon, nine by two inches (22x5 cm), using a palette knife, and wrap the ribbon around the cake. Press the top of the ribbon towards the middle of the cake, see image on page 218, for white chocolate decoration. Set in refrigerator.
26. Make feathers out of the remaining chocolate, to decorate with in the middle of the cake, see chocolate decorations on page 61.
27. Place cake on a doily paper and carefully remove the plastic ribbon, so the chocolate doesn't crack.
28. Allow to thaw at room temperature for one hour or three hours in the refrigerator. Dust with a little confectioners' sugar right before serving.

King Cake

This is a pistachio strawberry cake with a crown made out of vanilla bavaroise – can a birthday party get any more festive than this? This beautiful cake is composed of delicious vanilla, a luscious pistachio base and strawberry compote and it's well worth all the work. It's also beautiful to behold.

Treat yourself and pair the cake with a tasty dessert wine or sweet champagne, for a festive feel.

12 PIECES

One cake ring, 2x9-inch (5x22 cm) or a springform pan with the same diameter measurement

Pistachio Bottom
3 tbsp unsalted butter (40 g)
½ cup pistachio (80 g)
¼ cup sugar (50 g)
4 ¼ oz almond paste 50/50 (120 g)
⅕ cup (50 g/about 1)
3 oz, or about 4, egg yolks (80 g)
¾ cup corn starch (90 g)
⅓ cup egg whites (80 g/about 3)
1 tsp lemon juice (5 g)
2 tbsp sugar (30 g)
3 oz white chocolate (80 g), preferably Valrhona Ivoire for brushing of the cake base

Vanilla Bavaroise
⅕ oz gelatine leaves (6 g/about 3)
1 vanilla bean, preferably Tahiti
1 cup milk, 3% (250 g)
⅓ cup sugar (75 g)
2 oz, or about 3, egg yolks (60 g)
8 ⅓ fl oz whipping cream (250 g) 40%

Strawberry Compote
⅕ oz gelatine leaves (6 g/about 3)
17 ½ oz strawberries (500 g)
⅔ cup sugar (125 g)
1 ¾ tbsp lemon juice (25 g)

⅓ recipe strawberry syrup, see page 73

Whipped Cream
8 ⅓ fl oz 40% whipping cream (250 g)
2 tsp sugar (10 g)
1 tsp pure vanilla extract (5 g)

½ recipe jelly roll cake bottom, see page 24
1 recipe apricot preserve, see page 45
2 tbsp toasted and sliced almonds (20 g)
2 tbsp chopped pistachios (20 g)

For decoration of the finished cake
9 oz whole strawberries (250 g)
3 ½ oz neutral gelatine glaze (100 g), see page 43

Pistachio Bottom
1. Preheat the oven to 375°F (190°C). Place a cake ring or a springform pan on a baking sheet lined with parchment paper.

2. Melt butter and set aside.
3. Sift the corn starch on a paper.
4. Make a tpt by mixing the pistachios with a quarter of a cup of sugar into a powder in a blender.
5. Add the almond paste and egg and blend into a cream.
6. Pour the mixture into a bowl and add egg yolks. Whisk it all for about 10 minutes into firm foam.
7. Whisk the egg whites, lemon juice and two tablespoons of sugar into a firm meringue. Start whisking on medium speed and increase the speed at the end, until it's a firm meringue.
8. Fold the egg yolk foam and corn starch into meringue using a spatula.
9. Mix a few tablespoons of the mixture with the butter and fold back into the batter.
10. Add the mixture to the cake ring and spread it on the sides of the ring to ensure that the cake bottom is flat when baked.
11. Bake bottom until golden brown for about 25 minutes. Check that it is thoroughly baked by sticking the tip of a knife into it.
12. Sprinkle a little sugar on top and place on a baking sheet lined with parchment paper. Turn the bottom upside down. Place a plate over the cake, so that it doesn't dry out.

Vanilla Bavaroise
13. Soak the gelatine in cold water for at least 10 minutes.
14. Cut the vanilla bean lengthwise and scrape the seeds out into a saucepan. Add the rod, milk and half of the sugar. Bring to a boil. Put the pan aside and let it steep for 10–15 minutes.
15. Beat the egg yolks with the remaining sugar into a light and fluffy batter.
16. Remove the vanilla rod. Pour the hot mixture into the egg mixture. Mix well.
17. Pour the mixture into a saucepan and gently heat while constantly stirring using a whisk or spoon until it starts to thicken. It should reach a temperature of 185°F (85°C). If you don't have a thermometer, you can perform a spoon test.
18. Pour the batter through a fine sieve, a so-called chinoise.
19. Remove the gelatine from the water and let the remaining water on the leaves follow into the mixture. Stir until gelatin is melted.
20. Cool in a cold water bath to 70°F (20°C).
21. Lightly whip the cream. Fold the mixture into the cream in two rounds.

Strawberry Compote

22. Soak the gelatine in plenty of cold water for at least 10 minutes.
23. Rinse and drain the strawberries. Cut them into slices and mix with sugar and lemon juice.
24. Bring to a boil and add the drained gelatine leaves. Stir until melted.
25. Pour the compote into a tin foil pan, 9 inches in diameter. Allow to cool.
26. Freeze for at least 6 hours.

Assemblage

27. Cut the cake base out of the ring. Divide it into two equally thick bottoms using a serrated knife.
28. Chop and melt the chocolate to 113° F (45° C) in the microwave or in a water bath.
29. Brush chocolate on one side of one of the bottoms. Set in the fridge to harden.
30. Place a cake ring or springform pan on a tray covered with parchment paper. Line the ring with plastic cake wrap.
31. Place a chocolate-covered bottom in the ring with the chocolate side facing down.
32. Add half of the vanilla bavaroise.
33. Remove the compote from the tin foil pan and push it down in the bavaroise.
34. Top it up with more bavaroise and add the second bottom.
35. Add a layer of strawberry syrup and freeze the cake for at least 6 hours.

Completing the cake

36. In a chilled bowl, whip the cream, sugar and vanilla extract to solid foam.
37. Spread whipped cream on the sides and on top of the cake using a palette knife.
38. Fill a plastic pastry bag with the remaining whipped cream. Use a flat nozzle no. 12 or cut a hole in the tip.
39. Pipe twelve balls of cream, equally spaced out on top of the cake. Transfer the cake onto a cake plate.
40. Spread apricot on the jellyroll base using a brush and sprinkle the top with sliced and toasted almonds and chopped pistachios.
41. Divide the base lengthwise into two parts, using a sharp knife dipped in hot water. Cut the lengths into twelve pointed pieces, as shown in the image, each one being just over four inches long.
42. Bend the pieces over the balls of cream and apply them so that the cake resembles a crown. Shape a bottom to place in the middle, using a drinking glass or a cookie-cutter.
43. Melt the jelly and dip the strawberries in it. Decorate the cake with glazed strawberries.
44. Allow the cake to thaw for about one hour at room temperature or three hours in refrigerator.

Champagne Cake with Raspberry Jelly and Almond Biscuit

Serve this tasty cake for someone's special day. The light almond base and the contrast between the smooth bavaroise and the tart jelly really is something else. Spray the cake with white chocolate and garnish it with a fresh rose and a few raspberries. If one is tired of champagne, they are tired of life, in my opinion.

I once worked with Richard Juhlin, Sweden's foremost Champagne expert. That time we mixed champagne with chocolate, which is also a wonderful combination.

12 PIECES

One cake ring, 2x9-inch (5x22 cm) or a springform pan with the same diameter measurement

For decoration
One acetate sheet
1 ½ oz white chocolate (40 g), preferably Valrhona
    Ivoire
3 oz dark chocolate (80 g), Valrhona Grand Cru Pur
    Caribe 66.5%

Raspberry Jelly
⅛ oz gelatine leaves (4 g/about 2)
17 ½ oz raspberries (500 g)
½ cup sugar (80 g)

Champagne Bavaroise
⅕ oz gelatine leaves (6 g/about 3)
2 oz, or about 3, egg yolks (60 g)
½ cup sugar (80 g)
1 cup dry champagne (200 g)
1 ¾ tbsp lemon juice (25 g)
1 ¾ tbsp brandy (25 g)
8 ⅓ fl oz 40% whipping cream (250 g)

One duchesse bottom, see page 21

Chocolate Spray
6 oz white chocolate (175 g)
1 cup cocoa butter (75 g)

One fresh red pesticide-free rose

Chocolate decoration
1. Temper both of the chocolate types for the decorations, see tempering on page 52. Spread the two chocolate types on an acetate sheet using a palette knife, into a marbled pattern. Place in fridge under pressure, so that the chocolate doesn't warp.

Raspberry jelly
2. Soak the gelatine leaves in plenty of cold water for at least 10 minutes.
3. Mix raspberries and sugar in a bowl and place in a simmering water bath. Let stand for 45 minutes.
4. Strain the juice through a sieve cloth. There should be about seven fluid ounces of juice.
5. Remove the gelatine from the water and place in the juice. Let the water that's left on the leaves follow into the mixture. Stir until gelatin is melted.
6. Pour the jelly into a tin foil pan, nine inches in diameter, lined with with plastic film. Allow to cool.
7. Freeze the gel for about 6 hours.

Champagne Bavaroise
8. Soak the gelatine leaves in plenty of cold water for at least 10 minutes.
9. Whisk yolks and sugar until light and fluffy.
10. Bring the champagne and lemon juice to a boil and beat the boiling mixture over the egg foam. Stir well.
11. Heat, stirring to 185°F (85°C), if you don't have a thermometer you can perform a spoon test.
12. Pass it through a fine sieve, a so-called chinoise.
13. Remove the gelatine leaves and let the water that's left on the leaves follow into the egg mixture.

14. Stir until the gelatine is melted, add the brandy and stir.
15. Cool the cream in a 70° F (20° C) cold water bath.
16. Whip the cream to light foam.
17. Fold the cream in two batches to a light and porous Bavaroise.

Assembling the cake

18. Place a cake ring on a tray covered with parchment paper and line the ring with plastic cake wrap.
19. Divide the cake base into three equally thick pieces using a serrated knife. Freeze one bottom for another occasion.
20. Fill half of the ring with bavaroise. Remove the jelly from the foil pan and press it down on the bavaroise.
21. Fill the ring with bavaroise and add a cake base.
22. Freeze the cake for about 6 hours.

Completing the cake

23. Loosen the cake from the ring and plastic cake wrap and place it on a container covered in parchment paper.
24. Melt the chocolate to 110° F (45° C) for drizzling. Melt the cocoa butter to 110° F (45° C).
25. Mix the cocoa butter with the chocolate and pass it through a fine sieve, a so-called chinoise. Pour it into an electric paint sprayer or an olive oil sprayer.
26. Spray the cake with the chocolate until it's completely covered.
27. Place the cake on a cake plate and garnish with the leaves from a pesticide-free rose as shown in image and place the marbled chocolate pieces around it.
28. Let thaw for 1 hour at room temperature or for about 3 hours in the refrigerator.

Spanische Windtorte

Austrian confectioners call meringue "Wind Masse", light as the wind. This construction is characteristic of the baroque - both the concept and the execution – and it's perhaps the most beautiful among Vienna's famous cakes. The cake can only be ordered at Hofzuckerbäckerei Demel on Kohlmarksgasse, the prettiest and most exclusive place to go for Viennese pastry.

Some exclusive and extremely elegant products are known in Vienna as "Spanish". Maybe it has to do with the Spanish Riding School? The actual meringue cake can be prepared several weeks in advance, so the recipe isn't as bad as it looks. The cake is filled with whipped cream, vanilla, sugar and fresh berries and the outside is garnished with candied violets. I've placed a swan made out of meringue on the top layer, to make it look especially pretty.

1 CAKE, 9 INCHES IN DIAMETER
12–15 PIECES

For the bottom and rings
10 ½ oz, or about 10, egg whites (300 g)
2 tsp lemon juice (10 g)
1 ½ cup sugar (300 g)
2 ¾ cups confectioners' sugar (285 g)
1 tbsp pure vanilla extract (15 g)

Decoration of the rings, lid and swan
7 oz, or about 6–7, egg whites (200 g)
1 tsp lemon juice (5 g)
1 cup sugar (200 g)
2 cups confectioners' sugar (190 g)
2 ⅓ tsp pure vanilla extract (10 g)

Filling
⅙ oz gelatine leaves (4 g/about 2)
1 vanilla bean, preferably Tahiti
1 ½ oz, or about 2, egg yolks (40 g)
¼ cup sugar (50 g)
16 ⅘ fl oz 40% whipping cream (500 g)
¼ cup dark rum or Kirschwasser (50 g)
9 oz fresh raspberries (250 g)
9 oz fresh blueberries (250 g)
9 oz fresh strawberries (250 g)

1. Preheat the oven to 210° F (100° C).
2. Draw two circles on each of the three baking sheets that are lined with parchment paper; a total of six rings.
3. Beat the cold egg whites with the lemon juice until the foam begins to lift.
4. Add half of the sugar (three quarters of a cup) and whisk on medium speed.
5. Sprinkle the remaining sugar while whipping and increase the speed until you have a firm meringue foam.
6. Sift the confectioners' sugar and vanilla extract into the meringue and turn it into the foam using a spatula.
7. Put the meringue mixture into a plastic pastry bag with a flat nozzle no. 14, or cut a hole in the tip.
8. Pipe four circles, one twelfth of an inch thick, and two bottoms that will be used as the base and the lid. Pipe from the inside out until the circle is filled, see image on page 36.
9. Pipe two swans, as shown on page 36.
10. Let the meringue dry in the oven for about 90 minutes, remove them from the oven and let cool.

Garnishing the rings, lid and swan

11. Make a meringue in the same manner as above.
12. Turn the swans with the flat side up and pipe a little meringue. Place them together into a whole swan and place on the baking sheet to dry next to the cake.
13. Place a bottom on a baking sheet lined with parchment paper. Put the meringue into a plastic pastry bag with a flat nozzle no. 12, or cut a hole in the tip.
14. Pipe a circle of meringue on the outside of the cake base and add a meringue ring.
15. Repeat the procedure three more times. Spread around the sides of the cake using a palette knife.
16. Pipe a border around the bottom part, as shown in the image. Add the remaining meringue to a plastic pastry bag with a fluted nozzle no. 10.
17. Garnish around the cake and make a border around the top.
18. Decorate the lid with a fluted nozzle as shown in the image (save 2 tablespoons of meringue in the refrigerator, which will be used to attach the swan). Garnish with candied violets on the cake and lid.
19. Let dry in oven for another 90 minutes.
20. Take out the lid, scoop a small hole in the middle using a spoon and place a little of the extra meringue into the hole. Set down the swan and make sure that it's straight.
21. Turn the oven off, but leave the bottom to dry for a little while longer until the swan is properly secured.

Filling

22. Soak the gelatine in plenty of cold water for at least 10 minutes.
23. Cut the vanilla bean lengthwise and scrape the marrow out of the rod.
24. Place the vanilla marrow in a round bowl together with the egg yolk and sugar.
25. Place the bowl in a simmering water bath and heat while constantly whisking to about 105–115° F (40–45° C).
26. Using a hand blender, whisk the egg mixture until cool into solid foam.
27. Whip the cold cream in a chilled bowl to firm foam.
28. Remove the gelatine from the water and leave the remaining water the leaves. Melt it in a saucepan to 110–120° F (45–50° C).
29. Beat in the liquor and fold the gelatine mixture into the whipped cream along with the egg foam and mix into a light and fluffy mousse.
30. Fold in the rinsed and hulled berries at the end.
31. Place the bottom on a cake plate, fill it with plenty of the berry cream and add the lid.
32. Serve immediately, with a large bowl of strawberry coulis, see recipe on page 75.

Decorate with a beautiful purple silk ribbon on the side, which enhances the elegance of this lavish pastry. It is Maria Escalante, the champion of bows, who tied the bow.

Scottish Cake

This tasty Swedish cake is becoming more rare, and I don't understand why. It has a really tasty almond paste and it goes well with wine and is perfect at a dessert buffet. At Conditori Lundagård in Lund, we received a lot of "Scottish cake" orders, especially during Christmas. The Scottish cake should be served as fresh as possible, as the fruit will dissolve the almond paste if it's left for a long time.

It is traditionally baked on a wafer, but don't despair if you can't find the wafer. Instead, make a thin shortcrust pastry bottom (refer to the basic recipe). Back in the old days it always used to be decorated with preserved fruits: pineapple, pears and cherries, but nowadays there are many fresh fruit choices – use them instead, to make the cake less sweet.

12 PIECES

One wafer sheet (Stockholm essence factory), or one
    half-baked shortcrust pastry bottom, see page 40
28 oz almond paste 50/50 (800 g)
3 oz, or about 3, egg whites (90 g)

Glaze
1 tbsp egg whites (15 g/about ½)
½ cup confectioners' sugar (60 g)
½ tsp vinegar, white vinegar or lemon juice

fresh berries, such as strawberries
confectioners' sugar

1. Draw a nine-inch circle on a wafer and cut out a bottom. Place on a baking sheet lined with parchment paper.
2. Heat the almond paste to room temperature, preferably in a microwave, and gradually add egg whites until it's a smooth batter.
3. Move half of the mixture to a plastic pastry bag with a fluted nozzle no. 12.
4. Add a little more egg white into the remaining paste, until the mixture is spreadable.
5. Spread the softened almond paste using a palette knife on the bottom wafer (or on the shortcrust pastry bottom) as evenly as possible, approximately three inches thick.
6. Pipe the remaining almond paste, start by making a grid in the center of the bottom and then decorate it around it with daubs, as shown in image.
7. Allow to dry on the surface for at least one hour.
8. Preheat the oven to 445° F (230° C).
9. Bake the cake until golden brown for about 8–10 minutes. Make sure that it isn't too hard, you want the almond paste to retain its soft texture. Immediately move it to a rack to cool.

Glaze
10. Mix egg white, confectioners' sugar and vinegar until fluffy, using a hand blender. Add it to a paper cone and cut a small hole in the tip.
11. Pipe the glaze as shown in the picture, preferably when the cake is hot, as it will solidify immediately.
12. Decorate with fresh berries and dust a little confectioners' sugar on top.

Budapest Cake

You will have to look a long time before you find this tasty long cake or pastry in Budapest.

The origin is actually Swiss, but there you fill it with chocolate buttercream and brandied cherries. In Sweden, this is a light and tasty cake, and with its rollable crunchy meringue and creamy filling, it's a real delicacy.

It should be rolled up when it has cooled, and it should be filled and served fresh, not frozen, because the meringue won't be as crispy as it should.

We always used to make two versions at Patisserie Hollandia in Malmö, one with vanilla and one with cocoa. Pastry Chef Rolf Augustsson was happy to eat the edges of the cake with his coffee.

Filling them with tangerines out of a jar, like many people do, is an abomination in my opinion. Fill them with fresh berries instead. Raspberries are my favorite, and these days they are available year-round. Never use frozen berries, it just gets wet.

For the chocolate version, replace half of the corn starch with cocoa powder.

2 CAKE LENGTHS

Rollable Meringue
⅔ cup roasted and peeled hazelnuts (100 g)
½ cup sugar (90 g)
2 ⅓ tsp pure vanilla extract (10 g)
½ cup corn starch (70 g)
7 oz, or about 7, egg whites (200 g)
1 tbsp lemon juice (15 g)
1 cup sugar (200 g)

Filling
1 cup vanilla cream (250 g), see page 46
⅕ oz gelatine leaves (6 g/about 3)
11 ¾ fl oz 40% whipped cream (350 g)

9 oz fresh raspberries (250 g) for the filling

1. Preheat the oven to 355° F (180° C).
2. Start off by making a tpt by mixing nuts, sugar, vanilla extract and corn starch into a powder in a food processor or blender.
3. Beat the egg whites at medium speed with lemon juice and a quarter of a cup of sugar.
4. Add the remaining three quarters of a cup of sugar while constantly whipping into a solid meringue.
5. Fold the tpt into the meringue using a spatula. Move the meringue into a plastic pastry bag with a flat nozzle no. 12, or cut a hole in the tip.
6. Place a parchment paper on a baking tray and pipe lengths of meringue side by side. Bake for about 20 minutes. Open the oven door from time to time to aerate the oven.

7. The meringue is ready when it feels firm, yet soft, and has a golden brown color. It it's baked too long, it will crack when rolling. Let cool on baking grid.

Filling
8. Bring the cream to a boil and let cool.
9. Soak the gelatine in plenty of cold water for at least 10 minutes.
10. In a chilled bowl, whip the cream to solid foam.
11. Pass the vanilla cream through a sieve.
12. Remove the gelatine and let the remaining water stay on the leaves. Melt in a saucepan to 110–120° F (45–50° C).
13. Add half of the vanilla cream to the gelatine and mix well.
14. Add the remaining vanilla cream and fold it into the whipped cream using a spatula.

Assemblage
15. Turn the Budapest bottom upside down on a parchment paper and remove the top paper.
16. Apply the filling using a palette knife and sprinkle with raspberries.
17. Roll it into a tight roll and tighten it a little using a ruler.
18. Place the roll in the freezer for 30 minutes.
19. Cut the roll into two lengths and polish the cut surface using a saw blade knife.
20. Dust with confectioners' sugar.

DECORATING INSPIRATION

I n this field, everything is possible!
Below you will find a couple of suggestions for
cake decorations, for holidays and other festivities.

*Modern Three Layer Cake wrapped in White
Chocolate and fresh Raspberries*

This is how I usually wrap wedding cakes (see image
on page 217) or birthday cakes, in a thin layer of white
or dark chocolate depending on the customer's request.
See image of how to wrap cakes in chocolate decor on
page 218. Use the cake of your choice depending upon
taste preference.

Spread tempered white chocolate, see tempering, p.
52, onto a soft plastic cake wrap, 3 inches (7 cm) wide
and a half of an inch (1 cm) longer than the length of the
cake. Wrap the plastic and chocolate around the cake and
seal the seam. Fold it using your thumbs and push in the
plastic. Let the cake set in the fridge for 15 minutes.

Carefully loosen the plastic from the chocolate and
place the cake on the cake dish.

Fill the center with raspberries or the berries of your
choice and sprinkle with confectioners' sugar. Center
the cake on the cake stand.

A cake that is 8 inches (20 cm) in diameter needs approximately three and a half ounces (100 g) of chocolate, a 8 ½ inch (22 cm) cake needs approximately five
ounces (150 g) of chocolate and a 9 ½ inch (24 cm) cake
needs approximately six ounces (180 g) of chocolate.

*Karin and Jessica with a wedding cake at Olof Viktors,
ready for delivery (see image on page 216)*

This Joconde style cake is filled with raspberry mousse
and passion fruit mousse. It is wrapped in a white
chocolate ribbon that is placed around the frozen cake.
Next, it's garnished with small white chocolate rolls
and fresh roses.

Karin, here with an English cake with orchids

Karin, trained in cake decor in England, is displaying a
beautiful example of pastillage flowers, dressed up and
threaded onto a string. A cake of your choice is covered
in thinly rolled out pastillage and then encircled with a
ribbon of icing.

Confirmation Cake

In this image I have dressed a cake with one tenth of an inch (2.5 mm) thick marzipan rolled out with confectioners' sugar. The church window is made of tempered chocolate, with the help of a small plastic pastry bag. I use the same pastry bag to write the gothic scripture on the piece of marzipan, as well as the squiggles behind the marzipan roses. Use chocolate to glue the marzipan roses and leaves to the cake.

The bible is made of golden yellow marzipan and decorated with chocolate. I've added some shadow below the scripture using chocolate.

Cake with a Monkey

A regular Princess Cake is dressed in white marzipan, instead of green. The name Björn and the dots are piped with tempered dark chocolate.

Pipe a little glaze around the edges of the cake.

The monkey is made out of two brown marzipan legs, weighing one third of an ounce (10 g) apiece. The tail weighs one fifth of an ounce (6 g) and the arms one quarter of an ounce (7 g). The body itself weighs one ounce (25 g) and the white stomach consists of one sixth of an ounce (5 g) white marzipan. The ear weighs one tenth of an ounce (3 g) and it has a bead, weighing one fourteenth of an ounce (2 g), which is mounted on

each ear. The banana consists of one fourteenth of an ounce (2 g) white marzipan and a tiny amount (1 g) of yellow marzipan that's attached as leaves on each side. The head, one seventh of an ounce (4 g) of brown marzipan, is rolled into a ball.

Attach a one fourteenth of an ounce (2 g) bead of yellow marzipan to make the nose and attach a small bead of brown marzipan. Create nostrils by making two indentations with a stick. Attach a bead of red marzipan and use a stick to form it into a mouth. Shape a pair of glasses from one fourteenth of an ounce (2 g) of marzipan.

Assemble the monkey by moistening the parts with egg whites; it will make them stick together more easily.

Children's Cake "Bo 8 years" with Elephant

This cake is dressed with a layer of yellow marzipan one tenth of an inch (2.5 mm) thick, which has been rolled out with confectioners' sugar and lightly sprayed with green food coloring using an airbrush sprayer.

I have laid out a stencil of an elephant on a one tenth of an inch (2 mm) thick piece of pastillage, bought at a craft store, and sprayed it with blue food coloring, again using the airbrush sprayer.

Create the lettering by using a plastic pastry bag filled with tempered chocolate and frame the elephant with a thin border of chocolate. Add two small flowers using white and yellow marzipan formed into beads and put together.

The Merry Christmas Cake

The cake of your choice is dressed in a one tenth of an inch (2.5 mm) layer of red Christmas marzipan. Roll out

one ounce (25 g) of yellow marzipan into a thin layer and cut out stars using star cutters. Roll out three ounces (100 g) of pastillage, see recipe on page 69. Stab or draw a star and cut it out using a knife. Make a glaze, see page 69.

Put it into a plastic pastry bag and cut a tiny hole at the end. Attach the stars with the glaze and decorate the cake with glaze, as shown in the image.

Form a Santa body using one ounce (30 g) of red marzipan and two arms, each weighing one fifth of an ounce (6 g). Make the hands with pastillage, one fourteenth of an ounce (2 g) for each hand, using a small knife. The bag with the string is made up of one fourteenth of an ounce (2 g) brown marzipan, the head is made of one third of an ounce (8 g) faint orange marzipan and the beard of one sixth of an ounce (5 g) pastillage. A tiny piece (½ g) is shaped into a mustache and a small bead of red marzipan is attached as the mouth.

The hat is shaped into a cone using one fifth of an ounce (6 g) of red marzipan and one fourteenth of an ounce (2 g) of pastillage for the brim, plus a small bead of pastillage for the pom pom.

Moisten the parts of the Santa with a little egg white and assemble.

Christmas Cake with Angels
Dress the cake of your choice with brown marzipan and decorate with glaze, see recipe on page 69, using

a small plastic pastry bag, see image. Roll out yellow marzipan thinly, cut out a couple of stars out and attach to the cake with glaze.

Roll out three ounces (75 g) of white pastillage, see recipe on page 69, cut out a piece 3 inches (8 cm) in diameter, and mark it with a knife. Attach to the cake with glaze and frame it with glaze. Make a heart, using one third of an ounce (8 g) of red marzipan. Shape two pieces of white marzipan, one and a half ounce (40 g) each, into bodies. Make arms out of one fifth of an ounce (6 g) white marzipan and attach to the bodies after moistening them with egg whites. Shape two books, one seventh of an ounce (4 g) and attach with egg whites.

Use 1/15x1/3 ounce (2x8 g) of faintly colored orange marzipan to make the head. Mark the mouth, nostril and eyes with the use of a pick. Shape 1/15x1/6 (2x6 g) of yellow marzipan by rolling them into cigar-like shapes and nudging them. Place them on the head to make it resemble hair and attach the head with some egg white.

Roll out two ounces (50 g) of yellow marzipan and cut out two hearts with a cookie cutter. Moisten them with egg white and attach as wings. Place the angels on the cake.

Green Princess Cake with Christmas motif of Joseph, Mary and baby Jesus
Roll out one sixteenth of an inch (1.5 mm) thin white marzipan, cut out a round piece and place it on top of the stencil.

Temper the chocolate and transfer it to a small plastic pastry bag and cut a hole at the top. Follow the lines of the stencil and let the chocolate set.

Make a glaze, see page 69. Place the marzipan picture on the cake and frame it in pearls using the glaze. Garnish with snow crystals made of glaze and dust with a little confectioners' sugar.

Happy Easter Cake

This old-fashioned motif is still appropriate today, in my opinion.

Dress a Princess Cake with one tenth of an inch (2.5 mm) thin piece of yellow marzipan. Make a glaze, see page 69. Using food coloring, color a couple of tablespoons of the glaze yellow for the chickens, and a little orange for the legs and beaks.

Temper dark chocolate, see tempering on page 52. Fill a plastic pastry bag with chocolate and cut a small hole at the end of the tube. Pipe Happy Easter and draw some lines for the willow twig. Pipe white drops of glaze onto the twigs as shown in the picture and cover with some chocolate using the pastry bag.

Pipe drop-shaped chicken formations in yellow glaze and use orange glaze for the feet and legs. Pipe on a head and a wing using the pastry bag. Pipe a beak using orange glaze and a small bead of tempered chocolate for the eye.

Easter Cake with a Marzipan Lent-lily and Marzipan Eggs

Dress the cake of your choice in a one tenth of an inch (2.5 mm) thin layer of green marzipan. Make eggs out of different colored pieces of marzipan, one sixth of an ounce (5 g) each. Make glaze, see page 69.

Lent-lily: Place beads of yellow marzipan, one sixth of an ounce (5 1/2 g) each, underneath a plastic bag and smoothen them out into leaves (the marzipan will not stick to the plastic) using a spoon. Shape a bead out of the yellow marzipan and create a cup by wrapping it around your index finger. Make a mark inside using a knife. Attach pieces with glaze.

Roll out one sixteenth of an inch (1.5 mm) of white marzipan and place it on top of the picture. Fill the plastic pastry bag with some tempered chocolate and cut a small hole at the tip. Pipe chocolate according to the lines of the stencil and let set. Cut out the chocolate picture, place on top of the cake and attach the eggs with some glaze. Fill a small plastic pastry bag with glaze and cut a small hole at the tip. Pipe a line of beads around the edges using the glaze.

Pentecost Cake, see image on the right

I remember that we used to make a lot of these cakes for Pentecost and plenty of birch trees for decoration.

Dress the cake of your choice with approximately one tenth of an inch (2.5 mm) of brown marzipan. Make a glaze, see page 69. Pipe five birch trees using a slightly more loose glaze and let set for 3 minutes. Melt one third of an ounce (10 g) of dark chocolate, dip a thin

brush in the chocolate and draw very thin lines over the birch trees.

Thicken the remaining icing by whisking it and color it with yellow and green food coloring.

Pipe the grass and birch branchlets onto the cake using a small plastic pastry bag.

Shape two thirds of an ounce (20 g) of light brown marzipan into a birdhouse and make a hole in the middle using a pen. Make the roof out of one sixth of an ounce (5 g) brown marzipan and attach house and roof to cake with glaze. Make a small perch out of brown marzipan. Shape a small speckled bird out of one sixth of an ounce (5 g) sloppily mixed brown and white marzipan, to create a two-colored bird.

Princess Cake as a Christening Cake

Make a classic Princess Cake and place a piece of marzipan, 5 x 1/10 inch (12 cm x 2.5 mm) thick, on the center top of the cake before dressing it in a traditional green marzipan coat. Using a sharp knife, cut open the top layer of marzipan as far as the bottom layer

extends. Fold back the tabs as shown in the image, revealing the white marzipan underneath.

Make the baby's head using one ounce (25 g) of light orange marzipan. Make the eyes by inserting a small pointed pen into the head. Make two marzipan ears, one fourteenth of an ounce (2 g) each, by shaping them into beads. Moisten the ears with egg whites and attach with a small pointy stick. For the hair, shape one fourteenth of an ounce (2 g) of yellow marzipan into a drop. Moisten it with egg whites and attach.

Shape two beads of white marzipan, one weighing one fourteenth of an ounce (2 g) and the other weighing half of that (1 g), into a pacifier. Moisten it with egg whites and attach to the face. Moisten the head with egg whites and attach to the cake. Make a bow tie out of one fourteenth of an ounce (2 g) white marzipan and half the amount (1 g) of red marzipan. Moisten with egg whites and attach to the cake.

Make a glaze, see page 69. Put it in a plastic pastry bag and cut a small hole at the tip. Pipe a border of beads around the cake and the baby's head. Decorate with a marzipan rose with green leaves, see instructions on page 70.

Good Luck Wedding Cake

Dress the cake of your choice with approximately one tenth of an inch (2.5 mm) thin piece of white marzipan. Roll out two ounces (50 g) pastillage, see recipe on page 69, as thinly as possible and place it on top of the stencil. It should be thin enough for you to see the marked lines through it.

Temper the dark chocolate, put it into a small plastic pastry bag and cut a small hole in the front. Pipe along the marked lines and let the chocolate harden.

Make a glaze, see page 69, and attach the layer to the cake and frame with glaze.

Garnish with a red marzipan heart, one third of a ounce (10 g), five red marzipan roses, see instructions on page 70, and green leaves with nerves marked with a knife.

Cake with Crown Princess Victoria

When it comes to cocoa painting, the possibilities are endless, and it's not as difficult as you may think. The cake is dressed with a one tenth of an inch (2 mm) thick layer of pastillage, the roses and leaves are made of marzipan and the crowns and coat of arms are made with shapes of sulfur that I used to make at the pastry trade school in Uppsala, when I received my journeyman's certificate about 40 years ago.

Cocoa Painting

Cocoa Painting is a really old-fashioned way of decorating and master confectioner Curt Andersson was

a genius at it. The Christmas display of Christmas cakes is a tribute to Curt, who is a renowned confectioner in Malmö. The picture is done on pastillage and is painted with cocoa and olive oil, the snow is made of glaze and it is also framed in glaze. The angels are made of pastillage.

Cocoa Painting is a type of paining that consists of various colors that are developed from the one color. The mixture consists of finely sieved cocoa powder and olive oil or cocoa powder dissolved in alcohol. In the world of art it is called a wash.

Cocoa painting should be light and porous. You can trace a design using a pen on parchment paper. To prevent the subject from being inverted, you must turn the translucent paper over and fill it in using a charcoal pencil. When it comes to cocoa painting, you should always start with the lightest color tones and finish with the darker ones. One can also use a more modern method and transfer the image from the computer directly onto the pastillage or marzipan.

Roll out the marzipan or the pastillage using talc (can be purchased at the pharmacy). Cut out a circle of an appropriate size. Remove excess talc by using a dash of a white spirit, such as vodka, and let dry until the next day.

Place the drawing on a parchment paper. Place a one sixteenth of an inch (1.5 mm) thick layer of marzipan or pastillage on top before you start to paint. Using a small spatula, mix the finely sieved cocoa with oil into a smooth mixture. Use a thin brush and draw the lines that are visible through the layer.

Dilute the cocoa mixture with the oil and paint the light areas first. Paint as beautifully as you can and let dry for 1 hour.

Book Cake

This is a typical cake for occasions like company celebrations or confirmations. You can satisfy most wishes using the cocoa painting.

The king statue is located in the middle of Stortorget in Malmö. Hotel Kramer is right behind it, where I worked during a summer when I was 15.

Dress the cake of your choice in yellow marzipan and make indentions using a knife to resemble the pages of a book. Dress the cake with brown marzipan and frame it with glaze.

Cake with a Crayfish motif

When I was young, pastry shops usually had Ice Cream and cakes with crayfish motifs on display, so why not start the trend again? A tasty cake is perfect after the salty crayfish.

Dress the cake of your choice with one tenth of an inch (2.5 mm) thin layer of yellow marzipan. Spray it with a little green food coloring using an airbrush sprayer. Make a glaze, see page 69. Cut out a half moon using one tenth of an inch (2 mm) yellow marzipan and position it on a one tenth of an inch (2 mm) thin white marzipan layer. Frame it with a line of beads made of glaze and do the same to the edges of the cake.

Color some glaze light green and a little yellow. Put it in two small plastic pastry bags and cut holes in the tips. Pipe a couple of dill heads.

Color three and a half ounces (100 g) of marzipan red and shape a crayfish. Try to make it resemble the one in the image. Pipe legs out of the red glaze and eyes out of brown glaze.

The Golfer's Cake

Dress the cake of your choice with one tenth of an inch (2.5 mm) layer of orange marzipan and garnish with carnations and marzipan leaves, see instructions on page 70.

Roll out the one sixteenth of an inch (1.5 mm) white marzipan and place it on top of the stencil. Temper the chocolate, add it to a small plastic pastry bag and cut a hole in the tip. Follow the lines as accurately as you can and let the chocolate harden. Spray it lightly with a little green food coloring using an airbrush sprayer.

Cut out a circle. Place it on the cake and make a glaze, see page 69. Put it in a small plastic pastry bag and cut a hole in the tip. Pipe a line of beads of glaze around the subject.

The Skier's Cake, see image on page 226

Dress the cake with a one tenth of an inch (2.5 mm) thick black licorice marzipan layer. Make a filling of your choice.

Piping

1 Cut a sheet of waxed paper.
2 Make a cone out of the paper.
3–4 The finished cone.
5 Piping with tempered chocolate.

Fill in the outlines of a white marzipan circle using tempered chocolate in a small plastic pastry bag.

Write "skiing holiday" with chocolate.

Make a glaze, see page 69. Color it with blue, red and orange. Fill the selected areas with the colored glaze as shown in image and place the circle on the cake. Pipe a line of beads around the subject using the glaze.

Large Pink Christening Cake

Cut out a one fifth of an inch (5 mm) thick piece of paper according to the stencil with a box-cutting knife.

Roll out the yellow pastillage until it's one tenth of an inch (2 mm) thick, using confectioners' sugar, and cut out the parts of the cradle. Allow to dry until the next day. Assemble the cradle with glaze and decorate around it using glaze. Allow to dry. Spray it lightly in yellow with an airbrush sprayer.

Make a baby's head out of one ounce (25 g) of light orange-colored marzipan and shape the face using a small stick. Add on two balls of marzipan for ears and open the mouth using a small stick. Shape a blanket out of pink marzipan with a white border and place it on top.

Dress a cake of your choice with one tenth of an inch (2.5 mm) thin layer of white marzipan or pastillage.

Roll out a tenth of an inch (2 mm) thick layer of pastillage and cut out butterflies (the cutter is sold at certain houseware stores). Let the butterflies dry between the two sticks for 1 hour, to make them slightly bent.

Cut out pieces, 3 inches (80 mm) in diameter, using a cookie cutter, fold them in your hand and place on parchment paper for about 1 hour.

Make a glaze, see page 69.

Place the cakes on a cake stand and use glaze in a small plastic pastry bag to pipe a line of beads around the cakes. Pipe glaze over the cake and make a child's

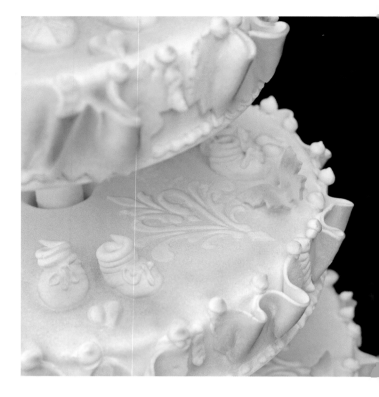

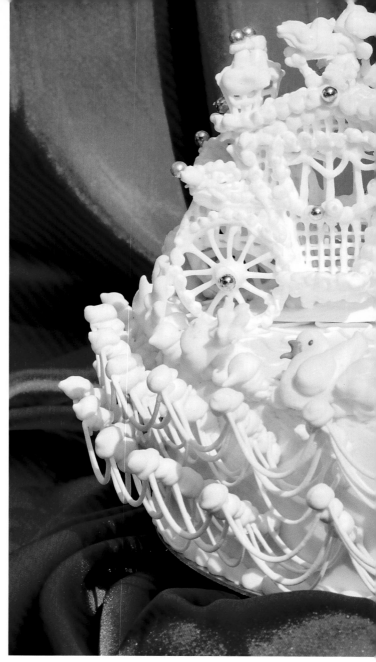

shoes by piping a little ball with a few rings on top - try to pipe laces on the front.

Attach the butterflies with glaze and attach the bent pieces around the edges of the cake, using glaze.

Spray the whole cake slightly pink, the American way, using pink food coloring. Assemble the cake on the cake stand. Garnish with the cradle on top.

Graduation Cap

This traditional Swedish cake usually consists of a Princess cake as the base. The cake is covered with a one tenth of an inch (2.5 mm) thick layer of white marzipan. Roll out and shape the brim out of the black marzipan, as shown in the image, and cut it with a knife.

Place a few roses and marzipan leaves on the edges; see instructions on page 70.

Temper dark chocolate and put it in a small plastic pastry bag, cutting a hole in the front. Pipe "the

graduate" on top of the hat and decorate with some chocolate music notes.

Roll out two and a half ounces (75 g) of yellow marzipan and two and a half ounces (75 g) of blue marzipan and form a long strip, 9 inches (22 mm) thick, and form a bow, as shown in the image. Assemble it by moistening with egg white.

Cake with Zerni, 50 years, and a Boxing Hare

Dress the cake with marzipan and lightly decorate it using an airbrush sprayer and yellow food coloring.

Add an acetate sheet over the stencil and tape it on, to ensure that it stays still.

Temper the dark chocolate, see tempering on page 52. Make a plastic pastry bag and cut a small hole in the tip. Fill in the contours of the character using dark chocolate.

Temper the white chocolate and milk chocolate, add to two plastic pastry bags and cover the sections with the chocolates. Let stand. Wait 30 minutes before

removing and turning the subject around. You can make most subjects using this technique, which is very useful for cake decorations.

Horse Carriage made of Glaze for a Wedding Cake

This beautiful, nostalgic horse and carriage is romance at its best for the confectioner. It doesn't get much more elegant than this. At the International Sugar School in Zurich, Willy Pfund made us produce many of these carriages for cakes that were ordered from other bakeries.

The carriage, the horse cavalier, the doves and the horses are piped according to a stencil. One must have great patience when putting together the carriage.

The cake consists of plum cake dressed in pastillage and it is decorated with dots of glaze around the sides. The cakes are piped with thin pendants along the sides that are left to dry for 1 hour. Another row of dots are piped and a new series of pendants are piped on top,

which will be left to dry for another hour. Repeat the procedure four times.

The dried doves are secured with glaze and are placed around the cake and the entire cake is piped in an irregular pattern. The carriage is garnished with small silver balls.

Decoration of English Wedding Cakes

I'm really fond of this classic cake style. Cakes should be sturdy, like the Plum Cake, the Sacher Cake Bottom or mazarin bottom, and covered in apricot preserve with a one tenth of an inch (2.5 mm) thick layer of pastillage, see recipe on page 69.

Whisk the glaze without using acid. The glaze is whisked until it's pipeable and resilient.

Place parchment paper on top of the stencils and secure them with tape to prevent the paper from moving.

Fill a plastic pastry bag with the glaze and cut a small hole at the tip. Pipe on top of the pattern, as accurately as possible, and repeat twice. Allow to dry until the next day.

Garnish the cakes with piped glaze, as shown in the image, and attach the dried doves around it. Move the cakes onto cake doilies and attach the ornaments using the glaze.

Garnish with pastillage roses, made in the same manner as marzipan roses, see page 70.

The cake with the free-floating pendants is piped with dots made of glaze and is left to solidify for 1 hour. Pipe on the pendants and pipe a new dot, see image.

Pipe beads made of glaze and let solidify before the next round of piping.

ABCDEFGHIJKLMN
OPQRSTUVWXYZ
abcdefghijklmnop
-qrstuvwxyz-
1234567890

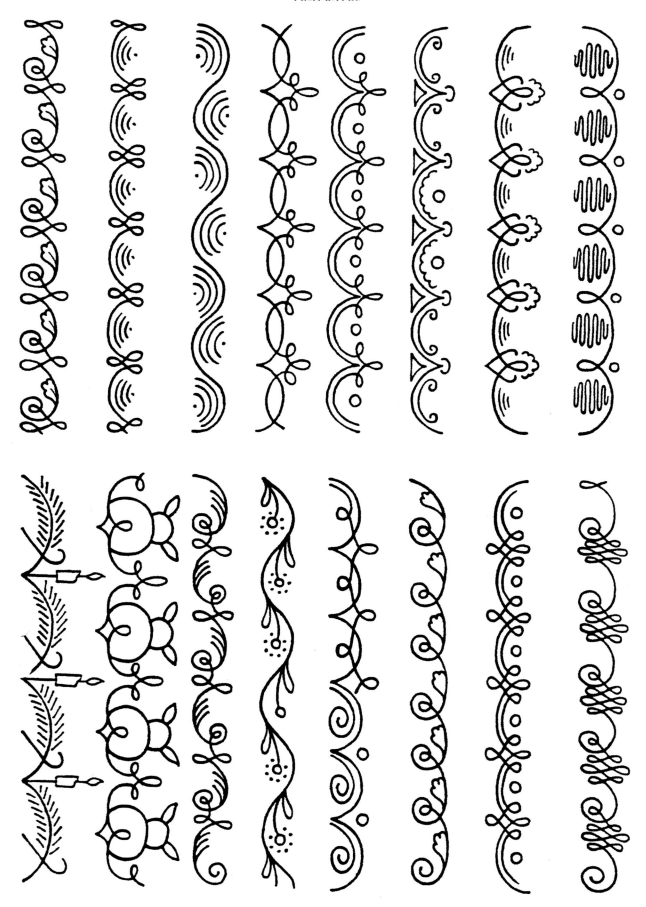

Wedding cakes with pastillage, baked by Karin at Olof Viktors.